James Chapman is Professor of Film Studies at the University of Leicester, UK. His previous books include *The British at War: Cinema, State and Propaganda, 1939–1945* (1998), *Licence to Thrill: A Cultural History of the James Bond Films* (2nd edition 2007) and *Inside the Tardis: The Worlds of* Doctor Who *– A Cultural History* (2006, new edition 2013), all from I.B.Tauris. He is the editor of the *Historical Journal of Film, Radio and Television*.

Nicholas J. Cull is Professor of Public Diplomacy in the Annenberg School for Communication and Journalism at the University of Southern California in Los Angeles. His previous books include *Selling War: British Propaganda and American Neutrality in the Second World War* (1995), *The Cold War and the United States Information Agency: American Propaganda and Public Diplomacy, 1945–1989* (2008), *The Decline and Fall of the United States Information Agency: American public diplomacy, 1989–2001* (2012), and (with James Chapman), *Projecting Empire: Imperialism and Popular Cinema* (I.B.Tauris, 2009). He is President of the International Association for Media and History.

'I very much enjoyed the background that Chapman and Cull produced on these films . . . I managed to learn something new in every chapter. The authors did a masterful job in the selection of examples – a mix of the essential and the surprising – which nevertheless manage to cover many of the key periods in the genre's evolution on the screen. They make a strong case for why SF films need to be considered in their own right and not simply as an extension of the literary version of the genre. All told, I suspect this book is going to be well received by fans and academics alike.'
– Henry Jenkins, co-author, *Spreadable Media: Creating Value and Meaning in a Networked Culture*

Cinema and Society series
GENERAL EDITOR: JEFFREY RICHARDS

JAMES CHAPMAN & NICHOLAS J. CULL

PROJECTING TOMORROW

Science Fiction and Popular Cinema

I.B. TAURIS

LONDON · NEW YORK

Published in 2013 by I.B.Tauris & Co Ltd
6 Salem Road, London W2 4BU
175 Fifth Avenue, New York NY 10010
www.ibtauris.com

Distributed in the United States and Canada
Exclusively by Palgrave Macmillan
175 Fifth Avenue, New York NY 10010

ISBN: 978 1 78076 409 2 (HB)
       978 1 78076 410 8 (PB)

A full CIP record for this book is available from the British Library
A full CIP record is available from the Library of Congress

Library of Congress Catalog Card Number: available

Printed and bound by TJ International Ltd, Padstow, Cornwall

For David Culbert

Contents

Illustrations

Acknowledgements

This book has developed from the authors' previous collaboration, *Projecting Empire*, and, like its predecessor, comprises a series of case studies of important films, including both American and British, in the cinema of science fiction. These films have been chosen according to several criteria, including their narrative and visual representation of the future, their significance in shaping the genre, and, not least, the availability of archival collections documenting their production and reception. *Projecting Tomorrow* has been written to a set of agreed criteria and principles. James Chapman wrote the Introduction and Chapters 2, 3, 4, 6, 7 and 9, while Nick Cull wrote Chapters 1, 5, 8, 10, 11 and 12, and the Afterword.

Like *Projecting Empire*, to which it is to some extent a companion volume, *Projecting Tomorrow* draws upon extensive research in US and British film archives. We are indebted to many archivists and librarians whose unstinting assistance and exemplary professionalism is only too rarely acknowledged. Therefore, we would like to record our thanks and appreciation to: Nathalie Morris, Jonny Davies and the Special Collections Unit of the British Film Institute, London; Jacqueline Kavanagh and the BBC Written Archives Centre, Caversham, Reading; Richard Daniels and the Stanley Kubrick Archive, University Archives and Special Collections Centre, University of the Arts, London; Barbara Hall, Jenny Romero and the Special Collections Department at the Margaret Herrick Library, Academy of Motion Picture Arts and Sciences, Los Angeles; Ned Comstock and the Cinematic Arts Library, University of Southern California; Sona Basmadjian of the David L. Wolper Center for the Study of the Documentary at the University of Southern California; Julie Graham and the Performing Arts Special Collection, University of California Los Angeles; Harold L. Miller and the Center for Film and Theater Research, Wisconsin Historical Society, University of Wisconsin, Madison; and the staff of the New York Library of the Performing Arts, Lincoln Center, New York City. Nick Cull is grateful to David F. Miller and Robert Cohen of the 20th Century-Fox legal department for their kind permission to work on the legal files associated with *Just*

Imagine, more especially as these records have subsequently been closed.

Many friends and colleagues have provided information, suggested sources and offered their constructive criticism and encouragement. Our thanks are due in particular to Philippa Brewster, our commissioning editor at I.B.Tauris, Professor Jo Fox, Dr Mark Glancy, Professor Michèle Hilmes, Professor Tobias Hochscherf, Professor Henry Jenkins, Clive Kennedy, Peter Krämer, John Muto, Professor Jeffrey Richards and Professor Tony Shaw. Valued informants have included Walon Green, director of one of the films and screenwriter of a sequel to another; Peter Weller, who brought RoboCop to life, and Mike Arnerich. Nick Cull gratefully acknowledges the help of his research assistant Sarah Myers at USC and of his wife Karen Ford Cull. His three sons – Sandy, Magnus and Oliver – generally allowed his hijacking the TV remote to watch and re-watch the films mentioned in the book.

James Chapman's visit to archives in Los Angeles and Madison, Wisconsin in 2010 was funded by a Small Research Grant from the British Academy. Nick Cull's visits to Madison, Wisconsin, the British Film Institute in London and Lincoln Center in New York were supported by the Annenberg School for Communication and Journalism.

It is a pleasure to dedicate this book to David Culbert, John L. Loos Professor of History at the University of Louisiana, Baton Rouge, our valued colleague on the Council of the International Association of Media and History, and long-serving editor of the *Historical Journal of Film, Radio and Television*. David's contribution to the fields of film and media history has set an example for us all.

General Editor's Introduction

As Dr Louis Judd wrote in his classic work *Anatomy of Atavism:* 'Visions of Yesterday or Dreams of Tomorrow, who is to say which exerts the strongest pull in the psyche of man?' That dynamic duo of cinematic scholars, Chapman and Cull, have now explored both sides of that perennial question. In their previous collaboration, *Projecting Empire* (I.B.Tauris, 2009), they examined the changing representation of imperialism in the cinemas of Hollywood and Britain between the 1930s and the early twenty-first century.

In the present volume they have turned their attention to dreams of tomorrow, the imagined futures of science fiction films, both British and American. They have adopted the same approach in this book as in the earlier one-contextual cinematic history. So they scrupulously locate their chosen films in their individual industrial, economic, political, social and cultural contexts. They trace the films' often fraught and complex production histories and their critical and box office reception. They relate the films to the fiction both of celebrated writers like H. G. Wells and Arthur C. Clarke and the army of authors of pulp fiction and comic strips who have contributed so much to the ideas and themes of science fiction cinema. Their fourteen chosen films range from *Just Imagine* (1930) with its trip to an inhabited Mars and its satire on prohibition to *Avatar* (2009) with its unsparing critique of American imperialism and capitalist exploitation. They demonstrate how – appropriately enough – the evolution of the science fiction genre has benefited from the development of more and more advanced cinematic technology, so that epics such as *Things to Come* in 1936 or *Star Wars* in 1977 or *Avatar* in 2009 represent the state of the art.

Crucially Chapman and Cull highlight the extent to which contemporary cultural anxieties have been projected onto the future in science fiction cinema: the Cold War and fear of Soviet invasion, the destructive potential of super-weapons, concern about changes in gender relations, the ruthless onward march of corporate capitalism, fear of man-made machines running out of control.

We should never underestimate the power of these dreams of tomorrow to influence the audiences of today. Thousands of people now describe themselves on census forms as Jedi knights after the warrior caste in *Star Wars* and recently a group of Palestinians painted themselves blue and dressed like the Na'vi in *Avatar* to protest against Israel's construction of a barrier. In this lovingly researched, thoughtfully argued and vividly readable volume, Chapman and Cull help us to understand better why and how science fiction cinema has extended such power over the imagination of its audiences.

Jeffrey Richards

Introduction

The history of cinema and the history of science fiction have run in parallel ever since their simultaneous points of origin at the end of the nineteenth century. The first recorded public exhibition of motion pictures occurred in Paris on 22 March 1895 when Louis and Auguste Lumière unveiled their new Cinématographe to a meeting of the Société d'Encouragement à l'Industrie Nationale.[1] H. G. Wells's *The Time Machine* – often regarded as the first modern SF story – was serialized between January and May 1895 before its publication in book form by William Heinemann of London in May.[2] Cinema and science fiction were both products of the technological revolution of the late Victorian period. The cinematograph was the 'last machine' of the Victorian age, following the telephone (1876), internal combustion engine (1876), cathode ray tube (1878), phonograph (1878) and wireless telegraphy (1894).[3] Science fiction also reflected this interest in technology and modernity. What differentiated Wells's work from previous examples of what at the time was known as 'scientific romance' was its insistence on explanatory frameworks based on scientific and philosophical principles (particularly Darwinism) rather than fantasy or magic. To this extent cinema and science fiction were products of the same historical and technological contexts.

There were close parallels between Wells's writing and early cinema. Wells has been claimed as a 'proto-cinematic' writer. His work is replete with 'optical speculations' such as the disappearing protagonist of *The Invisible Man* and the Martian death rays in *The War of the Worlds*.[4] A tradition of optical 'trick' effects permeated early cinema, particularly in the fantasy films of the French pioneer Georges Méliès, such as *The Vanishing Lady* (1898) and *A Voyage to the Moon* (1902). The giant public entertainment screens that Wells describes in the futuristic city of *When the Sleeper Wakes* anticipated the Paris Exposition of 1900 when the Lumière brothers projected films onto a screen some twenty metres square. Wells's fiction also demonstrates an affinity with cinema in its narration. In *The Time Machine*, for example, he describes the sensation of time travel as if from the perspective of a cinema spectator:

The laboratory got hazy and went dark. Mrs Watchett came in and walked, apparently without seeing me, towards the garden door. I suppose it took her a minute or so to traverse the place, but to me she seemed to shoot across the room like a rocket. I pressed the lever over to its extreme position. The night came like the turning of a lamp, and in another moment came tomorrow. The laboratory grew faint and hazy, then fainter and even fainter.[5]

One does not need to subscribe to the fashionable cult of Deleuze to recognize that cinema is based around temporal and spatial contraction. Wells's narration here anticipated such filmic devices as the fade and the dissolve, used to indicate temporal and/or spatial ellipsis, as well as the illusion of accelerated motion that results from changing the speed of the projector.

Indeed, *The Time Machine* was not only the first SF story but might have become the first SF film. The British pioneer R. W. Paul was quick to realize the cinematic potential of Wells's novel. Paul was a manufacturer of scientific instruments who turned to filmmaking when he was commissioned to produce films for Thomas Edison's kinetoscope. On 24 October 1895 Paul filed a patent application for a device he described as 'a novel form of exhibition whereby the spectators have presented to their view scenes which are supposed to occur in the future or past, while they are given the sensation of voyaging upon a machine through time'.[6] The idea was that spectators would stand on a platform with their attention directed towards a screen on which the films were being projected: it might be seen as a precursor of today's amusement park rides and attractions. It is probable that Wells collaborated with Paul on the 'Time Machine patent' – their retrospective accounts suggest this was so – though in the event it went no further than the drawing board.[7]

Wells is often described as the 'father of science fiction': the American writer Robert Silverberg, for example, called him 'the father of us all'.[8] He is certainly the most oft-filmed SF author: there have been over forty films based on Wells's stories.[9] In particular his novels of 'scientific romance' – *The Time Machine*, *The Island of Doctor Moreau*, *The Invisible Man*, *The War of the Worlds* and *The First Men in the Moon*, all published between 1895 and 1901 – have all been made into major motion pictures in Hollywood and Britain.[10] Unlike many intellectuals of his generation, Wells was interested in cinema and recognized its potential as a vehicle for communicating ideas: this would lead to his collaboration with Alexander Korda on the production of *Things to Come* in the 1930s. Other SF writers, however, have fared less well at the hands of the film industry. Isaac Asimov, for example, is represented only by a travesty of a film that borrows just the title of his seminal *I, Robot*.[11] Robert Heinlein, too, is represented by just one film, though at least

Paul Verhoeven captured something of the militaristic flavour of *Starship Troopers*.[12] There have been superior films of Richard Matheson's *I Am Legend* and *The Shrinking Man* and Ray Bradbury's *Fahrenheit 451*.[13] Of three major films adapted from Philip K. Dick – *Blade Runner*, *Total Recall* and *Minority Report* – only the first bears any resemblance to its source.[14] British writer John Wyndham has been well served by two films based on *The Midwich Cuckoos* – *Village of the Damned* and its sequel *Children of the Damned* – if rather less so by the film of *The Day of the Triffids*.[15] And several seminal works of science fiction remain unfilmed, including Karel Capek's *R.U.R.*, Aldous Huxley's *Brave New World* and Arthur C. Clarke's *Childhood's End* – though the producer George Pal toyed with the idea of filming all three – and series such as Isaac Asimov's *Foundation* trilogy and Ray Bradbury's *The Martian Chronicles*.[16]

Why has SF literature been so poorly served by the cinema? One reason is that until the mid-twentieth century the major form of SF literature was the short story rather than the novel. In addition to his half dozen novels of 'scientific romance', Wells wrote over eighty short stories between the 1880s and the 1920s. And the short story was also the favoured medium of the American 'pulp' magazines that popularized science fiction in the 1920s and 1930s. The most significant of the 'pulps' were *Amazing Stories* and *Science Wonder Stories*, both founded by Hugo Gernsback in the late 1920s, and *Astounding Stories*, founded in 1930, and which, from 1937, under editor John W. Campbell Jr, published early work by Isaac Asimov, Robert Heinlein, Clifford Simak and Theodore Sturgeon.[17] The short story is difficult to adapt for cinema as a feature film of around 90–120 minutes invariably requires padding out.[18] Another reason is that SF literature often focuses on speculative ideas and concepts that do not always translate well into the narrative medium of film. Wells himself recognized this. In his introduction to the published screenplay of the film *Things to Come* – which he adapted from his speculative 1933 book '*The Shape of Things to Come* is essentially an imaginative *discussion* of social and political forces and possibilities, and a film is no place for argument. The conclusions of that book are therefore taken for granted in this film, and a new story has been invented to display them.'[19]

While SF literature has dealt largely in ideas – some critics prefer the term 'speculative fiction' – SF cinema has followed a different trajectory. The history of SF cinema is inextricably linked with the history of film technology. More than any other genre, science fiction depends upon the technology of the medium: it relies upon special effects to create images of future civilizations and alien worlds. From the 'trick' films of Méliès to effects-driven blockbusters such as George Lucas's *Star Wars* (1977) and James Cameron's *Avatar* (2009), science fiction has always been at the cutting edge of film technology. As one critic put it: SF films 'reflect the technology that makes them possible'. [20] It has been suggested, however, that cinema's preference for spectacle has prevented it from engaging with the underlying ideas of science fiction. Barry Keith Grant, for example, argues that the prevalence of spectacle has 'been at the root of the genre's general failure to express fully the ideas and concepts found in the best science fiction literature'.[21]

The history of SF cinema can be divided into several periods or cycles. In the 1920s and 1930s there were very few major science fiction films. As those were products of different national cinemas – the Soviet Union (*Aelita*, 1924), Germany (*Metropolis*, 1926), America (*Just Imagine*, 1930) and Great Britain (*Things to Come*, 1936) – they cannot be said to constitute a cycle as such.[22] These films were all expensively produced and were notable for their detailed representation of futuristic urban spaces and ordered societies. They were also somewhat earnest and ponderous: critics admired their technical achievements but were less persuaded by their melodramatic narratives. At the other end of the production scale, however, science fiction flourished in Hollywood's serials (or 'chapter plays') of the 1930s and 1940s: *The Phantom Empire*, *The Lost City*, *Undersea Kingdom*, *Flash Gordon* (and its two sequels), *Buck Rogers*, *Brick Bradford*, *King of the Rocket Men* and *Captain Video*.[23] The serial represented an alternative mode of film practice produced with juvenile audiences in mind. Their sources were the 'pulps' and comic strips, and what they lacked in production values they made up for in zest and breathless pace. The emergence of television in the 1950s killed off the serials but they were remembered with affection. George Lucas's inspiration for *Star Wars* came from the *Flash Gordon* and *Buck Rogers* serials he saw as a child.

The first major cycle of SF films came from Hollywood in the 1950s. This period is now regarded as a 'golden age' of science fiction cinema with films including *Destination Moon*, *The Thing from Another World*, *The Day the Earth Stood Still*, *When Worlds Collide*, *The War of the Worlds*, *Invaders from Mars*, *It Came from Outer Space*, *20,000 Leagues Under the Sea*, *This Island Earth*, *Conquest of Space*, *Forbidden Planet*, *Invasion of the Body Snatchers*, *Journey to the Center of the Earth* and *The Time Machine*.[24] There were several reasons for the emergence of science fiction as a major production trend at this time. One was that science fiction was an ideal genre for the new technologies such as widescreen (*20,000 Leagues Under the Sea*, *Forbidden Planet*) and 3D (*It Came from Outer Space*) that the film industry turned to in its efforts to counter the rise of television. Another was that science fiction offered film-makers a medium for exploring the political and cultural anxieties of Cold War America. Peter Biskind remarks that the 1950s 'established that science fiction, whether in film or in the mainstream literature of the genre, could provide an important vehicle for articulating cultural anxieties and for commenting in a serious way on those concerns'.[25] These ranged from the right-wing fears of the Soviet Union expressed in the hawkish politics of some alien invasion films (*The Thing from Another World, Invaders from Mars*) to liberal tracts warning against the dangers of nuclear proliferation (*The Day the Earth Stood Still*) and ideological conformity in the face of McCarthyism (*Invasion of the Body Snatchers*). Other films prophesied catastrophe, whether from natural causes (*When Worlds Collide*) or atomic warfare (*This Island Earth*), while a cycle of 'creature features' (*The Beast from 20,000 Fathoms, Them!, It Came from Beneath the Sea*) warned against the possible effects of radiation and the consequences of nuclear testing.

Science fiction was less prominent in the 1960s, but the success of two major films in 1968 – *Planet of the Apes* and *2001: A Space Odyssey* – kick-started another cycle that lasted until the mid-1970s, including *The Forbin Project, THX 1138, The Andromeda Strain, Silent Running, The Omega Man, Slaughterhouse Five, Soylent Green, Westworld, Zardoz, Dark Star, Rollerball, Futureworld, The Man Who Fell to Earth* and *Logan's Run*. [26] The recurring motif of these films is a dehumanized, dystopian future where individual liberty and freedom of thought have been suppressed by technology. The pessimistic vision of the future in 1970s SF cinema has been understood as an expression of the mood of disillusion and despair that affected America following Vietnam and Watergate. Collectively these films marked a decisive shift away from the basically optimistic outlook that characterized SF cinema before the 1970s. The films were a mixed bag in terms of quality and popular appeal, though they all demonstrated, once again, how SF cinema functioned as a vehicle for social commentary.

The emergence of SF cinema as a mainstream genre coincided with the reformulation of the industrial practices and aesthetic strategies of the film industry that has been termed 'New Hollywood'.[27] Hitherto the received wisdom of the film industry was that science fiction was a marginal genre with limited appeal: even the one genuine blockbuster SF film prior to the late 1970s, *2001*, was regarded as something of an exception. However, the *annus mirabilis* for SF cinema was in 1977 when the extraordinary impact of two films – George Lucas's *Star Wars* and Steven Spielberg's *Close Encounters of the Third Kind* – transformed the prevailing view of the genre's popular appeal. *Star Wars* (with record-breaking domestic rentals of $193 million) and *Close Encounters of the Third Kind* ($84 million) became two of the most successful films in cinema history. Since then SF films have consistently been among the biggest-grossing films, including *E.T.: The Extra-Terrestrial, Jurassic Park, Independence Day, The Matrix, The War of the Worlds, Avatar* and the six *Star Wars* sequels and prequels.[28] These super-blockbusters, with their state-of-the-art film technology, represent the culmination of the trend towards the cinema of spectacle that had begun with Méliès: indeed the promotional discourses of these films usually focus on their special effects rather than their plots. The advances in film technology that have facilitated the rise of the SF blockbuster were themselves a consequence of the success of the genre: George Lucas founded the special effects company Industrial Light and Magic on the back of the profits of *Star Wars*.

There is of course an extensive body of critical literature on SF cinema. Much of the existing scholarship falls into one of two schools. One approach, exemplified by the work of John Baxter, John Brosnan and Christine Cornea, has been to map the history of the genre, identifying the major production trends and analysing the recurring themes.[29] Such histories tend to deal in broad brush strokes: they usually have little space for the detailed consideration of individual films and sometimes marginalize films that do not fit easily into wider thematic patterns and production trends. The other approach, exemplified by Brooks Landon, Vivian Sobchack and J. P. Telotte and in volumes edited by Annette Kuhn, Ziauddin Sardar and Sean Cubitt, draws upon the discourses of cultural theory: the modern and the postmodern, simulacra and hyper-reality, the self and the other, the human and the monstrous.[30] The emphasis here is often on close readings of films: but there is a tendency to return to the same narrow range of examples (*Alien, Blade Runner, The Terminator*) that best support a particular theoretical interpretation rather than expanding the field of enquiry. *Alien* and its sequels are also key points of reference in a growing body of feminist readings of SF cinema that focus on themes of gender politics and sexual difference.[31]

Projecting Tomorrow combines aspects of these two schools but is different from both. As in our previous book together, *Projecting Empire*, our approach is historical and case-study based.[32] We have selected a dozen SF films, mostly American but including several British examples to represent Britain's important contribution to the genre, from the 1930s to the early twenty-first century. Our examples include several classics of the genre but also some that have been marginalized or neglected in other histories. We have ranged across the full range of SF templates and themes, including the 'history of the future' (*Things to Come*), space travel and extra-terrestrial encounters (*Forbidden Planet, 2001*), the invasion narrative (*The War of the Worlds, The Quatermass Experiment*), space opera (*Star Wars*), planetary romance (*Avatar*), future apocalypse (*Planet of the Apes*), utopia/dystopia (*Logan's Run*), cyborgs (*RoboCop*), documentary (*The Hellstrom Chronicle*) and even an SF musical comedy (*Just Imagine*).[33] We have included films based (however loosely) on SF literature and films written specifically for the screen. Two of our case studies – *Things to Come* and *2001* – reveal what happened when leading SF writers (H. G. Wells and Arthur C. Clarke) were lured into collaborating with the film industry.

We do not claim that these are necessarily the best or the most historically significant SF films – though several, including *Things to Come*, *Forbidden Planet*, *2001* and *Star Wars* would undoubtedly be recognized as landmarks of the genre. Nevertheless all the films are of interest for their narrative and visual representations of the future (or as in the case of *Star Wars*, a technologically advanced mythical past) and for their role in shaping the genre. We could have written the book with an entirely different selection of case studies. An alternate list might include *The Day the Earth Stood Still*, *Invasion of the Body Snatchers*, *The Time Machine*, *Fahrenheit 451*, *THX 1138*, *The Omega Man*, *Westworld*, *Dark Star*, *Close Encounters of the Third Kind*, *Blade Runner*, *The Terminator* and *Starship Troopers*. Perhaps this is to anticipate a sequel: *Projecting Tomorrow 2*?

As film historians our methodology is that of empirical investigation and analysis. We seek to locate SF films in their historical contexts – industrial, economic, political, social, cultural – and to document their production and reception histories. To this end we have drawn upon a wide range of primary sources including scripts, studio records, personal papers, censors' reports, publicity materials, autobiographies, trade papers, and contemporary newspaper and journal reviews. In particular we are interested in how and why the films were as they were: this involves the sometimes conflicting inputs of producers, writers and directors, and a variety of other factors such as censorship policy, studio politics, and (as often as not) budgetary constraints. Our method therefore owes nothing to voguish trends in cultural theory and everything to the evidence of the archives. As with our previous study of the cinema of empire, *Projecting Tomorrow* shows how the content of films is shaped by the agencies involved in their production and the conditions under which they were made.

The theme that links all our case studies is how the futuristic narratives and images of SF cinema are determined by the circumstances of their production. It is often said that science fiction is as much about the present in which it is created as the future in which it is set: to this extent SF cinema functions in a similar way to the historical film as a commentary on the times in which it is produced and consumed. While this is hardly a new insight, it is one that hitherto has largely been taken for granted in both the historical and the theoretical literature. We would maintain that the truth of this assumption can be proven only through archival research and the nitty-gritty accounts of production and reception that are grist to the film historian's mill. *Projecting Tomorrow* therefore seeks to show how cinema's imagination of the future has also functioned as a mirror of the present.

Notes

[1] Kristin Thompson and David Bordwell, *Film History: An Introduction* (New York: McGraw-Hill, 1994), p.9.

[2] Harry M. Geduld (ed.), *The Definitive Time Machine: A Critical Edition of H. G. Wells's Scientific Romance* (Bloomington: Indiana University Press, 1987), pp.5–6.

[3] Ian Christie, *The Last Machine: Early Cinema and the Birth of the Modern World* (London: British Film Institute, 1994), p.65.

[4] Keith Williams, *H. G. Wells, Modernity and the Movies* (Liverpool: Liverpool University Press, 2007), p.1.

[5] H. G. Wells, *The Time Machine* (London: Penguin Classics, 2005 [1895]), pp.18–19.

[6] Quoted in Terry Ramsaye, *A Million and One Nights: A History of the Motion Picture* (New York: Simon and Schuster, 1926), p.155.

[7] Wells recalled the collaboration in his introduction to *The King Who Was A King: The Book of the Film* (London: Ernest Bell, 1929), p.10. See also John Barnes, *The Beginnings of the Cinema in England 1894–1901, Volume 1: 1894–1896* (Exeter: University of Exeter Press, rev. edn 1998), pp.38–41; and Williams, *H. G. Wells*, pp.24–31.

[8] Robert Silverberg, 'Introduction', in Glenn Yeffeth (ed.), *The War of the Worlds: Fresh Perspectives on the H. G. Wells Classic* (Dallas: Benbella, 2005), p.1. The Paramount DVD 'Special Collector's Edition' of the 1953 film *The War of the Worlds* includes a supporting documentary entitled *H. G. Wells: The Father of Science Fiction*.

[9] Don G. Smith, *H. G. Wells on Film: The Utopian Nightmare* (Jefferson NC: McFarland, 2002). Smith identifies forty-three theatrically released feature films based either directly or indirectly on Wells between 1909 and 1997. This figure includes adaptations of his social realist fiction such as *Kipps*, *The History of Mr Polly* and *The Passionate Friends*. See also Paul Jensen, 'H. G. Wells on the Screen', *Films in Review*, 18/9 (1969), pp.521–7.

[10] *The Time Machine* has been filmed twice, directed by George Pal for MGM in 1960 and by Simon Wells (Wells's great-grandson) for Warner Bros. in 2002. There have been three films of *The Island of Doctor Moreau*, directed by Erle C. Kenton for Paramount in 1932 (as *Island of Lost Souls*), by Don Taylor for American International Pictures in 1977 and by John Frankenheimer for New Line Cinema in 1996. *The Invisible Man* was directed by James Whale for Universal in 1933: there were four sequels in the 1940s (five if we include 1951's *Abbott and Costello Meet the Invisible Man*) that had little to do with Wells. There have been two theatrically released films of *The War of the Worlds*, directed by Byron Haskin for Paramount in 1953 and by Steven Spielberg for Dreamworks in 2005. *The First Men in the Moon* was directed by Nathan Juran for Columbia in 1964, and *The Food of the Gods* by Bert I. Gordon for AIP in 1976. *Sleeper* (Rollins-Joffe, dir. Woody Allen, 1973) is very loosely derived from *When the Sleeper Wakes*. In addition, feature films based on Wells's short stories include *The Man Who Could Work Miracles* (London Films, dir. Lothar Mendes, 1936) and *Empire of the Ants* (AIP, dir. Bert I. Gordon, 1977).

[11] *I, Robot* (20th Century-Fox, dir. Alex Proyas, 2004).

[12] *Starship Troopers* (Buena Vista, dir. Paul Verhoeven, 1997).

[13] The three films of *I Am Legend* are *The Last Man on Earth* (AIP, dirs. Ubaldo Ragana and Sidney Salkow, 1964), *The Omega Man* (Warner Bros., dir. Boris Sagal, 1971) and *I Am Legend* (Warner Bros., dir. Francis Lawrence, 2007); *The Shrinking Man* was filmed as *The Incredible Shrinking Man* (Universal, dir. Jack Arnold, 1957); *Fahrenheit 451* was filmed under its own title by François Truffaut for Anglo-Enterprise in 1966.

[14] *Blade Runner* (Warner Bros., dir. Ridley Scott, 1982) was an adaptation of Dick's novel *Do Androids Dream of Electric Sheep?*; *Total Recall* (Carolco, dir. Paul Verhoeven, 1990)

was supposedly based on his short story 'We Can Remember It for You Wholesale'; and *Minority Report* (Dreamworks, dir. Steven Spielberg, 2002) was based on a story of the same title.

15 *Village of the Damned* (MGM, dir. Wolf Rilla, 1960); *Children of the Damned* (MGM, dir. Anton M. Leader, 1963); *The Day of the Triffids* (Philip Yordan, dir. Steve Sekely, 1963).

16 The BBC dramatized *R.U.R.* (*Rossum's Universal Robots*) in 1938 and again in 1948: these were live broadcasts and no longer exist. There have been two television films of *Brave New World*: by Universal in 1980 with Keir Dullea (*2001: A Space Odyssey*) as Grambell and for USA Network in 1998 with *Star Trek*'s Leonard Nimoy as Mond. In 2008 it was announced that Ridley Scott would direct a film of *Brave New World* with Leonardo di Caprio: at the time of writing this project seems to have stalled. NBC produced a three-episode television mini-series of *The Martian Chronicles* in 1980.

17 See Gary Westfahl, *Hugo Gernsback and the Century of Science Fiction* (Jefferson NC: McFarland, 2007).

18 In contrast short SF stories proved a fertile ground for television anthology dramas in the 1950s and 60s. The British series *Out of This World* (ABC, 1962) and *Out of the Unknown* (BBC2, 1965–71) included adaptations of Isaac Asimov, Ray Bradbury, Frederick Pohl and John Wyndhan. In America Richard Matheson wrote several episodes of *The Twilight Zone* (1959–64), and Harlan Ellison contributed to *The Outer Limits* (1963–5).

19 H. G. Wells, *Things to Come: A Film by H. G. Wells* (New York: Macmillan, 1935), p.viii.

20 J. P. Telotte, *Science Fiction Film* (Cambridge: Cambridge University Press, 2001), p.25. The argument is best developed by Garrett Stewart, 'The "Videology" of Science Fiction', in George E. Slussen and Eric S. Rabbin (eds), *Shadows of the Magic Lamp: Fantasy and Science Fiction in Film* (Carbondale: Southern Illinois University Press, 1985), pp.159–207.

21 Barry K. Grant, 'Looking Upward: H. G. Wells, Science Fiction and the Cinema', *Literature/Film Quarterly*, 14: 3 (1986), p.154.

22 *Aelita* (Mezhrabpom, dir. Yakov Protazanov, 1924); *Metropolis* (UFA, dir. Fritz Lang, 1926); *Just Imagine* (Fox, dir. David Butler, 1930); *Things to Come* (London Films, dir. William Cameron Menzies, 1936).

23 *The Phantom Empire* (Mascot, dirs. Otto Brauer & B. Reeves Eason, 1935); *The Lost City* (Krellberg, dir. Harry Revier, 1935); *Undersea Kingdom* (Republic, dirs. B. Reeves Eason & Joseph Kane, 1936); *Flash Gordon* (Universal, dir. Frederick Stephani, 1936); *Flash Gordon's Trip to Mars* (Universal, dirs. Ford Beebe & Robert Hill, 1938); *Buck Rogers* (Universal, dirs. Ford Beebe & Saul A. Goodkind, 1939); *Flash Gordon Conquers the Universe* (Universal, dirs. Ford Beebe & Ray Taylor, 1940); *Brick Bradford* (Columbia, dir. Spencer G. Bennett, 1947); *King of the Rocket Men* (Republic, dir. Fred Brannon, 1949); *Captain Video* (Columbia, dir. Spencer G. Bennett & Wallace Grissel, 1951).

24 *Destination Moon* (George Pal, dir. Irving Pichel, 1950); *The Day the Earth Stood Still* (20th Century-Fox, dir. Robert Wise, 1951); *The Thing from Another World* (RKO, dir. Christian Nyby, 1951); *When Worlds Collide* (Paramount, dir. Rudolph Maté, 1951); *The War of the Worlds* (Paramount, dir. Byron Haskin, 1953); *Invaders from Mars* (Edward L. Alperson, dir. William Cameron Menzies, 1953); *It Came from Outer Space* (Universal, dir. Jack Arnold, 1953); *20,000 Leagues Under the Sea* (Disney, dir. Richard Fleischer, 1954); *This Island Earth* (Universal, dir. Joseph Newman, 1955); *Conquest of Space* (Paramount, dir. Byron Haskin, 1955); *Forbidden Planet* (MGM, dir. Fred M. Wilcox, 1956); *Invasion of the Body Snatchers* (Allied Artists, dir. Don Siegel, 1956); *Journey to the Center of the Earth* (20th Century-Fox, dir. Henry Levin, 1959); *The Time Machine* (MGM, dir. George Pal, 1960).

25 Peter Biskind, *Seeing is Believing: How Hollywood Taught Us to Stop Worrying and Love the Fifties* (London: Pluto Press, 1984), p.127. See also Susan Sontag's widely-cited essay

'The Imagination of Disaster', in which she argues that 1950s SF films both 'reflect world-wide anxieties and ... serve to allay them'. Sontag, *Against Interpretation and Other Essays* (New York: Dell, 1966), pp.212–28.

[26] *Planet of the Apes* (20th Century-Fox, dir. Franklin J. Schaffner, 1968); *2001: A Space Odyssey* (MGM, dir. Stanley Kubrick, 1968); *The Forbin Project* (aka *Colossus: The Forbin Project*, Universal, dir. Joseph Sargent, 1969); *THX 1138* (Warner Bros., dir. George Lucas, 1970); *The Andromeda Strain* (Universal, dir. Robert Wise, 1970); *Silent Running* (Universal, dir. Douglas Trumbull, 1971); *The Omega Man* (Warner Bros., dir. Boris Sagal, 1971); *Slaughterhouse Five* (Universal, dir. George Roy Hill, 1972); *Soylent Green* (MGM, dir. Richard Fleischer, 1973); *Westworld* (MGM, dir. Michael Crichton, 1973); *Zardoz* (20th Century-Fox, dir. John Boorman, 1974); *Dark Star* (Jack H. Harris, dir. John Carpenter, 1974); *Rollerball* (United Artists, dir. Norman Jewison, 1975); *Futureworld* (AIP, dir. Richard T. Heffron, 1976); *The Man Who Fell to Earth* (British Lion, dir. Nicolas Roeg, 1976); *Logan's Run* (MGM, dir. Michael Anderson, 1976).

[27] See Geoff King, *Spectacular Narratives: Hollywood in the Age of the Blockbuster* (London: I.B.Tauris, 2000); Peter Krämer, *New Hollywood: From Bonnie and Clyde to Star Wars* (London: Wallflower Press, 2005).

[28] *Star Wars* (20th Century-Fox, dir. George Lucas, 1977); *Close Encounters of the Third Kind* (Columbia/EMI, dir. Steven Spielberg, 1977); *E.T.: The Extra-Terrestrial* (Universal, dir. Steven Spielberg, 1982); *Jurassic Park* (Universal, dir. Steven Spielberg, 1993); *Independence Day* (20th Century-Fox, dir. Roland Emmerich,1996); *The Matrix* (Warner Bros., dirs. Larry & Andy Wachowski, 1999); *The War of the Worlds* (Dreamworks, dir. Steven Spielberg, 2005); *Avatar* (20th Century-Fox, dir. James Cameron, 2009). *Star Wars* prompted two sequels – *The Empire Strikes Back* (dir. Irvin Kerschner, 1980) and *Return of the Jedi* (dir. Richard Marquand, 1983) – and three prequels, all directed by Lucas: *The Phantom Menace* (1999), *Attack of the Clones* (2002) and *Revenge of the Sith* (2005). Other big-budget SF films produced in the wake of the *Star Wars* 'boom' included *Star Trek: The Motion Picture* (Paramount, dir. Robert Wise, 1979), *The Black Hole* (Disney, dir. Gary Nelson, 1979) and *Flash Gordon* (Dino de Laurentiis, dir. Mike Hodges, 1980).

[29] John Baxter, *Science Fiction in the Cinema* (London: Zwemmer, 1970); John Brosnan, *Future Tense: The Cinema of Science Fiction* (Macdonald and Jane's, 1978); Christine Cornea, *Science Fiction Cinema: Between Fantasy and Reality* (Edinburgh: Edinburgh University Press, 2007). See also Phil Hardy (ed.), *The Aurum Film Encyclopedia: Science Fiction* (London: Aurum Press, 1985). Other works that touch on science fiction from a historical perspective include Christopher Frayling, *Mad, Bad and Dangerous? The Scientist and the Cinema* (London: Reaktion, 2005) and Andrew Tudor, *Monsters and Mad Scientists: A Cultural History of the Horror Movie* (Oxford: Blackwell, 1989).

[30] Brooks Landon, *The Aesthetics of Ambivalence: Rethinking Science Fiction Film in the Age of Electronic (Re)production* (Westport: Greenwood Press, 1992); Vivian Sobchack, *Screening Space: The American Science Fiction Film* (New York: Ungar, 1987); J. P. Telotte, *Replications: A Robotic History of the Science Fiction Film* (Urbana: University of Illinois Press, 1995); Annette Kuhn (ed.), *Alien Zone: Cultural Theory and Contemporary Science Fiction Cinema* (London: Verso, 1990); Annette Kuhn (ed.), *Alien Zone II: The Spaces of Science Fiction Cinema* (London: Verso, 1999); Ziauddin Sardar and Sean Cubitt (eds), *Aliens R Us: The Other in Science Fiction Cinema* (London: Pluto Press, 2002). See also Sean Redmond (ed.), *Liquid Metal: The Science Fiction Film Reader* (London: Wallflower Press, 2004) and Gregg Rickman (ed.), *The Science Fiction Film Reader* (New York: Limelight Editions, 2002).

[31] Barbara Creed, *The Monstrous Feminine: Film, Feminism, Psychoanalysis* (London: Routledge, 1993); Mary Jacobus, Evelyn Fox Keller and Sally Shuttleworth (eds), *Body/*

Politics: Women and the Discourses of Science (London: Routledge, 1990); Patricia Melzer, *Alien Constructions: Science Fiction and Feminist Thought* (Austin: University of Texas Press, 2006).

32 James Chapman and Nicholas J. Cull, *Projecting Empire: Imperialism and Popular Cinema* (London: I.B.Tauris, 2009).

33 These categories are adapted from those outlined in David Pringle (ed.), *The Ultimate Encyclopedia of Science Fiction* (London: Carlton, 1996), pp.21–61.

1

DRY FUTURE: *JUST IMAGINE* (1930)

The city shone. Gleaming white towers formed broad avenues laid out with ribbons of garden. Bridges arched gracefully between the ranks of buildings, carrying trains and speeding lines of automobiles; some streets plunged into tunnels through the larger towers. Between the skyscrapers neat formations of aircraft crisscross the city. We notice two single-seat monoplanes in particular. They pull to a standstill and hover next to each other using propellers mounted horizontally in the wing. The young male pilot of one jumps onto his wing and hops nimbly across onto the wing of the other. A young woman smiles up from the controls and the action begins...

It was a scene unlike anything in American motion pictures to that point. A vision of a possible future realized with a level of detail had been seen only once previously, in Fritz Lang's lavish German masterpiece *Metropolis* (1927). This was the first sight of the future New York in Fox Metrotone's *Just Imagine*, the film with the distinction of being Hollywood's first major SF film. Here for the first time were many elements that would become commonplace in the decades to come, the most obvious being contemporary comment. *Just Imagine* was a genre piece before the cinematic genre had fully formed: a paradox that led to a flurry of allegations of plagiarism from writers who considered themselves to be the only possible originators of its ideas. Other films would seek to impress the audience with lavish spectacles of the future and space travel, and beguile them with speculation in risqué fashions in the future, but *Just Imagine* would remain unique in one regard: it would be the only SF musical.

The origins of *Just Imagine* lie not in America's traditions of experimental fiction or genuine social or scientific speculation, but on that familiar epicentre of American fantasy: Broadway. *Just Imagine* plundered the emerging aesthetics of the imagined future to serve the ends of musical entertainment and make a political point – satirizing Prohibition – along the way. It was the creation of Fox Metrotone studios and the highly successful team of lyricists Buddy DeSylva and Lew Brown and composer Ray Henderson.[1] Individually, each of the three had already made a mark with songs that became part of the American landscape. The team first came together on Broadway in 1925. Their collective output included standards like 'Button up your Overcoat', songs showcasing African-American entertainers including 'Black Bottom', and songs for 'Minstrel' entertainers like Al Jolson for whom they wrote 'Sonny Boy'. In October 1929 they scored a massive hit with the film musical *Sunny Side Up* for Fox. It was a cheerful 'cross town' romance set in New York City. Tunes included the highly hum-able title song 'Keep your Sunny Side Up'. The director of *Sunny Side Up*, David Butler, attracted attention with mobile camera work and experimental colour sequences. The film's real success lay in its being available at the very moment that the bottom dropped out of the American economy. It became America's escape from the Wall Street Crash. The film did well enough to guarantee studio demand for a swift follow-up. The follow-up would become *Just Imagine*.

In seeking to repeat the success of *Sunny Side Up*, DeSylva, Brown and Henderson sought an amalgam of the previous film's successful elements: music, romance and comedy. The new future setting added a dose of escapist fantasy. It was a promising strategy to show a comfortable future in the midst of a distressed present. Studio documents reveal that *Just Imagine* was a pet project of DeSylva particularly. He had long since noticed the potential for a musical set in the future – some of the ideas seen in *Just Imagine* were road-tested on stage in *The George White Scandals* of 1926. In fact he recalled raising the idea of a 'futuristic musical comedy' when he first began contract negotiations with Fox studio executive Sol Wurtzel, long before *Sunny Side Up*.[2]

The core plot of *Just Imagine* concerned a standard pair of lovers divided, but that still left the need for comic relief. In *Sunny Side Up* the humour had been provided by one of the most popular screen comedians of the era, El Brendel, who played the poor girl's downstairs neighbour Eric Swenson. The new film would place his talents front and centre. Brendel was a dialect comedian whose screen persona was a hapless thickly-accented Swede with a propensity for phrases like 'yumping yiminy'. Born in Philadelphia from a German/Irish family, Brendel had begun a career in vaudeville in 1913 with a German dialect routine. With the wave of anti-German feeling that surged across America during the Great War, Brendel judiciously evolved his Swedish persona and prospered, performing with his wife Flo Bert. The humour was gentle and played on the anxieties of an immigrant nation whose citizens found understandable release in laughing at someone less adjusted to life in the new world than themselves.[3] The same dynamic was

1. The city of 1980 as realized for *Just Imagine* (1930)
(Source: British Film Institute).

seen at work in the 'greenhorn' tradition in Jewish comedy.[4] By 1921 Brendel
was a regular on Broadway. His success was such that even before the
coming of sound he had a contract in Hollywood, joining Famous Players in
1926. He signed with Fox in 1929. In the wake of *The Jazz Singer* Brendel was
ideally placed to exploit the new technology with its demand for amusing
audio to match the pictures. His speaking roles included the rookie flyer
turned mechanic Herman Schwimpf in *Wings* (1927) and in 1930, the comic
role of Gus the Swede in *The Big Trail* (1930).[5] In *Just Imagine* Brendel played
an Everyman from the present revived fifty years in the future – a take on
the familiar idea of the sleeper waking in the future familiar from Edward
Bellamy's utopian novel of 1888 *Looking Backward* or William Morris's
British response *News From Nowhere* (1890), or H. G. Wells's *When the Sleeper
Wakes* of 1899. There was no particular plot reason for making him a Swede,
though the characterization made a certain sense if one imagined a modern
man fifty years adrift in time as the ultimate greenhorn immigrant.

The most exciting element of *Just Imagine* would be its future city
settings. These were the work of the set designer and art director, a former
architect named Stephen Goosson. As James Sanders has noted, Goosson
drew inspiration from the work of the late Italian futurist Antonio Sant'

Elia, the New York architect Harvey Wiley Corbett and most especially the drawings that Corbett commissioned from Hugh Ferriss, which reached a wider public as a result of his book of illustrations, *Metropolis of Tomorrow*, which appeared in 1929.[6] These influences had already shaped Fritz Lang's *Metropolis*. With an unprecedented budget and a dirigible hanger in Arcadia, California to work in, Goosson, together with the mechanical effects director Ralph Hammeras and their team, began the process of creating the city of the future. The fan magazine *Photoplay* reported:

> It took 205 engineers and craftsmen five months to build it, at a cost of $168,000…. It was designed after long conferences with noted artists and scientists who dare to peer far into the future. Seventy-four 5,000,000 candle power sun arcs light the set from above. Fifteen thousand electric light bulbs illuminate its buildings and streets.[7]

The production was complex. The scenes set on Mars required casting multiple sets of identical twins. The film needed elaborate costumes, sets, miniature work and the brand new process of back projection, which worried studio managers. A studio lawyer wrote anxiously to Wurtzel:

> It is my understanding that plans are being made for some trick photography in the new Butler production. If this is the case, I think that we should be sure what method is going to be used and whether or not we are laying ourselves open to any claim for damages by reason of existing patents.[8]

The production was apparently fairly uneventful. When interviewed in his later years the director's only major recollection concerned the leading man John Garrick being stranded above the set in his mock-up aircraft during an earthquake.[9]

Just Imagine began with a preface in invoking the world of fifty years previously – 1880 – it depicted a sleepy street corner in horse-drawn New York City and then flashed forward to the same corner in 1930 following a hapless jaywalker and his attempt to cross the street without being hit by a car. With the distance to the past established, a narrator invited the audience to 'Just Imagine' the world of fifty years into the future: 'If the last fifty years made such a change, *just imagine* the New York of 1980 … when everyone has a number instead of a name and the government tells you whom you should marry. *Just Imagine* … 1980!' The scene shifts to the skies above the future New York where two lovers hovering in adjacent aircraft steal a conversation. The young man, an airline pilot named J-21 (John Garrick), has bad news for the woman LN-18 (Maureen O'Sullivan); the state marriage tribunal has ruled against his petition to marry her and instead favoured her father's choice, an obnoxious newspaper proprietor named MT-3 (Kenneth Thompson), on the grounds that MT-3 has achieved more in his life. J-21's appeal date is set for four months' time.

Later, at home, J-21 confides his despair to his friend RT-42 (Frank Albertson). As a distraction, RT-42 and his girlfriend D-6 (Marjorie White) take J-21 to witness a medical experiment at D-6's place of work: the revival of man who has been dead since he was struck by lightning on a golf course in 1930. At the lab they find an astonishing array of technology and ranks of impassive scientists. A mysterious ray revives the corpse (El Brendel) but the scientists have no further plans for the man and even offer to kill him again. Concerned, J-21 volunteers to help him find his feet in the new world. Noting that he predates the alpha-numeric naming schema of the day, they resolve to call him 'Single O'.

Single O is disoriented by the sights of 1980, though fascinated by the revealing women's fashions. When he realizes that food has been replaced by one kind of pill and illicit cocktails by another, he mourns 'give me the good old days'. He makes the same remark when he sees a couple obtain a baby from a vending machine rather than through the traditional method.[10] He cheers himself up by getting drunk on pills.

MT-3 forces LN-18 to reject J-21 and he wanders the city alone. A mysterious stranger finds him and offers to give the flyer his heart's desire. J-21 is taken to meet a great inventor named Z4 (Hobart Bosworth), who reveals that he is looking for someone to pilot his rocket plane to Mars. J-21 recognizes his opportunity to distinguish himself beyond MT-3 and thereby get the court to rule in his favour. RT-42 agrees to join him as his co-pilot and the flyers celebrate their departure with an illicit drinking party on the airship Pegasus. They go to the launch site. As their rocket blasts away from earth Single O emerges as stowaway, under the impression that he was going to J-21's 'Ma's' rather than the planet Mars.

Landing on Mars a month later, the three friends encounter exotically costumed Martians, many of whom appear to be dancing girls. They are welcomed by the Martian queen, Loo Loo (Joyzelle Joyner). Single O is befriended by a large, camp, Martian male named Boko (Ivan Linow). The Earthmen are entertained to a bath and a show by performing Martian monkeys. As the show reaches its climax, they are attacked and captured by a second group of Martians led by Boo Boo (also Joyzelle Joyner) and Loko (also Ivan Linow), who are the physical doubles of the first. J-21 realizes that every Martian has an evil twin who becomes part of a parallel hostile civilization. The three Earthmen are flogged into jail by Martian girls and witness a ritual 'victory dance' in front of an idol. J-21 realizes that time is

2. Rocket to Mars: the spacecraft from *Just Imagine* (1930) later recycled for *Flash Gordon* (1936) and other projects (Source: British Film Institute).

running out to get back to Earth for his appeal tribunal, but fortunately Boko springs them from jail. After a chase, which entails much confusion between Boko and his evil double, Single O saves the day and carries his friends to freedom. They blast off for the return journey and make it back to earth just in time for J-21's court hearing. Recognizing that J-21 has proved his worth, the judge grants his marriage license. A bearded old man appears, claiming to be Single O's son. With a delighted paternal cry of 'climb up on my knee sonny boy' Single O whisks the old man onto his lap and they strike a final tableau before the end title.

Just Imagine was built to be a stage for contemporary comment. Its core objective was to satirize Prohibition. Congress had passed the constitutional amendment to control the sale of alcohol in the United States in 1919 and given it draconian reach through the Volstead Act of the same year, which banned the sale of almost all intoxicating drink. By 1930 Prohibition had little credibility. Because the law outlawed the sale of even fairly weak beer and wine it seemed unfairly indiscriminate. It had plainly created an opportunity for organized crime and was regularly flouted by people who were supposed to be the guardians of public morals. Pressure groups campaigned for a change as ardently as their forebears had called for restrictions. The issue of alcohol was introduced in the first seconds of the film. The flashback to 1880 concludes with a drunk exiting a bar and the narrator's comment 'We also had this ...' Waking in 1980 Single O is amazed to learn that Prohibition is still in effect. RT-42 promises, 'It looks like in a year or two we're going to get a little light wine and beer', which Single O notes was also the expectation in 1930. Single O swiftly takes to the intoxicating pills that are the alcohol substitute for many in 1980. It is clear that the law is still routinely flouted. At the party on the Pegasus the assembled pilots sing their drinking song with the refrain: 'If they want the world dry, we'll obey/we'll just drink it that way.' More than this, the marriage law subplot is also a comment on Prohibition in as much as it is a case of government over-reaching and intruding in the personal lives of its citizens, rendered on an absurd scale. The link is explicit. When RT-42 complains about the law to a government census official, she strikes a pose and declares: 'Like the Volstead Act, it is a noble experiment ...' borrowing the famous phrase that President Herbert Hoover had used to defend the legislation while running for the White House in 1928.[11] *Just Imagine* can be seen as a part of the death-throws of Prohibition: making the point when criticism of that law could be a subject for mainstream popular culture, and the flouting of that law could be depicted as the routine practice of the sympathetic characters.

Prohibition was not the only element of life in 1930 to attract comment. *Just Imagine* also dealt with anxieties around gender relations at the start of the 1930s. This is explicit in an early scene in which a female census inspector comes to call (as 1980, like 1930, is a census year). She is an officious, uniformed older woman. RT-42 speaks of his dislike for 'modern women' and teases her. J-21 responds by singing of his longing for an old-fashioned girl: 'the type that blossomed fifty years ago', RT-42 dreamily imagines a succession of flappers shaking a cocktail, abandoning resistance to a kiss and simultaneously smoking and reading a book entitled 'Ex-Wife' (which itself is suggestive), while rocking the cradle with her foot. There are interesting hints at concern over technology intruding into reproduction. RT-42 tells the census taker that his parents were General Electric because he was an incubator baby. Later, Single O witnesses the baby delivered by vending machine.

There were other in-jokes about the politics of the period. When Single O learns that the cars and planes of the era all have obviously Jewish names – Rosenblatt, Pinkus and Goldfarbs – he quips 'It looks like someone got even with Henry Ford.' The remark turns on Ford's notorious anti-Semitism.[12] Unfortunately, the car names are the only indication of social diversity in the future. The Irish are still cops. All the scientists are old white and male with the exception of one who appears to be Japanese. No Black faces are seen.

The film may be pessimistic about government but it is unflinchingly optimistic about technology, not least because it promises that science might someday have the power to resurrect the dead. [13] Lesser innovations promised include videophones, video door viewers, beds and sinks that fold away. The ubiquity of aircraft in *Just Imagine* is very much of its era, with aviator Charles Lindbergh attaining an unprecedented celebrity following his solo Atlantic flight in 1927. *Just Imagine* traced such preoccupations into the future making aviation common place and obliging transatlantic pilot J-21 to venture into space in order to accomplish a Lindbergh-type breakthrough. We are told that everything else has been done.

Although the film mixes science fiction with humour, the humour is not at the expense of science fiction. Despite its heritage in literature with H.G. Wells and Jules Verne, the genre was not well enough established in film for the film to joke about its conventions. The world created within the film is treated fairly seriously with only limited use of the alpha-numeric names for puns.[14] The general approach is to have fun with the oddness of 1930 in 1980s eyes and 1980 to 1930s eyes and – no less – have fun with the similarities, as when Single O remarks: 'So women are still causing trouble? You'd have thought in fifty years they'd have found a good substitute for them.'[15] There are elements of the film that are designed to be funny in their own terms: El Brendel 'shtick' sometimes has nothing to do with the setting, as when he interrupts the action to deliver the comic monologue 'The Romance of Elmer Stremingway', which involves the rapid changing of hats. There is humour in the film's songs – sometimes quite racy humour as when D-6 and RT-42 urge their audience to 'Never swat a fly ...' because 'they want to make hay, hay the way I do ...'. Finally, DeSylva, Brown and Henderson can't resist in-jokes. The drunken Single-O sings a snatch of their song 'Sunny Side Up', and his final line 'Climb on my knee Sonny Boy' echoes the famous first line of their Al Jolson hit.

With the film complete Fox ran into a snag: how exactly to market a film so unlike anything seen before. The studio publicity material for *Just Imagine* avoided comment on the Prohibition element in the story, and made no promise of great comic or musical value beyond allusions to the success of *Sunny Side Up*. Instead they aimed for the lowest common denominator. The suggested tag lines in studio publicity include: '*Just Imagine* the necking, kissing, petting technique of 1980' and '*Just Imagine* youth on wings ... making love in the skies.' 'Get a load of this advance course in love making, sky-rocketing and thrill-hunting ... See what the girls will wear fifty years from now. Do you blush easily?'[16] Audiences wooed into the theatre by such come-ons would have been disappointed, more especially once America's censors had set to work on the film.

Just Imagine had one last hurdle before its distribution: the would-be moral guardians at the Motion Picture Distributors Association of America. As of 1930 the MPDAA was renewing efforts to pull film production into line promulgating a revised Production Code in February of that year. Their preview of *Just Imagine* left them a little uncomfortable. A memo written after the premiere of 10 October suggested that while the picture as a whole was 'quite delightful in its spontaneous fun' the studio might still usefully use the interval before its distribution to trim some of the cheekier scenes.[17] On 18 October Colonel Wilson from the Production Code Administration (PCA), wrote to Fox with suggestions for 'reconsideration' and a list of elements that were likely to be censored by local boards. His most substantial objections were to the 'Never Swat a Fly' number with its suggestive lines like: 'an ant may like to but it can't', close-ups of skimpy costumes, certain dance movements, and the gags around the character Boko/Loko on Mars:

> The line in which Single O says: 'She is not the queen, he is', after taking one look at Loko [*sic*], will probably be eliminated because of its implication. It is possible, too that some of the censors may want to eliminate from Loko's actions that which seems to make it appear that he is 'queer'.[18]

A further viewing in November raised further worries about the Mars sequences. Martians were shown at one point using nose thumbing as a greeting – a gesture that the PCA felt inappropriate for repeat viewing.[19] As predicted, many local censorship boards made substantial cuts. Targets included various combinations of cut multiple shots of skimpy garments on Earth and Mars, suggestive dance moves, the nose thumbing and the biggest laugh: Brendel's 'give me the good old days' response to seeing a baby arrive from a vending machine.[20] Major cuts to the version screened in New York included the risqué 'Never Swat a Fly' song. *Variety* felt that the film was much weaker as a result.[21] While the studio held out against the production code office's worries for several months, in December they finally agreed to make a number of cuts to render the film acceptable for screening to the Motion Picture Academy.[22]

The critical reaction was mixed. The *Los Angeles Evening Express* heralded the film as 'epochal', arguing that it 'Opens up new vistas of the power of the camera drama to release the ideas of authors for new flights…Its daring as an innovation never fails to arouse admiration.'[23] *Film Daily* hailed a 'wow comedy novelty, refreshing futuristic concoction packed with fanciful surprises and humor'.[24] The *Los Angeles Times* told readers: 'You daren't miss it.'[25] *Variety*, however, was underwhelmed, mourning that despite the engaging premise, the film failed to deliver. Its reviewer felt that the 'tunes' were 'not strong' and concluded: '*Just Imagine* cost heavy and is going to need impressive publicity outlay to help it on its way.'[26] The film performed disappointingly. It lasted only a week at its New York venue – The Roxy.

Explaining its early departure in his enthusiastic review for the *New York Times*, Mordaunt Hall reported: 'It is said that it did not find favor with the generation hovering around the twenties because a believable romance was absent.'[27]

During production, the Fox legal team had worried that they might be sued for patent violation over the innovative technical processes used. No such suits were filed, but the studio ran into a different sort of legal difficulty, which illuminates the novelty of the film's subject matter in 1930. Shortly after its release a writer named David Halperin sued Fox for $50,000 alleging that *Just Imagine* plagiarized his unproduced play *Starlight Gables*, which he claimed he had submitted to the studio the previous spring.[28] An internal investigation at the studio found that no one remotely connected with the production had seen this script but that a professional reader named Leonard Spiegelgass who sometimes worked for Fox had examined it as a favour to the author, rejected it but sent it on to MGM just to soften the blow.[29] Halperin's play (which survives in the studio's legal files) was a lacklustre work in which the inventor of a rocket called the Lunamobile receives a blow on the head from criminals and dreams that his craft makes a crazy trip to Mars. The script included excruciating personifications of the stars and planets.[30] Halperin claimed multiple similarities to the Fox film, including 'ultra-modernistic scenic effects' and a climax on Mars as he 'visualized and imagined, subjectively and perceptively, that planet to be'. He even claimed that the costumes and physique of Martians had been plagiarized from him. Quite apart from the *Just Imagine* team's complete ignorance of Halperin or his work, most of these elements were what would soon be recognized as standard conventions of the science fiction genre: a cigar shaped space vehicle, 'ultra-modern' setting and skimpy costumes for alien girls, rather than Halperin's own invention. On the idea of a trip to Mars, one Fox legal executive noted: 'the mere idea of a trip to Mars is an old one and has been repeatedly used in fiction since the days of Jules Verne'. He was able to recall prior use of the idea in film, noting: 'Universal released a picture in 1922 entitled *HELLO MARS* which deals with the adventures on that planet of a group of aviators.'[31] Another executive observed: 'There is utterly no similarity between Halperin's script and our picture excepting that a so-called "Lunamobile" in his story flies to Mars.' He concluded: 'This, of course, is such an ancient idea for use in fiction that I do not see any possibility of his being able to recover anything from Fox Film Corporation.'[32]

The Fox team had a brief moment of anxiety when it was pointed out that Halperin's script included reference to twins on Mars, but they were reassured to realize that this was simply a gag about Martian children all looking alike rather than a central focus of the culture in the same way as *Just*

Imagine's Jekyll and Hyde set-up. David Butler explained that he had devised the idea of twins on Mars as an easy way to suggest alienness 'to avoid expense of creating "eight-legged horses," strange animals and people, etc. etc'.[33] Full of confidence, the Fox team prepared to place both Butler and the film's originator Buddy DeSylva on the stand. The case never got to court. The existence of two other plagiarism complaints suggests that Halperin was not the only writer who could not tell where generic convention ended and their own creativity began.[34] The case opens fascinating questions of the understanding of genre at this juncture in Hollywood history.[35] As will be seen, the issue of originality would recur half a century later.

Just Imagine did not deliver the spectacular results that its creators had hoped for. It received Oscar nominations for Goosson and Hammeras for art direction, but lost (like many other nominees that year) to the RKO's epic Western *Cimarron*. In retrospect, the film was hardly deserving of great success. Its comedy was awkward and the romance painfully mechanical. The songs were not DeSylva, Brown and Henderson's best. The Martian sequences did not match the standard of the earlier scenes. The real star of the film – the elaborate cityscape – only appeared for a couple of seconds at the opening and then returned briefly later. Though the film soon disappeared from theatres, its aesthetics lived on in another way: Fox loaned out props and stock footage to other projects, including the serials of the later 1930s. The rocket miniature, some effects outtakes and the Martian idol sequence reappeared in *Flash Gordon* (1936) and *Flash Gordon Conquers the Universe* (1940), and the cityscape was seen in *Buck Rogers* (1939). In this way, glimpses of *Just Imagine* became part of the mainstream of American SF history.[36]

Despite its modest showing at the box office, the careers of the principal creative figures associated with the picture flourished. All had their contracts renewed at Fox.[37] Buddy DeSylva went on to be a co-founder of Capitol Records along with Johnny Mercer. In the 1950s DeSylva, Brown and Henderson were given the compliment of a Hollywood musical biopic of their careers called *The Best Things in Life Are Free* directed by Michael Curtiz. Their music lives on in the 'standard' repertoire though none of the *Just Imagine* songs remain in circulation. David Butler's later films included many Shirley Temple vehicles, and *Calamity Jane* (1953). Goosson became a great master of Hollywood art direction. His greatest triumph was to create the mythic realm of Shangri La for *Lost Horizon* (1937) at Columbia, for which he received an Academy Award. In contrast, of the *Just Imagine* cast, only Maureen O'Sullivan achieved real stardom – as Jane to Johnny Weissmuller's Tarzan in *Tarzan the Ape Man* (1932) and in subsequent films. El Brendel continued his unlikely career for many years ending as a guest star in 1960s TV.

Just Imagine dropped from view and was considered 'lost', becoming a legend among aficionados who knew it only from stills. The screening of the rediscovered film in the golden age of science fiction in the 1970s was something of an anticlimax. As 1980 approached, the studio had only a couple of letters requesting a re-release in the year in which the film was set, in order to compare prediction with reality. Clips surfaced in documentaries on science fiction, including *Looking Back at Tomorrow* for Disney's Epcot Center in Florida.[38] Art director Stephen Goosson, recalling the film in 1972, was struck by how far short of reality he and the architectural prophets of the 1920s had been. He wrote: 'What is being done now is far beyond anything thought of in those days, and I am pleased to see it.'[39]

Today *Just Imagine* is a fascinating document of the emergence of the genre and is readily compared by scholars to *Metropolis*.[40] Its value as a curiosity was sufficient to justify a release on DVD in 2008. The film's influence on the genre is hard to gauge, but seems limited. *Just Imagine*'s use of ideas that had already occurred to other writers was no sign of plagiarism, and in the same way, the later use of the ideas seen in *Just Imagine* is no indication of the film's influence. The later echoes of *Just Imagine* stand as an indicator of the emergence of generic conventions and shared reference to similar sources. The idea of evil doppelgangers on Mars loosely anticipates the 'mirror universe' created by Jerome Bixby for the original series of *Star Trek* and numerous other space age Jekyll and Hydes. Single O's story anticipates Woody Allen's *Sleeper* (1973) and Mike Judd's *Ideocracy* (2006), and directly inspired C. M. Kornbluth's story from 1951 'The Marching Morons'.[41] The number-for-name idea reappeared in George Lucas's first film, *THX 1138*, and in the names of the droids in the *Star Wars* films. The idea of an Art Deco future resurfaced in the future New York of Luc Besson's *The Fifth Element* (1997). The use of revealing women's costumes to connote the future would be a standard element of the genre: Single O would have appreciated the couture of *Forbidden Planet* (1956), *Barbarella* (1968), *Logan's Run* (1976), and the uniform designs of the original series of *Star Trek* (1966–9). But the memorial the filmmaking sought was not in celluloid imitation but in legislation. They plainly hoped that *Just Imagine* could be one more nail in the coffin of Prohibition. So it proved. Barely a year and half after the release of *Just Imagine*, the target of its satire – Prohibition – became a thing of the past. *Just Imagine* immediately became an anachronism, but doubtless, all concerned raised a glass regardless.

Notes

1. DeSylva's credits included the words to 'California here I come', and 'If you knew Susie'. Henderson had penned the tune 'I'm Sitting on top of the World', and in 1926, 'Bye-Bye Blackbird'. Brown was lyricist for the *George White Scandals*.

[2] John Tracey (Fox legal, Los Angeles) to Percy Heiliger (Fox NYC), 19 November 1931 in *Just Imagine* file, Box 806, 20th Century-Fox Legal Records (Collection 95) (hereafter FX LR). Performing Arts Special Collections, University of California Los Angeles (hereafter UCLA). David Butler concurred that most of the plot ideas were DeSylva's, though he had personally contributed the idea of the court appeal (to provide a motive for the trip to Mars) and the idea of twins on Mars.

[3] Margaret Herrick Library, Academy of Motion Picture Arts and Sciences (hereafter AMPAS), Core Collection biographical file on Brendel, especially Fox studio biography (Victor Shapiro, director of publicity at Fox), *c.*1930.

[4] On Greenhorn comedy see Esther Romeyn and Jack Kugelmass, *Let There Be Laughter! Jewish humor in America* (Chicago: Spertus Press, 1997), p.23. Contemporary incarnations of this comic form include Sacha Baron Cohen's Borat character.

[5] AMPAS Core Collection biographical file: Brendel.

[6] James Sanders, *Celluloid Skyline: New York and the Movies* (New York: Alfred A. Knopf, 2001), pp.110–11.

[7] Richard Griffith, *The Talkies: Articles and Illustrations from a Great Fan Magazine, 1928–1940* (New York: Dover, 1971), p.207 reprinting *Photoplay*, November 1930. Goosson recalled a budget of $250,000 in a letter written in 1972. University of Southern California Stephen Goosson Collection, Box 1, f.1, Goosson to Knutson (USC), 18 July 1972.

[8] UCLA FX LR 806, *Just Imagine*: Alfred Wright to Sol Wurtzel, 20 June 1930.

[9] Irene Kahn Atkins, *David Butler interviewed by Irene Kahn Atkins* (Metuchen NJ: Directors Guild of America/Scarecrow Press, 1993), pp.96–7. Butler incorrectly identifies this quake as the one that devastated Long Beach. That actually happened in 1933.

[10] David Butler recalled that this gag produced the biggest audience laugh in the film. Atkins, *David Butler,* p.98.

[11] 'Republicans ban stress on Prohibition', *New York Times,* 7 July 1928, p.1.

[12] On this aspect of Ford see Neil Baldwin, *Henry Ford and the Jews: The Mass Production of Hate* (New York: PublicAffairs, 2002).

[13] J. P. Telotte, *Science Fiction Film* (Cambridge: Cambridge University Press, 2001), pp.86, 211, n. 37.

[14] Other puns include parallels between 1930 given names and 1980 letter sequences: LN/Ellen, D/Dee, J/Jay and RT/Artie; MT puns with empty.

[15] One touch is that the airstrip used at the climax of the film is named Roosevelt Field, a probable tribute not to the 26th president (TR) but to the potential of the then governor of New York, FDR, to become the 32nd.

[16] New York Public Library, Lincoln Centre Library for Performing Arts, MFL+n.c. 132, (on microfilm reel *Zan-T8_23) *Just Imagine* publicity material.

[17] AMPAS PCA *Just Imagine* file: Memo by A.A.W., n.d. but *c.*October 1930.

[18] Ibid: Col. John V. Wilson (in Col. Joy's absence) to Yost, 18 October 1930. It is actually Boko who plays this scene.

[19] Ibid: Notes on screening by R. E. Plummer, 16 November 1930.

[20] Ibid: Joy to Wurtzel (Fox), 26 November, 1 December, 18 December 1930.

[21] *Variety,* 26 November 1930, p.18.

[22] Herrick, PCA files, *Just Imagine* file, Col. Joy's résumé (of conversation with Winfield Sheehan and Sol Wurtzel of Fox), 4 December 1930. The version of *Just Imagine* that has survived, includes most of the 'objectionable' material but lacks the suggestive close-ups during the idol dance and the multiple nose thumbing.

[23] *Los Angeles Evening Express,* 13 October 1930.

[24] *Film Daily,* 19 October 1930.

[25] Edwin Schallert, 'Just imagine fantasy hit', *Los Angeles Times,* 13 October 1930, p.11.

[26] *Variety,* 26 November 1930, p.18.

[27] Mordaunt Hall, 'A Clever Film Fantasy', 30 November 1930, p.X5.

[28] 'Author sues Fox company', *Los Angeles Times*, 21 December 1930, p.5.

[29] UCLA FX LR 806, *Just Imagine* file, statement by Leonard Spiegelgass, 19 December 1931.

[30] Ibid: Script: David Halperin, *Starlight Gables*, 1928.

[31] Ibid: Edwin P. Kilroe (Fox NYC) to John Tracey (Fox CA), 18 December 1930. *Hello, Mars* (Universal, dir. Alfred J. Goulding, 1922). Other films of the era dealing with Mars include two animations by pioneer Max Fleischer: *Trip to Mars* (1924) and *Up to Mars* (1930).

[32] Ibid: Alfred Wright (Fox legal dept.) to Sheehan, 23 December 1930.

[33] Ibid: John Tracey to Percy Heiliger (Fox NYC) 19 November 1931; Heiliger to Tracey, 2 December 1931; Tracey to Heiliger, 15 December 1931.

[34] AMPAS PCA files, *Just Imagine*. The file includes a note from the Production Code office to Robert Yost at Fox, 25 August 1930, reporting a visit from an irate author named Peter Adams with a similar complaint. The office declined to become involved. FX LR 806, *Just Imagine*: Freston and Files law office (LA) to Fox, 5 June 1931, is a claim on behalf of a writer called Helen Maher that *Just Imagine* plagiarized her story *Starlight, Starbright*. The studio found that as in the Halperin case the author had been mistaken in thinking that the people who had seen the story worked for Fox. In this case it was seen only by personnel at the Joyce Selznick agency and had never reached the Fox studio.

[35] My USC colleague Henry Jenkins reports similar plagiarism disputes in the genre of comedy at this time around the originality or otherwise of slapstick routines. There is clearly a subject here for further research.

[36] Roy Kinnard, Tony Crnkovich and R. J. Vitone, *The Flash Gordon Serials, 1936–1940: A Heavily Illustrated Guide* (Jefferson, NC: McFarland, 2008), pp.8, 9, 28, 142, 169; Michael Benson, *Vintage Science Fiction Films, 1896–1949* (Jefferson, NC: McFarland, 1984), p.94.

[37] UCLA FX LR 708, DeSylva file; FX LR 1026 Lew Brown file; FX LR 54, Henderson file; FX LR 984 David Butler and El Brendel files.

[38] UCLA FX LR 806, *Just Imagine* file, agreement with WED productions, 7 June 1983. Fox made no charge for this use. Other films using footage included *The Shape of Things to Come* (Film Ventures International, dir. George McCowan, 1980).

[39] USC Goosson Box 1 f.1: Goosson to Knutson (USC), 18 July 1972.

[40] See, for example, Vivian Sobchack, 'Cities on the Edge of Time: The Urban Science Fiction Film', *East-West Film Journal*, 3: 1 (1988), pp.4–9; and J. P. Telotte, '*Just Imagine*-ing the *Metropolis* of Modern America', *Science Fiction Studies*, 23: 2 (July 1996), pp.161–70.

[41] The link is noted in Frederick Pohl's introduction to *The Best of C. M. Kornbluth* (New York: Taplinger, 1977).

THE PROPHET AND THE SHOWMAN: *THINGS TO COME* (1936)

The 1930s have been called 'the Wellsian decade' in SF cinema.[1] In Hollywood there were films of *The Island of Doctor Moreau* – filmed by Paramount as *Island of Lost Souls* in 1932 – and Universal's *The Invisible Man* (1933), which in the hands of British director James Whale became a macabre comedy that so pleased the author he said 'that it gave me a great desire to associate myself more wholeheartedly with the screen'.[2] In Britain, the Gaumont-British Picture Corporation announced in 1932 that it planned a film of *The War of the Worlds* from a screenplay by Ivor Montagu and Frank Wells, though it was never put into production.[3] However, it was Alexander Korda's London Films which produced the major Wellsian screen adaptation of the decade: *Things to Come*. *Things to Come* is unique in that it marked the only occasion where Wells was involved in the production of a film of one of his own works. However, the collaboration between the visionary author and the flamboyant producer would turn out to be anything but an easy experience.

Wells had maintained his interest in the cinema since his association with R. W. Paul and their putative film of *The Time Machine* in 1895. He was a founding member of the Film Society in London in 1925, alongside such figures as George Bernard Shaw, film critics Ivor Montagu and Iris Barry, film directors Anthony Asquith and Adrian Brunel, theatre director John Strachey and actor Ivor Novello. The Film Society was at the forefront of an intellectual film culture emerging in Britain in the 1920s that championed the European avant-garde in preference to the commercial products of the British and American studios.[4] Wells also had a peripheral involvement with the film industry at this time. In 1927 he wrote the scenario for a film entitled *The Peace of the World*, promoting his idea of a world state – a project that collapsed when the producer, Edward Godal, went bankrupt – and in 1928 he lent his name to a trio of comedy shorts produced by Ivor Montagu and Adrian Brunel: *Bluebottles*, *Daydreams* and *The Tonic*, starring Elsa

Lanchester and Charles Laughton.[5] Although he was disappointed with most of the films of his work that he lived to see – *The Invisible Man* was the one exception – Wells nevertheless recorded in his diary in 1935: 'I was and am still interested in the film as a means of expression rather than entertainment.'[6]

Wells's fullest involvement in the film industry came through his association with Alexander Korda in the mid-1930s. Korda, an Anglophile Hungarian *émigré*, had established himself as a major force in the British film industry with *The Private Life of Henry VIII* in 1933. The success of that film prompted Korda to embark upon an ambitious, though highly profligate, production programme with a series of expensive films including *Catherine the Great* (1934), *The Private Life of Don Juan* (1934), *The Scarlet Pimpernel* (1934), *Sanders of the River* (1935), *The Ghost Goes West* (1935), *Rembrandt* (1936), *Elephant Boy* (1937), *Knight Without Armour* (1937) and an uncompleted film of *I, Claudius*.[7] Korda was prepared to take both economic and aesthetic risks in his quest to produce films that could compete with the best Hollywood had to offer. *Things to Come* was the culmination of this strategy. It was expensive – its final cost of around £250,000 made it the most expensive British film up to that point – and it was intellectually ambitious.[8] *Film Weekly* saw it as nothing less than an attempt to elevate the status of the author in the film industry: 'Mr Wells has become the first writer to receive what is known in the entertainment business as "top billing". He has written something which he calls a film scenario, and although there has never been a scenario like it before, it is gratefully accepted as a work of genius.'[9]

There had indeed never been anything quite like *Things to Come*. It was unusual in so far as it was a hybrid of a literary adaptation and an original screen story. Wells adapted the scenario from his own book *The Shape of Things to Come*, published in 1933. *The Shape of Things to Come* is characteristic of Wells's later work in that it is not a conventional novel but a philosophical and historical treatise. It is a speculative history of the future, in the guise of a 'dream book' left behind by one Dr Philip Raven, an adviser to the League of Nations, chronicling world events from 1930 to 2105. It describes the collapse of the world economic system following the Wall Street Crash and the secret re-armament of Germany, leading to the outbreak of the Second World War in January 1940. The war lasts until 1949 when social breakdown, uprisings and the spread of disease force the warring nations to cease hostilities. In 1956 an outbreak of 'maculated fever' wipes out half the world's population. Wells then describes the rise of the Modern State. The surviving scientists, meeting at Basra in 1965, lay down the principles on which the Modern State will be built, including the centralization of economic planning and the abolition of nation states and private property.

The Air Police employ 'pacifin', a new peace gas, to overcome opposition and impose the rule of law. An era of 'Puritan Tyranny' follows, in which a scientific elite leads the task of reconstruction. In 2059, when war, poverty and disease have all been abolished, the World Council is dissolved – there is no further need for it – and 'there remains no single human being upon the planet without a fair prospect of self-fulfilment, of health, interest and freedom'.[10]

It will be clear that *The Shape of Things to Come* was no ordinary book. It can be seen as a summary of Wells's views on politics, society, economics and religion. Most discussion of the book has tended to focus on its speculative qualities – Wells accurately predicted the immediate cause of the Second World War as a dispute between Germany and Poland over Danzig and foresaw the strategic role of air power – though its real significance resides in its ideas about historical process. It develops themes that Wells had already explored elsewhere, including in *The Outline of History* (1920), *A Short History of the World* (1922) and *The Work, Wealth and Happiness of Mankind* (1931), into a manifesto for the future of humanity. In particular it expresses his belief in a system of world government and, controversially, his advocacy of an altruistic dictatorship by a scientific and intellectual elite. It asserts that nation states and organized religion are obstacles to progress and should be abolished. And it argues that technocracy – the organization of society according to rational scientific principles – represents the key to achieving future peace and prosperity.[11]

The challenge in adapting *The Shape of Things to Come* for the screen was to turn Wells's polemical manifesto into a dramatic and coherent film story. Wells recognized that the film would need to be different from the book. In his preface to the published film story he wrote: '*The Shape of Things to Come* is essentially an imaginative *discussion* of social and political forces and possibilities, and a film is no place for argument. The conclusions of that book are therefore taken for granted in this film and a new story has been invented to display them.'[12] Korda paid Wells £10,000 for the screen rights and adaptation. Wells was also contracted to write *The Man Who Could Work Miracles*, from one of his early short stories, though in the event this was largely the work of Korda's regular contributor Lajos Biró.[13]

Wells was very much involved, however, in the preparation of *Things to Come*, or *Whither Mankind?* as it was originally known. His first treatment, which does not survive, was rejected by Korda and director William Cameron Menzies as being 'quite impracticable for production'.[14] His second treatment, however, is recognizable as the blueprint of the final film. This treatment abandons the framing device of the 'dream book' and omits most of the asides on intellectual and scientific developments that occupy whole chapters of *The Shape of Things to Come*. The complex historical processes described in the book are represented through archetypal characters, and whereas the book offers a broad-brush account of world events, the treatment narrows the focus to the British city of 'Everytown'. Wells included detailed notes on particular sequences, especially regarding aspects of design, and suggested that instead of credits at the beginning, the audience should be presented with a printed programme: 'This is a long needed innovation upon cinema practice. It is in the interest of everyone ... Few people remember the names that are just flashed on the screen.'[15]

Whither Mankind? opens in Everytown at Christmas against a background of growing international tensions. The three principal characters – engineer John Cabal, idealistic doctor Edward Harding and businessman 'Pippa' Passworthy – are introduced discussing the worsening international crisis. War breaks out and Everytown is subjected to heavy aerial bombardment followed by a gas attack. Cabal, a pilot, shoots down an enemy airman who, fatally wounded, gives his gas mask to a little girl ('I've given it to others, why shouldn't I have a whiff myself?'). War continues, through a montage of newspaper banners, until 1968, when we are reintroduced to Harding, who is trying to find a cure for the pestilence known as the Wandering Sickness, 'which is destroying mankind'. Everytown is now ruled by a gangster known as the Boss. Society has regressed politically and technologically: the Boss has an air force of unserviceable planes and his army wear rag-tag uniforms. In 1975 Cabal arrives back in Everytown in a futuristic aeroplane. He represents the World Transport Board (which in the film becomes the rather more impressive-sounding 'Wings Over the World'), an organization that comprizes 'we who are all that is left of the old technical services, the old engineers and industrial machinists ... We alone can pull the world together.' Cabal is imprisoned by the Boss, but escapes and subdues the Boss and his men with peace gas. Wells then describes the rebuilding of Everytown. In 2054 Cabal's descendant, Oswald Cabal, is President of the Council. He and Raymond Passworthy discuss the Space Gun that is about to fire the first human beings to the Moon: Cabal's daughter and Passworthy's son are among the crew. An artist called Theotocopulos (the only character who also features in the book) opposes the launch. He rouses a mob to destroy the Space Gun but is too late. The treatment ends with Cabal pontificating on the choice for humanity: 'If we are no more than animals – we must love and suffer and pass and matter no more – than all the other animals do or have done. It is that – or this? All the universe – or nothingness. Which will it be, Passworthy?'

It is evident from the treatment that Wells, for all his inexperience as a screenwriter, nevertheless had a coherent vision for the shape and structure of the film. He described it in musical terms and suggested that it should be understood as being like an opera:

> The film consists of four main parts. The first part (*Pastorale*) represents *A Christmas Party* under (practically) PRESENT CONDITIONS. No date. War breaks out and the chief character reappears in the second part (*Marche Funèbre*), *The Episode of the Two Aviators* (1940). A series of short exposures then shows war, degenerating into SOCIAL CHAOS, leading to the third part, which begins in *The Darkest Hour of the Pestilence*, shows *The Wandering Sickness at its Climax* (1960), and the revolt of the airmen, technicians and men of science, who achieve *Resurrection amidst the Ruins*. The third part is set in A SPECTACLE OF IMMENSE RUIN. Everything is done to summon up a vision of our present world *smashed*. Then comes a rapid series to convey WORK, leading up to the counter vision of what can be done with our world ... The fourth part (*Chorale*) is THE WORLD IN 2054. This concentrates on fresh spectacular effects. If they are not surprising and magnificent and REAL the whole film falls down. The interest of this latter part brings the drama of creative effort versus the resistances of jealousy, indolence and sentimentality, to a culmination.[16]

Wells added a note to the effect that the dates in the treatment 'are merely rough indications': the finished film would set its climax in 2036, a hundred years in the future.

It is instructive to consider what Wells's treatment omits from the book and what it adds. The major omissions are the critique of democratic government and the suppression of organized religion. The omission of these themes would almost certainly have been necessary in order to meet the strictures of censorship: the British Board of Film Censors forbade any criticism of institutions such as Parliament and the Church.[17] Censorship would also account for the fact that the identity of the country which attacks Britain is not revealed. (In the book the Second World War begins with a pre-emptive Polish attack on Germany: Britain remains neutral.) The main additions are the sequence depicting Everytown under the dictatorship of the Boss, and the climax involving the Space Gun. The Space Gun now seems the most risible aspect of the film: it is not clear why Wells adopted this quaint throwback to Jules Verne and George Méliès at a time when rocket technology was becoming a reality.

There were also some themes in the treatment that did not make it into the finished film. It includes more discussion of the social organization and technology of the future. It also includes unusual references to Hindu deities – unusual in the sense that Wells himself was not religious – that are overlaid onto the characterizations. It suggests that the dramatic structure was based on the Hindu trinity – Brahma the Creator, Siva the Destroyer and Vishnu the Possessor – which 'express the main forces in the world about us'.[18] This reflects Wells's intellectual ambition, but in the event Korda's commercial instincts prevailed and the idea was discarded. It would seem unlikely that many British or American cinema-goers in the 1930s would have been sufficiently well versed in Hindu theology to understand it.[19]

Things to Come went before the cameras early in 1935: such was the scale of the film that it occupied sets at two studios (Elstree and Worton Hall), while exteriors were shot at Denham Studios, Korda's state-of-the-art new complex still in the process of being built. The production employed 'every resource and discovery of modern film technique'.[20] Korda assembled a top-drawer creative team including William Cameron Menzies, the leading Hollywood production designer, to direct; special effects supervisor Ned Mann (known at Denham as 'The Mann Who Could Work Miracles'); French cinematographer Georges Périnal, who had shot *The Private Life of Henry VIII* and *Sanders of the River*; and Korda's brother Vincent as art director. It was Wells's initiative to hire British composer Arthur Bliss, despite Bliss never having written a film score before, after attending a lecture at the Royal Academy of Music. 'Something that I said on this occasion must have caught Wells's attention,' Bliss recalled in his autobiography, 'for he invited me to lunch, and there and then spoke of his projected film based on his book *The Shape of Things to Come*, and asked me whether I would like to collaborate with him by writing the musical score.'[21]

Wells's interest in the music of *Things to Come* demonstrates how he tried to impose his *impramatur* on every aspect of its production. On one occasion, for example, he wrote to Bliss: 'I am not sure about the Finale ... It's good – nothing you do can fail to be good – but it is not yet that exultant shout of human resolution that might be there – not the marching song of a new world of conquest among the atoms and stars.'[22] Yet despite Wells's interventions, Bliss succeeded in writing what by common consent was the first masterpiece of British film music. His score, the first to be issued on gramophone disc, combines aspects of the musical avant-garde such as discordant melody and off-beat syncopation with classical compositions reminiscent of Elgar (the triumphalist 'Building of the New World') and Holst (the famous March depicting the outbreak of war has echoes of 'Mars – Bringer of War').[23]

Wells had been promised that he would be consulted at every level of the production and that the film would be a faithful translation of his ideas. Publically, at least, he praised Korda and expressed his satisfaction with the finished film. In an interview for *Film Weekly* he said: 'Alexander Korda

3. The Prophet and the Showman: H. G. Wells (right) and Alexander Korda on the set of *Things to Come* (1936). It was an uneasy collaboration (Source: British Film Institute).

offered to make a film which was, as far as humanly possible, exactly as I dictated ... The film has emerged spiritually correct, despite the fact that it now embodies many alterations suggested by Alexander Korda, William Cameron Menzies, and a score of other people.'[24] Privately, however, he was profoundly disappointed. In his diary he called the film 'a huge disappointment'. Menzies, he averred, was 'an incompetent director' who 'had no grasp of my ideas'. He felt that his own participation had been 'ineffective'. 'I did not take Korda's measure soon enough or secure an influence over him soon enough,' Wells reflected. 'I grew tired of writing stuff into the treatment that was afterwards mishandled or cut out again.' He thought the film had failed in his intention to educate the public and feared that it 'would damage my prestige, perhaps irreparably'.[25]

Wells's growing dissatisfaction with the filmmaking process is evident from a memo he circulated 'to everyone concerned in designing and making the costumes, decorations, etc. for the concluding phase of *Things to Come*', which he subsequently released for publication. 'There are certain principles in this undertaking to be observed, which as yet do not seem to be as clearly grasped as they must be,' he began tetchily. In particular he was concerned that the costume design should not be too 'extravagant or silly'. Here, and elsewhere, he was keen to differentiate *Things to Come* from *Metropolis*, which he described as 'balderdash'.

> As a general rule you may take it that whatever Lange [*sic*] did in *Metropolis* is the exact contrary of what we want done here ... You will not see people rushing about in a monstrous rig, all goggles and padding and gadgets like the early aviators ... Men and women of the future will carry the equivalent of the purse, pocket book, fountain pen, watch, etc. etc. of to-day, but these things will be unobtrusive and subservient in a graceful decorative scheme.[26]

Wells particularly disliked *Metropolis*, which he had seen in 1927 and considered 'the silliest film ... It gives in one eddying concentration almost every possible foolishness, cliché, platitude, and muddlement about mechanical progress and progress in general served up with a sauce of sentimentality that is all its own.'[27] To some extent his hostility towards Lang's film arose from his view that it had taken ideas from his own novel *When the Sleeper Wakes* (1899) without acknowledgement; but it also reflected his concern that *Things to Come* should imagine a future that seemed both real and functional.

Korda, for his part, also had cause for concern. *Things to Come* was one of several expensive films in production in 1935 – alongside *Rembrandt* and *The Man Who Could Work Miracles* – while the completion of Denham Studios had been delayed by a fire.[28] Korda's ambitious production and studio-building programme had been bankrolled by the Prudential Assurance Company, which by the autumn of 1935 was becoming increasingly concerned over rising costs and was looking for ways to rein Korda in.[29] *The Man Who Could Work Miracles* had been completed before *Things to Come* but was held back as it was deemed the lesser film.[30] A great deal was riding, therefore, on the success of *Things to Come*, which opened in the West End of London in February 1936. Among those attending the première at the Leicester Square Cinema was the actor Ernest Thesiger, originally cast as Theotocopulos, who discovered only then that his scenes had been reshot with Cedric Hardwicke.[31]

Thesiger's scenes were not the only ones to end up on the cutting room floor. Some ten minutes were cut between the trade show (an advance screening for critics) and the film's première. The cuts – which can be identified by comparing the release script with the finished film – removed several of the remaining asides about social and technological developments in the future, including improvements in health and the engineering of the Space Gun.[32] One omission is particularly significant: a long discussion between Mary Gordon (Ann Todd) and the Boss's mistress Roxana (Margaretta Scott) about the place of women in society. Wells had long been an advocate of women's rights: his novel *Ann Veronica* (1909), for example, has been claimed as proto-feminist for its characterization of a socially emancipated heroine. Also cut at the last minute were scenes featuring Oswald Cabal's wife Rowena, supposedly a descendant of Roxana, though Margaretta Scott is credited with both roles on the film titles. The effect was to remove from the film a sub-theme about changing gender roles with the result that its gender politics remain static and highly conservative: women are portrayed either as dutiful wives (John Cabal's wife) or as a duplicitous temptress (Roxana).

The critical response to *Things to Come* was largely positive: it was recognized as a major production achievement for the British cinema, and reviewers rhapsodized about its technical qualities even if some had reservations about the stilted dialogue and declamatory performances. *Kinematograph Weekly*, for example, declared: 'Technically the production is the greatest thing that has ever happened in the history of the kinema, and histrionically it yields to none, in spite of the fact that acting is forced to play second fiddle to stagecraft.'[33] *Film Weekly* similarly thought it a 'great screen spectacle ... so astounding – even terrifying – that the heaviness of the subject and the stodginess of much of the dialogue do not seem to matter very much'.[34] For the *Monthly Film Bulletin* it was 'a film which because of its conception and technical achievements demands to be seen and deserves careful and discriminating attention'.[35] The *Morning Post* considered it 'incomparably the greatest achievement of filmcraft to date, and in scope and sincerity sets a mark for film producers to aim at for many years to come'.[36] The *Inquirer* heralded it as 'a triumph both of Cinema art and of the creative genius of H. G. Wells'.[37] C. A. Lejeune in the *Observer* declared that 'for the first time in its story, the cinema has replaced the pulpit, the stage, or even the printed word as the forum of the popular orator'.[38] A dissenting note was sounded, however, by the *Manchester Guardian*, which averred that '*Things to Come* fails both as entertainment and as education for peace'. [39] And the US trade paper *Variety* complained that it 'lacks warmth or feeling ... It's an impressive but dull exposition of a bad dream.'[40]

So much for the critics, but what about the public? It has become one of the myths of film history that *Things to Come* was a box-office flop. In fact, its net receipts of £119,500 (of which £71,757 came from the home market) were very good for a British film at this time.[41] *Kine Weekly* listed it as a 'hit', and according to John Sedgwick's statistical analysis of popular film preferences it was the ninth most successful film of the year in Britain and the second British film after Korda's *The Ghost Goes West*.[42] *Things to Come* should be seen, therefore, as one of those films, like *Cleopatra*, that was popular in its own right but because of its enormous expense failed to recoup its production costs. There is anecdotal evidence of its impact on audiences. Leslie Halliwell, who saw it on holiday on the Isle of Man, averred: 'The impression on that innocent, entertainment-seeking Monday night audience can hardly have been less sensational than the panic caused two years later in New York by Orson Welles's famous radio broadcast of *The War of the Worlds*, which caused millions of people to believe that Martians had actually landed.'[43]

Things to Come fared less well, however, in the US market, where audience apathy is generally explained by the comment (possibly apocryphal) of an unnamed distributor that: 'Nobody is going to believe that the world is going to be saved by a bunch of people with British accents.'[44] The film also ran foul of the chief censor, Joseph Breen, who was taken aback, after seeing it in Los Angeles, that it had been passed by the Production Code office in New York despite containing 'some profanity and certain expressions like "My God" – "Good God" – "God" – "Damn" – etc.' that he felt should not have been allowed.[45] Breen was assured that the film had been viewed and it had been felt these expressions 'were not used in a profane sense'.[46] However, Breen felt this was regrettable, as he explained:

> Already two of our companies here in Hollywood have spoken to us about it – have insisted that inasmuch as the Foreign picture was approved with these expressions in it, they ought to be allowed to use them here. I am very sorry that you made this decision. It is certain to complicate matters here. However, inasmuch as you have approved the picture, and the picture is playing throughout the country, I suppose there is little that can be done about it.[47]

The PCA may have been relieved, therefore, that *Things to Come* did only moderate business in the United States given that its approval seems to have been something of a mistake.

For all the travails of its production and mixed fortunes upon its release, however, *Things to Come* was undoubtedly a major landmark in the history of SF cinema. In hindsight its real historical significance resides not in its speculative narrative of the future – Wells predicted the outbreak of the Second World War but not its outcome – but in its relationship to various ideological currents in the 1930s. The first part of the film, for example, belongs to the lineage of pacifist cinema exemplified by films such as Lewis Milestone's *All Quiet on the Western Front* (1930), G. W. Pabst's *Kameradschaft* (1931) and Jean Renoir's *La Grande Illusion* (1937).[48] Wells, like many of his generation, had been profoundly affected by the Great War. He abhorred war on both moral and rational grounds. The theme of the futility of war is powerfully expressed in *Things to Come*, particularly in the incident that Wells called 'The Episode of the Two Aviators'. John Cabal (Raymond Massey) shoots down an enemy raider and then lands to comfort the dying pilot (John Clements) while asking rhetorically: 'Why does it have to come to this? God, why do we have to murder each other?' To this extent *Things to Come* can be seen as an expression of the zeitgeist. In the mid-1930s there were many indicators that public opinion in Britain was strongly anti-war. In 1933 the Oxford Union famously passed the motion that 'This House will in no circumstance fight for King and Country' and an independent candidate, John Wilmott, won the East Fulham by-election standing on an anti-war platform. In 1934 the Peace Pledge Union was founded; in 1935 10 million people signed a 'Peace Ballot' calling for a reduction of armaments; and in 1936 a group of documentary filmmaking produced the short film *Peace of Britain* urging people to write to their MPs to oppose the newly re-elected National Government's rearmament programme.

Another area in which *Things to Come* referred to contemporary anxieties was in its representation of air warfare. Wells had foreseen the strategic possibilities of air power since before the Great War in his novel *The War in the Air* (1908). By the early 1930s the spectre of aerial bombardment had become so great that the British Prime Minister Stanley Baldwin famously declared: 'There is no power on earth that can protect him [the man in the street] from being bombed ... the bomber will always get through.'[49] The most famous sequence of *Things to Come* is the bombing of Everytown – a superbly constructed montage sequence that shows anti-aircraft defences to be wholly ineffective and crowds panicking as the bombs fall. In hindsight the sequence has been seen as an apocalyptic prophecy of the Blitz of 1940, not least because Everytown is clearly meant to represent London with buildings resembling St Paul's Cathedral and the National Gallery. In 1936, of course, *Things to Come* remained an unrealized prophecy; but only a year later newsreels of the bombing of Guernica during the Spanish Civil War 'forcefully conveyed the full implications of aerial bombing to a British audience'.[50] *Things to Come* was reissued early in 1940, during the 'Phoney War' period: Mass-Observation reported that 'shots of thousands of planes crossing the coast caused some laughter, but shots of air raid panic, of gas masks being issued, of people running for shelter, and so on, were received in silence and with interest'.[51] It is tempting to speculate that the reissue may have been intended to prepare audiences for the anticipated Blitz.

Things to Come can also be seen as a response to the rise of Fascism in Europe. This is most evident in the middle sequence featuring the dictatorship of the Boss. Wells insisted 'that the Boss is not intended to be a caricature of a Fascist or Nazi leader ... He is something more ancient, more modern and more universal than any topical movements.'[52] In the film, however, the Boss was played by Ralph Richardson as a caricature of Italian dictator Benito Mussolini. This demonstrates how an actor's performance may influence the meaning of a film: it comes as no surprise that *Things to Come* was banned in Italy. Some commentators have also suggested that the airmen who form Wings Over the World bear some similarity to Fascists, not least because of their black uniforms and their insistence on discipline.[53] The Italian Fascists and the Nazis both saw the aviator as a heroic archetype, with Mussolini and Hermann Goering both associating themselves with the figure of the airman. And it is true, certainly, that Cabal's descent into Everytown in his futuristic flying machine resembles, in the shots and camera angles, Hitler's arrival at Nuremberg in *Triumph of the Will* (1935). However, upon closer examination this is not a persuasive reading. Fascism may have presented itself as modern but at its core was an intense nationalism that was emotional and regressive. Wings Over the World, in contrast, is internationalist, rational and progressive. Cabal explains that its aim is to harness science for the betterment of mankind. He refers to 'the brotherhood of efficiency, the free masonry of science ... We're the last trustees of civilization when everything else has failed.' And it is a much more benign regime than in the book: there is no mention in the film of the 'Air Dictatorship' or 'Puritan Tyranny'.

A further contemporary theme that can be identified in *Things to Come* is modernism. In particular the film draws upon the *moderne* movement in architecture to visualize the city of the future. To this extent the film needs to be understood in relation to the discourses of architecture and planning. The credit for transforming Wells's vague descriptions of the future – 'Moving platforms, spiral ways vanishing into tunnels, exposed lifts ... A vision of the city interior of the new age. General impression here of architecture and structure'[54] – belongs to Vincent Korda. Korda's influences included the designs of architect Le Corbusier and the avant-garde furniture of Oliver Hill.[55] The Everytown of 2036, with its gleaming towers, airy spaces and geometric angles, represents perhaps the most fully realized modernist future in the history of SF cinema. Along with *Just Imagine*, *Things to Come* established the definitive 'look' of shiny futuristic cityscapes that would remain the benchmark for the genre until *Blade Runner* (1982). Its influence extended beyond cinema. The promotional brochure for the World's Fair in New York in 1939 – billed as 'The World of Tomorrow', and the last great showcase of modernism before the Second World War – echoed the film in its declaration that: 'The eyes of the Fair are on the future – not in the sense of peering toward the unknown nor attempting to foretell the events of tomorrow and the shape of things to come, but in the sense of presenting

4. A modernist future, as imagined in the poster for *Things to Come* (1936) (Source: British Film Institute).

a new and clearer view of today in preparation for tomorrow; a view of the forces and ideas that prevail as well as the machines.'[56] While the sets of *Things to Come* drew extravagant praise from critics, however, there were reservations about the fashion sense of the future. Alistair Cooke remarked facetiously: 'It must be heartbreaking for Mr Wells to be told that the costumes he predicted they'd be wearing in 2030 are to be the very thing in beachwear this summer.'[57] This was precisely the reaction Wells had wanted to avoid when he had been issuing diktats regarding the costumes to the film makers.

Yet *Things to Come* still represents a distinctively Wellsian vision of the future. Most commentators have focused on the film's genuinely horrific representation of the destructive potential of air power; but just as technology has the power to destroy it also has the potential to rebuild. To this extent the film expresses Wells's belief in scientific and technological progress. The last third of the film is a celebration of technology as great machines undertake the task of reconstruction and a new Everytown emerges from the rubble. This sequence owes much to the techniques of the documentary film, regarded as the progressive sector of the British film industry in the 1930s. These sequences equate technology with progress and aesthetic beauty. As a child says to her grandfather in the brief 'history lesson' sequence: 'They keep on inventing things and making life lovelier and lovelier.' The technological utopia offered by *Things to Come* is very different from the technological oppression and social engineering that characterizes *Metropolis*. In this regard, at least, *Things to Come* fulfilled Wells's desire that it should be radically different from Fritz Lang's film.

H. G. Wells died in August 1946, a few weeks short of his eightieth birthday: he had lived long enough to witness the use of the atomic bomb, which he had anticipated in *The World Set Free* (1914). Before his death he had been developing ideas for a film sequel to *Things to Come*, entitled 'The Way the World is Going' and dealing with the aftermath of the Second World War.[58] Wells's legacy would persist in popular cinema, with Hollywood films of his seminal works including *The War of the Worlds* (1953 and 2005), *The Time Machine* (1960 and 2002), *The First Men in the Moon* (1964) and *The Island of Dr Moreau* (1977 and 1996).[59] Yet *Things to Come* remains the definitive Wellsian film on account of the author's close involvement in the production, no matter how unhappy the experience may have been, and its bold, if flawed, attempt to reconcile the philosophical and speculative nature of SF literature with the demands of the cinema for narrative and spectacle. *Things to Come* has suffered the fate of many SF films in that its idea of the future now looks very dated, but even so, there would not be another film to match its intellectual ambition and visual imagination until *2001*.

Notes

[1]   Jeffrey Richards, '*Things to Come* and science fiction cinema in the 1930s', in I. Q. Hunter (ed.), *British Science Fiction Cinema* (London: Routledge, 1999), p.28. On film adaptations of Wells, see James Chapman, 'H. G. Wells and Science Fiction Cinema', in Tobias Hochscherf and James Leggott (eds), *British Science Fiction Film and Television: Critical Essays* (Jefferson NC: McFarland, 2011), pp.11–27; Barry K. Grant, 'Looking Upward: H. G. Wells, Science Fiction and the Cinema', *Literature/Film Quarterly*, 14: 3 (1986), pp.154–63; Alan Wykes, *H. G. Wells and the Cinema* (London: Jupiter, 1977); and Kevin Williams, *H. G. Wells, Modernity and the Movies* (Liverpool: Liverpool University Press, 2007). For commentary on *Things to Come* see Timothy Travers, 'The Shape of *Things to Come*: H. G. Wells and Radical Culture in the 1930s', *Film and History*, 6: 2 (1976), pp.31–6; and, especially, Christopher Frayling, *Things to Come* (London: British Film Institute, 1995).

2   'I wrote this film for Your Enjoyment', *Film Weekly*, 29 February 1936, p.8.

3   'Mr H. G. Wells and the Screen', *The Times*, 3 November 1932, p.10.

4   See Jamie Sexton, *Alternative Film Culture in Interwar Britain* (Exeter: University of Exeter Press, 2008).

5   Sylvia Hardy, 'H. G. Wells and British Silent Cinema: The War of the Worlds', in Andrew Higson (ed.), *Young and Innocent? The Cinema in Britain 1896–1930* (Exeter: University of Exeter Press, 2002), pp.242–55.

6   H. G. Wells, *H. G. Wells in Love: Postscript to An Experiment in Autobiography*, ed. P. G. Wells (London: Faber and Faber, 1984), p.207.

7   On Korda's production strategies, see Charles Drazin, *Korda: Britain's Only Movie Mogul* (London: Sidgwick & Jackson, 2002); Karol Kulik, *Alexander Korda: The Man Who Could Work Miracles* (London: W. H. Allen, 1975); Rachael Low, *The History of the British Film 1929–39: Film Making in 1930s Britain* (London: George Allen & Unwin, 1985); and Sue Harper, *Picturing the Past: The Rise and Fall of the British Costume Film* (London: British Film Institute, 1994), pp.20–35.

8   British Film Institute (BFI) London Films Collection Box 5: Memorandum by Sir David Cunynghame, 7 January 1946.

9   'The Author on Trial', *Film Weekly*, 22 February 1936, p.3.

10 H. G. Wells, *The Shape of Things to Come: The Ultimate Revolution*, ed. Patrick Parrinder (London: Penguin, 2005 [1933]), p.444.

11 See John S. Partington, *Building Cosmopolis: The Political Thought of H. G. Wells* (Aldershot: Ashgate, 2003).

12 H.G. Wells, *Things to Come: A Film by H. G. Wells* (New York: Macmillan, 1935), p.viii.

13 Frayling, *Things to Come*, p.27.

14 *Things to Come: A Film by H. G. Wells*, p.ix.

15 BFI Unpublished Scripts Collection S6235: *Whither Mankind? A Film of the Future*. By H. G. Wells. Based on his two books, *The Shape of Things to Come* and *The Work, Wealth and Happiness of Mankind* (no date).

16 Ibid.

17 See James C. Robertson, *The British Board of Film Censors: Film Censorship in Britain, 1896–1950* (London: Croom Helm, 1985); Jeffrey Richards, 'The British Board of Film Censors and Content Control in the 1930s (1): Images of Britain', *Historical Journal of Film, Radio and Television*, 1: 2 (1981), pp.97–116; and Jeffrey Richards, 'The British Board of Film Censors and Content Control in the 1930s (2): Foreign Affairs', *Historical Journal of Film, Radio and Television*, 2: 1 (1982), pp.39–48.

18 BFI Unpublished Scripts S6235: *Whither Mankind?*

19 Leon Stover posits a reading of the film that equates the Hindu trinity with Plato's three soul-types: wisdom (Brahma the Creator), force (Siva the destroyer) and desire (Vishnu the Possessor). Stover, *The Prophetic Soul: A Reading of H. G. Wells's 'Things to Come'* (Jefferson NC: McFarland, 1987), pp.16–26. It is a reading that this author finds unconvincing in the extreme.

20 *Kinematograph Weekly*, 9 January 1936, p.80A.

21 Arthur Bliss, *As I Remember* (London: Faber and Faber, 1970), p.152.

22 Quoted in Frayling, *Things to Come*, p.39.

23 See John Huntley, *British Film Music* (London: Skelton Robinson, 1947), pp.39–40.

24 'I wrote this film for Your Enjoyment', *Film Weekly*, 29 February 1936, pp.8–9.

25 Wells, *H. G. Wells in Love*, pp.211–12.

26 *New York Times*, 12 April 1936.

27 H. G. Wells, *The Way the World is Going: Guesses and Forecasts for the Years Ahead* (London: Ernest Benn, 1928), p.87.

28 *Rembrandt* cost £140,236, *The Man Who Could Work Miracles*, £136,604.

29 Sarah Street, 'Alexander Korda, Prudential Assurance and British Film Finance in the 1930s', *Historical Journal of Film, Radio and Television*, 6: 2 (1986), pp.161–79.

30 Charles Drazin, *Korda: Britain's Only Movie Mogul* (London: Sidgwick & Jackson, 2002), pp.14–34.

31 Frayling, *Things to Come*, p.23.

32 BFI S6255 *Things to Come*. Release Script [n.d.]

33 *Kinematograph Weekly*, 27 February 1936, p.31.

34 *Film Weekly*, 29 February 1936, p.27.

35 *Monthly Film Bulletin*, 3: 26 (February 1936), p.25.

36 'Magnificence of "Things to Come"', *Morning Post*, 22 February 1936.

37 'Things to Come', *Inquirer*, 29 February 1936.

38 'The film that is a film', *Observer*, 23 February 1936.

39 'The New Wells-Korda Film', *Manchester Guardian*, 21 February 1936.

40 *Variety*, 22 April 1936.

41 BFI London Films Collection Box 5: Memorandum by Sir David Cunynghame, 7 January 1946.

42 John Sedgwick, *Popular Filmgoing in 1930s Britain: A Choice of Pleasures* (Exeter: University of Exeter Press, 2000), p.272.

43 Leslie Halliwell, *Seats in All Parts: Half a Lifetime at the Movies* (London: Granada, 1985), p.77.

44 Michael Korda, *Charmed Lives: A Family Romance* (London: Allen Lane, 1980), p.123.

45 Margaret Herrick Library, Academy of Motion Picture Arts and Sciences, MPPA PCA file on *Things to Come*: Joseph I. Breen to Vincent G. Hart, 1 May 1936.

46 Ibid: Hart to Breen, 4 May 1936.

47 Ibid: Breen to Hart, 5 May 1936.

48 See Andrew Kelly, *Cinema and the Great War* (London: Routledge, 1997).

49 Quoted in Michael Paris, *From the Wright Brothers to Top Gun: Aviation, nationalism and popular cinema* (Manchester: Manchester University Press, 1995), p.105.

50 Anthony Aldgate, *Cinema and History: British Newsreels and the Spanish Civil War* (London: Scolar Press, 1979), p.159.

51 The Tom Harrisson Mass-Observation Archive, University of Sussex, FR57: 'Audience Preference in Film Themes', 17 March 1940.

52 BFI S6235: *Whither Mankind? A Film of the Future*.

53 Travers, 'The Shape of Things to Come', pp.35–6; Richards, 'Things to Come and science fiction in the 1930s', p.21.

54 BFI S6235: *Whither Mankind? A Film of the Future*.

55 Frayling, pp.62–70.

56 Quoted in Peter Kurznick, 'Losing the World of Tomorrow: The battle over the presentation of science at the 1939 World's Fair', *American Quarterly*, 46: 3 (1994), p.342.

57 'Mr Wells Sees Us Through', *Listener*, 18 March 1936, p.545.

58 Don G. Smith, *H. G. Wells on Film: The Utopian Nightmare* (Jefferson NC: McFarland, 2002), p.183.

59 There was also a film entitled *H. G. Wells' The Shape of Things to Come* (Film Ventures International, dir. George McCowan, 1979), though this bore no relation either to Wells's book or Korda's film. Produced by Harry Alan Towers (under the pseudonym Peter Welbeck) it was one of the many cheapskate SF adventure films produced in the wake of *Star Wars*.

3

SCREENING WELLS FOR
COLD WAR AMERICA: *THE WAR*
OF THE WORLDS (1953)

No one would have believed, in the last years of the nineteenth century, that this world was being watched keenly and closely by intelligences greater than man's and yet as mortal as his own ... Yet across the gulf of space, minds that are to our minds as ours are to those of the beasts that perish, intellects vast and cool and unsympathetic, regarded this earth with envious eyes, and slowly and surely drew their plans against us.[1]

The opening of H. G. Wells's *The War of the Worlds* is probably the most famous in SF literature, while the novel itself became the foundational text of a whole lineage of alien invasion narratives. *The War of the Worlds* itself has been filmed twice for cinema (1953 and 2005) and adapted for radio (1938) and television (1988–9). Wells's novel was a commentary on the British *fin-de-siècle* experience, invoking contemporary anxieties around imperialism, invasion and social dislocation. Its serialization in 1897 coincided with the Diamond Jubilee of Queen Victoria, a self-conscious celebration of Britain's imperial greatness. In contrast Wells posited a nightmarish scenario where the seat of the British Empire is overcome by a ruthless and technologically superior invader. What is particularly striking about the major adaptations of *The War of the Worlds* is that they have appeared at moments of acute geopolitical tension: the Munich Crisis (1938), the Cold War (1953) and the War on Terror (2005). To this extent it is an example of a narrative that has been appropriated to meet different historical and ideological contexts.

With its combination of spectacle and melodrama, *The War of the Worlds* made ideal cinematic material. But it would be half a century before Wells's most famous story made its way to the screen. Paramount Pictures paid $50,000 for the film rights in 1926, seeing it as a potential vehicle for Cecil B. De Mille.[2] Roy Pomeroy, the studio's special effects supervisor who had parted the Red Sea for *The Ten Commandments* (1923), prepared a treatment that bore no relation to the book. Pomeroy set the story in Washington DC and overlaid onto it a romantic triangle involving Senator's daughter Celia Fenton, a young inventor called Robert Eliot (who has invented a ray 'which would make any country in secret possession of it the mightiest and safest in the world') and Secretary of Defense Freeman Jones (who holds the 'complacent opinion that America has nothing to fear from foreign invasion'). Pomeroy saw the story as a vehicle for the promotion of national preparedness: when the Martian invasion comes it is Eliot's secret weapon that saves the day. However, Pomeroy's chief inspiration were the lurid tales appearing in contemporary 'pulp' SF magazines. Thus the reason for the Martian invasion is 'to find beautiful women with whom they plan to breed and propagate a mixed Martian-Earth race which is to populate the earth anew'.[3] This idea did not impress Paramount's Script Department, which dismissed it as 'trite', though it felt the book had the potential to make a good motion picture: 'This amazing fantasy would cost a lot to make, but if a decent personal story could be woven into it, it would be worthwhile.'[4]

The next initiative to film *The War of the Worlds* came in the early 1930s. It was one of several projects considered by the Russian director Sergei Eisenstein during his brief visit to Hollywood in 1930.[5] It went no further than an idea – Eisenstein began the unfinished *Que Viva Mexico!* instead – but Ivor Montagu, the British cinephile who accompanied Eisenstein to California, and who knew Wells through the Film Society in London, would shortly later set to work on a script himself. In 1932 it was announced that Montagu and Wells's son Frank, who worked in several capacities in the British film industry during the 1930s, were to adapt *The War of the Worlds* for the Gaumont-British Picture Corporation and that Walter Forde would direct.[6] The Montagu-Wells treatment was a close adaptation, maintaining the book's British setting while updating it to include modern weapons (tanks, aeroplanes) and communications (radio). Wells's unnamed narrator became a GP called Dr Drage, while the role of the artilleryman who organizes an underground resistance movement was enhanced.[7] However, Paramount refused to sell the screen rights and the project went no further.[8] Gaumont-British made *The Tunnel* (1935), from a novel by Bernard Kellermann, instead.

In the United States the original serialization of *The War of the Worlds* had prompted several pirated versions in New York and Boston newspapers, which changed the location to the city concerned. However, it was in 1938 that *The War of the Worlds* imprinted itself indelibly upon the American consciousness, courtesy of another Welles: Orson Welles. The CBS radio network hosted *The Mercury Theater on the Air*, an anthology series produced by Welles and John Houseman, broadcast on Sunday evenings at 8 pm Eastern Standard Time. The series, consisting of adaptations of classic novels including *Treasure Island, Jane Eyre, Around the World in Eighty Days* and *Heart of Darkness*, was noted for its experimental and innovative use of the medium. *The War of the Worlds* was chosen for 30 October 1938, the night before Halloween, and the job of adapting it was handed to writer Howard Koch 'with instructions from Houseman to dramatize it in the form of news bulletins'.[9] The effect was extraordinary, as thousands of listeners were panicked into believing that Martians had actually landed in New Jersey.[10] The notoriety of the broadcast drew Welles to the attention of Hollywood and a contract with RKO that would lead to *Citizen Kane*, while Koch went to Warner Bros. and won an Academy Award for co-scripting *Casablanca*.

Many myths have arisen around the broadcast of *The War of the Worlds*. One of the most enduring is that it was intended as a Halloween hoax. This seems to have arisen from Welles's unscripted remark at the end of the broadcast that it had been 'the Mercury Theater's own radio version of dressing up in a sheet and jumping out of a bush and saying "Boo!"'.[11] However, this does not stand up to scrutiny: the programme makes no attempt to conceal that it is anything other than fiction, stating several times that it is an adaptation of *The War of the Worlds* presented by the Mercury Theater. Welles's comment was ad-libbed in response to the telephone calls that had jammed the CBS switchboard in New York during the broadcast. Another myth, propagated by Welles himself, was that he was responsible for both the concept and adaptation of *The War of the Worlds*. Anticipating the controversy over the script credit for *Citizen Kane*, Welles asserted that he, rather than Howard Koch, wrote the script of *The War of the Worlds*.[12] This was flatly contradicted, however, by John Houseman: 'The writing, most of it, was done by Howard Koch ... Orson Welles had virtually nothing to do with the writing of the script and less than usual to do with its preliminary rehearsals.'[13]

A comparison of Howard Koch's first working script and the programme as broadcast reveals that Koch was responsible not only for the structure but also for most of the incidental details. It was Koch who set the action in New Jersey and who turned Wells's narrator into astronomer Professor Richard Pierson of Princeton University (played by Orson Welles). And it was Koch who devised the idea of presenting the first part of the programme as a series of radio news bulletins and 'live' interviews with eyewitnesses. This device gave the broadcast a sense of immediacy and realism that in large measure accounts for the public response. The second part (following a station break for commercials) was more conventional, consisting largely of a first person narration by Pierson and just one dramatized scene involving another character (the artilleryman). Koch's first draft also included the book's encounter between the narrator and a curate who thinks the invasion represents God's punishment of mankind.[14] Koch generously acknowledged 'that Orson Welles and John Houseman ... made many valuable contributions to the development of the play to its final form' and that 'its impact on the air was due to their direction and production'.[15] But in essence it was his script that, with some refinements and the omission of the curate, was the basis of the broadcast.

The nature and extent of the panic caused by *The War of the Worlds* also requires qualification. For one thing *The Mercury Theater on the Air* attracted less than four per cent of the total listening audience: it was up against the popular *Edgar Bergen and Charlie McCarthy Show* that had an audience share of 35 per cent.[16] A contemporary study of the panic by sociologist Hadley Cantril – a valuable record in that it was undertaken shortly after the event – suggests that around 6 million people tuned in to *The War of the Worlds* but that it was those who switched from other stations during the broadcast who were most likely to think it was real. Cantril also found that the reaction was localized rather than nationwide: not surprisingly it was most intense in New Jersey and neighbouring states.[17] John Houseman, furthermore, suggested that the impact of *The War of the Worlds* was due to an accident of historical timing:

> It came within thirty-five days of the Munich crisis. For weeks, the American people had been hanging on their radios, getting most of their news no longer from the press but over the air. A new technique of 'on-the-spot' reporting had been developed and eagerly accepted by an anxious and news-hungry world. The Mercury Theater on the Air by faithfully copying every detail of the new technique – including its imperfections – found an already enervated audience ready to accept its wildest fantasies.[18]

This is not to suggest that Welles or Koch intended any parallel with the war scare in Europe. Rather, they were imitating the style of contemporary radio news reports, including scratchy transmissions and empty pauses, to achieve in broadcasting terms the same verisimilitude as Wells's matter-of-fact prose in the novel.

The real historical significance of the *War of the Worlds* broadcast was that it focused attention on the influence of the mass media. The liberal journalist Dorothy Thompson proved remarkably prescient when she wrote:

> If people can be frightened out of their wits by mythical men from Mars, they can be frightened into fanaticism by the fear of Reds, or convinced that America is in the hands of sixty families, or aroused to revenge against any minority, or terrorized into subservience to leadership because of any imaginable menace.[19]

A generation later America would fall victim to precisely this sort of hysteria whipped up by one Senator Joseph McCarthy. One of the victims of the witch hunts would be Howard Koch, blacklisted in 1951 under pressure from the House Un-American Activities Committee.

The notoriety of the 1938 broadcast would be indirectly responsible for Paramount's decision finally to produce *The War of the Worlds* for the screen. Early in 1951 the studio received a proposal from a writer called Mel Baber to produce a film based on the panic triggered by the Welles broadcast, entitled *The Martian Invasion*. Baber saw the film as a documentary-style reconstruction ('The picture should have a sense of complete reality. We should feel that actual people went through these experiences') and pitched it from the angle of Civil Defense. This was a time of heightened anxiety about the danger of nuclear war. It was the responsibility of the Federal Civil Defense Administration to prepare the American people for the possibility of nuclear attack and to persuade them that public services and institutions would be able to cope in the aftermath.[20] 'The A to Z bombs, bacterial warfare are fearful enough,' Baber averred, 'but what the authorities who are really on the job fear is panic.' A film dramatizing the hysteria around *The War of the Worlds* 'would be a real public service, possibly so great that it could save thousands of lives. 'A person who has seen this picture,' he suggested, 'will be just that much less likely to panic, that much more inclined to stop and think in an emergency.' He believed that such a film would receive official support, proposing that it would 'start with an introduction by a prominent psychologist or a top Civil Defense man'.[21] The proposal went no further: it was summarily rejected on the grounds that it was 'not ... a sound commercial idea'. However, it prompted one studio executive to suggest 'that a film of *War of the Worlds* itself (which we own and for which we happen to have production sketches) is a far better commercial idea – provided the cycle of science fiction films is not pretty well over'.[22]

The production season of 1950–1 had seen the emergence of science fiction, for the first time, as a major genre in Hollywood. The cycle began with two independent productions, *Rocketship X-M* and *Destination Moon*, and while the former quickly faded from memory, the latter won an Academy Award for Special Effects and was successful enough that Paramount brought its producer, George Pal, to the studio to make *When Worlds Collide*, which won another Academy Award.[23] *When Worlds Collide* had originally been bought as a property for Cecil B. De Mille in the 1920s. The old master congratulated Pal on his 'splendid producing job' and suggested that the timing was now propitious: 'When I bought it the atom bomb and long range rockets had not yet been developed, but the scientific progress of the last twenty years have given a plausibility which makes the story very exciting.'[24] While these films sent human beings into space, two major SF films in 1951 concerned aliens arriving on Earth. *The Thing from Another World* was the first of many SF/horror hybrids, while *The Day the Earth Stood Still*, in which the humanoid visitor is benign, challenged the mood of the early Cold War with its warning against the danger of nuclear proliferation.[25]

How can we account for the emergence of science fiction as a major genre at this time? There are three principal reasons. The first, as De Mille observed, was that the Second World War had accelerated the pace of scientific and technological development, especially nuclear physics (the atomic bomb) and rocketry (the German V2 missile). Super-weapons that only a decade before had been the stuff of pulp fantasy were now very much a reality. Another factor was the 'flying saucer' scare that began with the discovery of unidentified debris near Roswell, New Mexico, in 1947. The flying saucer phenomenon was a psychological side effect of the Cold War, famously expressed in the exhortation at the end of *The Thing from Another World* to 'Watch the skies – everywhere! Keep looking – keep watching the skies!'

The other reason for the emergence of SF cinema in the early 1950s was related to the changing nature of the film industry itself. The post-war period saw a precipitous decline in the habit of cinema-going: weekly cinema attendances in the United States fell away from a high of 90 million in the mid-1940s to 60 million in 1950 and 46 million in 1953.[26] The reasons for the decline in cinema attendances were complex – more leisure opportunities, the growth of home and car ownership, migration from cities to the suburbs – though the film industry identified the rise of television as the major factor. Hollywood's strategy for luring back the lost audience was to provide a level of spectacle that its new rival could not match: this meant colour and widescreen. A process of 'genre upscaling' occurred during the 1950s as films that hitherto had been regarded as B-movie fodder were treated to A-feature budgets and production values.[27] Science fiction was one of the genres that came of age during the 1950s (the other was the Western). The rise of the genre to A-feature status can be seen in the increasing budgets of George Pal's films: *Destination Moon* cost a modest $586,000, *When Worlds Collide* $936,000, while *The War of the Worlds* cost nearly $2 million.[28]

George Pal was the natural choice to produce *The War of the Worlds* following his previous genre films. Pal, a Hungarian émigré in Hollywood from 1939, had made his name as producer of an award-winning series of puppet-cartoon films for Paramount in the 1940s before turning to features, first as an independent producer with *The Great Rupert* (1949) and *Destination Moon* (1950), then as an in-house producer at Paramount. Pal was excited by the idea of filming *The War of the Worlds*, which he felt 'had withstood the advances of time remarkably well and remained today an exciting and visionary story of the future'.[29] The director was Byron Haskin, a former cinematographer who had headed the special effects unit at Warner Bros. in the 1940s before turning his hand to direction – his best-known film prior to *The War of the Worlds* was Walt Disney's *Treasure Island* (1950) – while the script was in the hands of Barré Lyndon, a British playwright who turned screenwriter in the 1940s. Pal adhered to the old Hollywood adage to put the budget on the screen: over half the cost of the film went on special effects.[30] This left little for star names – leads Gene Barry and Ann Robinson were very much from the second rank – though some *kudos* was had by hiring Sir Cedric Hardwicke as the narrator.

Lyndon followed the example of Howard Koch in locating the action in the United States (moving it to California) and updating the story to the present. In themselves these changes from the novel are cosmetic and do not significantly affect the story. Lyndon added a romantic subplot (this was at the behest of the studio: Pal later disavowed it) and introduced a geopolitical reason for the Martian invasion in so far as their home world is dying. His most significant contribution, however, was to introduce a strong religious dimension that does not feature in the book. The Martians are presented as godless and amoral:

> They want our earth with its warmth and water. They'll exterminate every living thing. They are a cold civilization from a cold world. They have degenerated as their civilization advanced. No spirituality. Our own culture was going the same way until scientists realized there was something beyond physics. Beyond electronics. Something, or Someone.[31]

In introducing this theme, Lyndon, whether consciously or not, was placing *The War of the Worlds* within the cultural discourses of the Cold War. A prominent theme of American Cold War propaganda was to present the United States as a society built on Christian values in contrast to the godless Soviet Union. For Lyndon, the defeat of the Martians became an act of God rather than biology, as in the book. He fashioned an ending in which the survivors of the human race are gathered in churches around the world: 'They're doing the only thing there is left to do. In the glow of candles and kerosene lamps they're praying for divine intervention. For deliverance. For God to lift His finger and perform a miracle, and save them.'

The script of *The War of the Worlds* went through several drafts that progressively downgraded the theme of class conflict and transformed the male protagonist from a conventional action-hero to a more intellectual character. Lyndon's first treatment, in June 1951, featured Greg Bradley, an oil company prospector described as 'a go-to-hell guy – rough, tough, ex-combat pilot', who meets Sylvia Ashton, a spoiled heiress who is

engaged to one George Ponsenby Vandenberg Jr. Greg and Sylvia find that
their initial antipathy towards one another turns to attraction as they are
thrown together during the crisis. By the first full screenplay in August
1951, however, this aspect had been dropped. The hero became Major
Greg Bradley of the Air Force Reserve, Sylvia Delano is his fashion model
girlfriend, and the class tension has been displaced onto Greg's father who
disapproves of Sylvia until she proves her mettle during the crisis.[32]

It was in this version of the screenplay that several key elements of
the film took shape. Lyndon changed Wells's insane curate into the heroic
character of Pastor Collins who tries to reason with the Martians: 'They're
living creatures ... If they're more advanced than us, then they should be
nearer the creator for that reason ... They are living creatures. And all life
comes from God.' Pastor Collins approaches the first Martian capsule

5. George Pal and Barré Lyndon added Pastor Collins (Lewis Martin) and
Sylvia Van Buren (Anne Robinson) to *The War of the Worlds* (1953)
(Source: British Film Institute).

reciting Psalm 23: he is killed by a heat ray. Lyndon added a scene in which a scientist analyses a Martian blood sample, acquired when Greg and Sylvia capture one of the Martians' mechanical eyes, which establishes the physical inferiority of the invaders: 'I've never seen blood as anaemic as this! They may be mental giants, but by our standards, they're physically degenerate.' The Air Force attempts to destroy the Martians with an atomic bomb: 'If it should fail, the Martians can conquer the earth in about six days. About the same length of time it took to create it!' The ending has Greg and Sylvia reunited with Greg's father, while a doctor explains the reason for the Martians' death: 'Everyone was praying for a miracle ... After everything men could do has failed – the Martians are being killed by the littlest things that God, in his wisdom, has put upon the earth.'[33]

The script continued to evolve. By October 1951 the hero had become Professor Clayton Forrester, a scientist from the California Institute of Technology, while heroine Sylvia Van Buren is no longer a glamorous fashion model but an ordinary girl of 'twenty-six, normal, nice' and Pastor Collins is her uncle. The theme of class antagonism has disappeared along with the hero's father, while the role of the military has been enhanced with a pitched battle between the US Air Force and the Martians.[34] This sequence was one of the casualties following a meeting held on 9 November to reduce the escalating costs of the film. Among other sequences to be dropped were cutaways to the Martians landing in other parts of the world. Haskin was concerned that the epic scope of the film would be lost if too many scenes were cut: 'We have so simplified the story that it is only the reaction of disaster on two people ... This is a documentary of Martians landing all around, and accumulated effects of world destruction and its being overcome.'[35] The 'Final White Script' of 18 December 1951 devised a cost-effective solution to the omission of some action sequences by adding a radio reporter (based on Ed Murrow) who describes the dropping of the atomic bomb.[36]

It was not only budgetary constraints that impacted upon the production of *The War of the Worlds*: as it neared shooting, the film also had to pass scrutiny from external agencies. It passed relatively unhindered through the Production Code Administration, whose main concerns were 'the need for the greatest possible care in the selection and photography of the costumes and dresses for your women' (this is a recurring theme in the PCA files at the time and seems to have been a routine directive to producers regardless of subject matter) and 'to avoid any excessive gruesomeness with reference to the portrayal of the men from Mars'.[37] However, the Pentagon was another story. The producers had hoped to secure the assistance of the Department of Defense in shooting the scenes involving the armed forces, only to be told 'that the picture would not qualify for official cooperation of the Military Department':

It is worth noting that the picture does nothing which could be said to have any public informational value to the Department of Defense or Army; but on the contrary it shows the Military to be inept and incapable of stemming the imaginary attack from Mars. Under these circumstances, it would not be possible to use real troops, or to film real troops in maneuvers, for use in connection with the production of the picture.[38]

In the 'First Preliminary Green Script' of 27 August 1951 the character of General Mann, the spokesperson for the military in the film, had indeed been an incompetent fool, and though he had become a more effective commander in later drafts, this was evidently insufficient for the Pentagon. In the event, Paramount secured the military hardware from the Arizona National Guard, supplemented by aerial footage from *Flying Leathernecks* (1951).[39]

Principal photography for *The War of the Worlds* was undertaken early in 1952, to be followed by a year of post-production and special effects work. Released in March 1953, the film enjoyed good reviews and box office returns. *Variety* thought it 'a socko science fiction thriller'.[40] The *Hollywood Reporter* called it 'a masterpiece, made with creative imagination and intelligence ... Not since "Dracula" has there been a film to cause such genuine terror as this filmization of a famous classic which as a radio play panicked the East and as a motion picture will cause uneasiness at the sight of a strange object in the sky.'[41] The *Los Angeles Examiner* found it 'a very superior picture, probably the best of the science fiction thrillers by George Pal ... The visual impact of the Technicolored destruction exceeds by far the spurious scare that the 1938 radio show threw into people.'[42] Some of the British critics disliked the 'Americanization' of the story, and *The Times* took against what it described as 'an offensive taste of false religiosity'.[43] But all reviewers admired its spectacle and special effects, for which the film won yet another Academy Award.

Pal's production of *The War of the Worlds* has typically been understood from a Cold War perspective. It was one of several Hollywood invasion narratives in the 1950s – others included *Invasion USA* (1952), *Invaders from Mars* (1953), *It Came from Outer Space* (1953) and *Invasion of the Body Snatchers* (1955) – that represented American society under attack from an external (alien/communist) threat. Mars has often functioned in SF cinema as a metaphor for the Soviet Union: there was even a film called *Red Planet Mars* (1952).[44] Yet, on closer inspection, *The War of the Worlds* is not without its ambiguities. We have seen, for example, that the US government declined to cooperate in the production, therefore positioning the film outside official Cold War propaganda. Furthermore, the transformation of the leading male protagonist from a pilot in early drafts of the script to a scientist in the finished film has the effect of detaching him from the military. The role of the scientist in SF cinema tends to be as an outsider who challenges the military: examples include *The Thing from Another World* (where the scientist is shown to be mistaken) and *Quatermass and the Pit* (where the scientist is proved correct). And, like *The Day the Earth Stood Still*, *The War of the Worlds* expresses unease about the major weapon in America's Cold War arsenal: the atomic bomb. The film's prologue refers ominously to 'the terrible weapons of super-science, menacing all mankind and every creature on earth'. Yet even the atom bomb is unable to stop the Martians: to this extent the film undermines the doctrine of Mutually Assured Destruction (MAD) that was the rationale for the existence of the nuclear deterrent.

The War of the Worlds became the definitive invaders-from-space film. Its cobra-like Martian war machines are one of the enduring images of the genre, while its representation of the Martians themselves, with their

6. Invaders from Mars: the iconic Martian war machines in *The War of the Worlds* (1953) (Source: British Film Institute).

enlarged heads and long spindly arms, influenced the 'look' of aliens in later films including Steven Spielberg's *Close Encounters of the Third Kind* (1977) and *E.T: The Extra-Terrestrial* (1982). Pal and Haskin followed *The War of the Worlds* with *Conquest of Space* (1955), a companion piece of sorts to *Destination Moon*, this time about an expedition to Mars. Pal would produce and direct another superior H. G. Wells adaptation, *The Time Machine* (1960), for MGM, while Haskin went on to direct episodes of the television anthology series *The Outer Limits* (1963–4) as well as a minor SF classic *Robinson Crusoe on Mars* (1964) and the supernatural thriller *The Power* (1968), the latter film reuniting him with Pal. In 1978 the composer Jeff Wayne turned *The War of the Worlds* into a 'concept rock' album featuring the vocal talents of David Essex, Justin Hayward and Julie Covington, with Richard Burton as the narrator.[45] Paramount made a 'sequel' to Pal's film in the form of the television series *War of the Worlds* (1988–9), set 35 years after the Martian invasion of 1953: the stored remains of the supposedly dead invaders are revived following exposure to radiation and they attempt to take over the world by stealth while seeking immunity from the germs that halted them the first time around.[46] And the super-blockbuster *Independence Day* (1996), noisily directed by Roland Emmerich, was more or less a remake of *The War of the Worlds*: here the alien invaders are finally defeated by introducing a computer virus into their command ship. In the twenty-first century Paramount has continued to milk Wells's formula in its expensively-produced *Transformers* film series (2007–11), while more diverse examples of the genre include the newly revived television series *Doctor Who* (2005–) and the recent low-budget British film *Attack the Block* (2011).

The continuing appeal and relevance of Wells's story was demonstrated in 2005, when no fewer than three films of *The War of the Worlds* were released. *H. G. Wells' War of the Worlds*, directed by David Michael Latt for Asylum Home Entertainment, was an updated version set in Washington DC and released straight to DVD. Also straight to DVD was *H. G. Wells' The War of the Worlds*, directed by Tim Haines for Pendragon Pictures, a period adaptation that maintained the Victorian setting and was shot in sepia tones to approximate the 'look' of early cinema.[47] Both these were entirely overshadowed, however, by Steven Spielberg's blockbuster *War of the Worlds*, which grossed $592 million worldwide. *War of the Worlds* is a characteristically Spielbergian film that balances visual spectacle with a narrative focusing on the restitution of the family. The screenplay by Josh Friedman and David Koepp turns the educated scientist of Wells's book into an emphatically blue-collar worker Ray Ferrier (Tom Cruise) who, during the crisis, learns to become a responsible parent to his neglected children. Spielberg's film locates itself in the lineage of previous adaptations through references to both the radio version (setting it in New Jersey) and the Pal-

Haskin film (Gene Barry and Ann Robinson make cameo appearances as Cruise's in-laws).

Spielberg's *War of the Worlds* does not entirely lose sight of its source, however. The alien tripods, the effect of the heat ray and the 'red weed' all appear as Wells described them, while Spielberg restores an important episode missing from the 1953 film by combining the characters of the curate and artilleryman into the deranged survivalist Ogilvy (Tim Robbins). And Spielberg is also alert to Wells's anti-colonial theme. As Kim Newman pointed out in his review of the film, the subtext here is the American-led invasion of Iraq in 2003:

> If Wells' Martians echo European imperialists in far-flung corners of the globe, then Spielberg's invaders – in their carapace-like machines, ignoring the native peoples except to imprison them and subject them to meaningless privations, so incapable of understanding the climate of the land they have conquered that a plan brewing 'for a million years' is undone because they didn't take elementary precautions against disease – stand less for Al-Qaeda or Saddam Hussein than for George W. Bush's America at work in Iraq.[48]

Thus, a tale that was originally a critique of Victorian attitudes towards 'inferior races' was turned into an allegory of American foreign policy at the start of the twenty-first century. *The War of the Worlds* is one of those narratives that have served the psychological and cultural needs of different historical periods and different national contexts. Each generation has produced its own version attuned to the ideological climate of the time. Consequently Wells's story continues to be as relevant to the world today as it was in 1897.

Notes

[1]   H. G. Wells, *The War of the Worlds*, ed. Patrick Parrinder (London: Penguin, 2005 [1898]), p.9. The story was serialized in *Pearson's Magazine* between April and December 1897, and published as a complete novel by William Heinemann in January 1898.

[2]   Steve Rubin, 'The War of the Worlds', *Cinefantastique*, 5: 4 (1977), p.4.

[3]   Margaret Herrick Library, Academy of Motion Picture Arts and Sciences (hereafter AMPAS), Paramount Pictures Scripts: *The War of the Worlds*: Treatment by Roy J. Pomeroy, 15 November 1926.

[4]   Ibid: 'Comment', undated, author unknown.

[5]   Ivor Montagu, *With Eisenstein in Hollywood* (Berlin: Seven Seas, 1974), p.71.

[6]   'Mr H. G. Wells and the Screen: "War of the Worlds" as a film', *The Times*, 3 November 1932, p.10.

7   British Film Institute, Ivor Montagu Collection, Item 25a: 'War of the Worlds' –
     Synopsis of Third Draft, n.d. This is a summary of a revised screenplay including six
     new sequences.

8   Montagu, *With Eisenstein in Hollywood*, p.36.

9   Wisconsin Center for Film and Theater Research (hereafter WCFTR) USS MS 50 AN
     Koch Box 1 f.2: Typescript by Howard Koch *c.*1962. This is a draft of the book *The Panic
     Broadcast: Portrait of an Event*, published in 1970.

10   The events surrounding the broadcast were dramatized in the television movie *The
     Night That Panicked America* (ABC, dir. Joseph Sargent, 31.10.1975).

11   A CD of the broadcast is included in Brian Holmstein and Alex Lubertozzi (eds), *The
     Complete War of the Worlds: Mars' Invasion of Earth from H. G. Wells to Orson Welles*
     (Napierville IL: Sourcebooks, 2001). It is also one of the Special Features on the
     Paramount 'Special Collector's Edition' DVD of *The War of the Worlds* (PHE 8726).

12   Simon Callow, *Orson Welles: The Road to Xanadu* (London: Jonathan Cape, 1995),
     pp.490–1.

13   John Houseman, 'The Men from Mars', *Harpers Magazine* (December 1948), pp.75–6.

14   WCFTR USS MS AN 50 Koch Box 1 f.3: Working script entitled 'Invasion from Mars',
     n.d.

15   WCFTR USS MS AN 50 Koch Box 1 f.1: Koch to David M. Knauf, 5 January 1964.

16   Callow, *Orson Welles*, p.402.

17   Hadley Cantril, with Hazel Gaudet and Herta Herzog, *The Invasion from Mars: A Study
     in the Psychology of Panic* (Princeton: Princeton University Press, 1940), *passim*.

18   Houseman, 'The Men from Mars', p.79.

19   Quoted in Holmstein and Lubertozzi, *The Complete War of the Worlds*, p.20.

20   Guy Oakes, 'The Family under Nuclear Attack: American Civil Defence Propaganda
     in the 1950s', in Gary D. Rawnsley (ed.), *Cold-War Propaganda in the 1950s* (London:
     Macmillan, 1999), pp.67–83.

21   AMPAS Paramount Scripts: *TWOTW*: Mel Baber to Erwin Gelsey, n.d.

22   Ibid: Bernard Smith to Don Hartman, n.d.

23   *Rocketship X-M* (Lippert Films, dir. Kurt Nuemann, 1950); *Destination Moon* (George
     Pal Productions, dir. Irving Pichel, 1950); *When Worlds Collide* (Paramount, dir. Rudolf
     Maté, 1951).

24   UCLA George Pal Collection Box 3 f.7: Cecil B. De Mille to Pal, 22 August 1951.

25   *The Thing from Another World* (RKO, dir. Christian Nyby, 1951); *The Day the Earth Stood
     Still* (20th Century-Fox, dir. Robert Wise, 1951).

26   John Belton, *American Cinema/American Culture* (New York: McGraw-Hill, 1994),
     p.257.

27   Kristin Thompson and David Bordwell, *Film History: An Introduction* (New York:
     McGraw-Hill, 1994), p.391.

28   George Pal, 'Filming "War of the Worlds" ', *Astounding Science Fiction* (October 1953),
     p.100. According to the Production Budget of 10 November 1951, the original budget
     was $1.6 million (AMPAS Paramount Production Records Box 229 f.2).

29   Pal, 'Filming "War of the Worlds" ', p.100.

30   ' "War" to have record special effects work', *Paramount News*, 21 April 1952.

31   AMPAS Barré Lyndon Papers Box 5 f.6: 'War of the Worlds' treatment, 7 June 1951.

32   AMPAS Paramount Scripts: *TWOTW*: First Preliminary Green Script, 27 August 1951.

33   This phrase is used by Wells's narrator but is no more than a passing comment in the
     book: it assumes greater significance in the film where it becomes the concluding line.

34   AMPAS Paramount Scripts: *TWOTW*: Limited Distribution Script, 9 October 1951.

35   AMPAS Paramount Production Records Box 231 f.9: 'War of the Worlds' – General
     Notes Meeting, 9 November 1951.

36   AMPAS Paramount Scripts: *TWOTW*: Final White Script, 18 December 1951.

37 AMPAS Motion Picture Producers of America: Production Code Administration file: *The War of the Worlds*: Joseph Breen to Luigi Luraschi (Director of Censorship, Paramount Pictures), 2 November 1951.

38 AMPAS Paramount Production Records Box 231 f.9: Lt Colonel Clair E. Towne (Motion Picture Division, Department of Defense) to Robert H. Denton, 24 October 1951.

39 Ibid: Donald Robb (Unit Production Manager) to Caffey, 21 November 1951.

40 *Variety*, 2 March 1953.

41 *Hollywood Reporter*, 2 March 1953.

42 *Los Angeles Examiner*, 26 November 1953, p.10.

43 *The Times*, 2 April 1953, p.12.

44 *Red Planet Mars* (United Artists, dir. Harry Horner, 1952). The film posits the discovery of a Christian civilization on Mars: the news prompts a religious revival on Earth that brings about the collapse of Communism.

45 Different versions of the album were released in Spain (with Anthony Quinn as the narrator) and Germany (with Curt Jürgens).

46 *War of the Worlds* ran for 43 episodes. After one season the series was 'rebooted' as *War of the Worlds: The Second Invasion* and dropped all continuity with the film.

47 Edward Gross, 'A War Over Worlds', *Cinefantastique*, 37 (April–May 2005), pp.48–68.

48 *Sight & Sound*, New Series 15: 9 (September 2005), p.84. See also Kirk Combe, 'Spielberg's Tale of Two Americas: Postmodern Monsters in *War of the Worlds*', *Journal of Popular Culture*, 44: 5 (2011), pp.934–53.

4

THE BRITISH INVASIONS:
THE QUATERMASS EXPERIMENT (1955), *QUATERMASS 2* (1957) AND *QUATERMASS AND THE PIT* (1967)

In the 1950s, as cinema attendances declined and box office revenues fell, the film industry responded in several ways. One strategy, exemplified by the Hollywood majors, was to turn to the production of fewer but bigger films that could be marketed as blockbuster attractions. Widescreen and high-definition colour offered levels of spectacle that cinema's new rival, television, could not match. Another strategy, pursued by independent producers such as American International Pictures, was the shift towards exploitation fare, especially horror and science fiction, targeted towards newly affluent teenagers rather than the traditional family audience. A similar tactic was adopted in Britain by Hammer Film Productions, a small and hitherto insignificant producer that suddenly emerged as a major force in the film industry.[1] In contrast to the Rank Organization, an ailing giant that responded sluggishly to structural change in the industry, or Ealing Studios, culturally a spent force by the mid-1950s, Hammer pursued a vigorous and innovative strategy of low-cost genre production that reaped rich rewards at the box office. It was the commercial success of *The Quatermass Experiment*, a science fiction-horror hybrid, that marked Hammer's entry into the premier league. The studio achieved this, ironically, by turning for inspiration to cinema's deadly rival: television.

Quatermass at the BBC

It is difficult today to appreciate the impact made by *The Quatermass Experiment* and its sequels on British television viewers in the 1950s. *The Quatermass Experiment* – billed as 'a thriller for television in six parts' – was broadcast in July and August 1953. An audience of 3.4 million for the first episode rose to 5 million for the final part, representing 13.6 per cent of the British population.[2] The BBC Audience Research Department found that it had a higher than average 'reaction index' and that viewers 'considered it a most unusual, exciting and ingenious serial', though a minority found it 'too fantastic' or 'too horrific'.[3] *Quatermass 2*, aired in October and November 1955, was produced in a newly competitive environment following the launch of the rival ITV network. Even so, its average audience of 8.2 million was significantly more than the first serial. This reflected both the rapid growth of television – the total number of television licences had doubled between 1953 and 1955 – and viewers' memories of the first *Quatermass*. Audience Research found that *Quatermass II* was if anything more popular than its predecessor: a majority thought it 'intensely thrilling and most exciting', though again some 'objected strongly to this serial on the grounds that it was too horrific, especially for Saturday night viewing when children would probably be watching'.[4] The third serial, *Quatermass and the Pit*, broadcast between December 1958 and January 1959, achieved an average of 9.6 million viewers with a high of 11 million for the final part. Audience Research found that viewers had expectations arising from the previous serials: for some *Quatermass and the Pit* 'had got off to a disappointingly slow start', but they stayed with it because its predecessors 'were remembered with pleasure'.[5]

All three Quatermass serials were produced by Rudolph Cartier, an Austrian *émigré* film-maker who joined the BBC after the Second World War, and written by Nigel Kneale, a BBC staff writer who had established a reputation as an expert in the craft of writing for the new medium of television. Kneale recognized television's visual possibilities rather than treating it as radio with pictures. All the serials were broadcast live: *The Quatermass Experiment* from the antiquated Alexandra Palace, *Quatermass II* from the recently acquired film studio at Lime Grove and *Quatermass and the Pit* from the new Riverside Studios in Hammersmith. The protagonist of all three serials is Professor Bernard Quatermass, Director of the British Experimental Rocket Group, though he was played by a different actor each time: Reginald Tate, John Robinson and André Morell. The Quatermass serials are set approximately ten years in the future – the first two posit the existence of a British space programme – and each presents a narrative in which Quatermass discovers and finally overcomes an alien threat to the Earth.

The Quatermass serials each represent different themes and templates of science fiction, including first contact with an alien life form (*The Quatermass Experiment*), invasion by stealth (*Quatermass II*) and an allegory of racial hatred (*Quatermass and the Pit*). Cartier averred that Kneale 'had all three stories in his mind from the start. We decided to do *Experiment* first because we thought it would give us less trouble with exteriors and things like that.'[6] This is contradicted, however, by Kneale himself, who always claimed that *The Quatermass Experiment* was conceived to fill a gap in the Saturday evening schedule.[7] Further evidence that Kneale had not planned all three stories from the outset is found in a memo he wrote to Cecil McGivern, the Controller of Television, regarding *Quatermass II*:

> I have tried to make this serial as effective as its predecessor, but in quite a different way: a logical extension. Given the publicly-expected components of the dogged professor, rocketry and Things from space, in terms of (substantially) live television, the possibilities are not infinite; but I eventually worked out a story that seemed more than mere repetition.[8]

Critical discussion of the Quatermass serials has tended to focus on their formal and aesthetic properties. They are seen as integral to a move to open up the 'intimate' screen of television by exploring the medium's potential for spectacle.[9] Cartier and Kneale disliked the dominant style of studio-bound plays and sought to incorporate some of the techniques of the film industry into television drama. Science fiction was an obvious genre in which to attempt this, despite the technological and budgetary limitations of early television.[10] But the serials can also be seen as an attempt to legitimate SF as a serious genre. As Cartier told the Air Ministry when requesting technical advice for *The Quatermass Experiment*: 'I am most anxious to lift this production above the level of strip-cartoons and magazine thrillers, and we have secured technical datae [*sic*] and scientific support from responsible quarters.'[11] The first serial, especially, asserted its distance from B-movie SF. The fourth episode (now 'lost') included a sequence where Victor Carroon, the astronaut who has been infected by an alien organism, hides in a cinema showing a 3D film called *Planet of the Dragons*. The film-within-a-film – described in production documents as 'the "Hollywood" picture' – is clearly intended as a spoof of the risible, juvenile nature of many contemporary SF films.[12] This was the first instance of what would become a dialogue between the film and television media that occurs throughout the Quatermass films.[13]

Kneale, for his part, saw Quatermass as a means of commenting on contemporary society: 'I try to give these stories some relevance to what is round about us today.'[14] *Quatermass II*, for example, expresses anxiety about the growth of state bureaucracy, while *Quatermass and the Pit* refers to social problems (it came in the wake of the Notting Hill race riots of 1958) and to the founding of the Campaign for Nuclear Disarmament (Quatermass calls nuclear weapons 'the dead man's deterrent'). The recurring theme of all the Quatermass serials is the relationship between science and society. Quatermass is an archetypal 'boffin' — Kneale took his first name from Bernard Lovell, Professor of Astronomy at the University of Manchester and designer of the pioneering radio telescope and observatory at Jodrell Bank – and represents the voice of scientific reason in contrast to blinkered characters like Inspector Lomax of Scotland Yard (*The Quatermass Experiment*) and the blimpish Colonel Breen (*Quatermass and the Pit*). However, the Quatermass serials also suggest a degree of ambiguity about science. Thus it is Quatermass's rocket that brings a deadly alien life form back to Earth (*The Quatermass Experiment*) and his design for a moon base that facilitates the incubation of alien invaders (*Quatermass II*). In the age of the atom bomb, science was no longer presented in such a positive light as in *Things to Come*.

The Enemy Outside:
The Quatermass Experiment (1955)

On 24 August 1953, two days after the conclusion of *The Quatermass Experiment*, the BBC's Head of Copyright reported: 'I have had a letter from Hammer Film Productions Ltd saying they would be interested in the purchase of film rights in "The Quatermass Experiment".'[15] Hammer was the production arm of Exclusive Films, a distribution company set up in 1935 by Enrique Carreras and Will Hinds. It was essentially a family business: James Carreras became its managing director in 1949 and Anthony Hinds acted as executive producer for most of its films. Hammer's interest in *The Quatermass Experiment* was consistent with its strategy of producing films adapted from other media including three Dick Barton adventures - *Dick Barton – Special Agent* (1948), *Dick Barton Strikes Back* (1949) and *Dick Barton at Bay* (1950) – *The Adventures of PC49* (1949), *The Man in Black* (1950), *Lady in the Fog* (1952) and *Life with the Lyons* (1953), all based on BBC radio serials. *The Quatermass Experiment* was regarded as just another adaptation of a successful property from another medium. It cost a modest £42,000 and principal photography took just five weeks. According to director Val Guest, this necessitated 'shooting the picture in a cinéma vérité, almost documentary style, sometimes using hand-held cameras to give it a newsreel quality'.[16]

The production of *The Quatermass Experiment* demonstrates the economic and cultural imperatives determining genre film-making in Britain in the 1950s. Exclusive Films had a co-production and distribution arrangement with Robert Lippert Productions, a minor American company specializing in second features. Evidence of the American partner's influence over the film can be seen in the casting of Margia Dean, a former beauty queen, in the role of Judith Carroon: Miss Dean happened to be the girlfriend of Robert Lippert Jr. American screenwriter Robert Landau, who had worked on several previous Hammer productions, including the SF melodrama *Spaceways* (1953), was brought in to ensure the film would be suitable for US audiences. Landau initially turned the character of Quatermass's assistant Dr Briscoe into an American in order to facilitate casting an American actor.[17] However, Briscoe reverted to being British (he is played in the film by David King Wood) when Brian Donlevy was cast as Quatermass. Donlevy's best known roles were as the sadistic sergeant in *Beau Geste* (1939) and in the title role of Preston Sturges's comedy *The Great McGinty* (1940), but by the 1950s his career was in decline: his favourite co-star by this time was Jack Daniel's. His performance as Quatermass is brusque and boorish – some critics complained that he played the role like an Irish-American cop – and entirely unlike the British 'boffin' of the television serials. In contrast the character of Quatermass's antagonist Chief Inspector Lomax was played by the avuncular Jack Warner.

However, the main obstacle to making *The Quatermass Experiment* was not its star's preference for a liquid lunch – in fact Guest said Donlevy was 'a delight to work with'[18] – but the British Board of Film Censors. In 1951 the film classification system had been modified with the introduction of the new 'X' certificate that prohibited exhibition to any person under sixteen. The 'X' was partly a replacement for the old 'H' (for 'horrific') category, but it was also intended for serious films that by dint of their subject matter were deemed unsuitable for children, such as *Women of Twilight* (1952), *Cosh Boy* (1953) and *I Am a Camera* (1955).[19] Most producers fought shy of the 'X' certificate, which they felt would limit their box office receipts, and some exhibitors even refused to show 'X' certificate films. The horrific content of *The Quatermass Experiment* meant that it was always likely to be an 'X', but even that was problematic, as Hammer found when they submitted the screenplay for pre-production scrutiny to the BBFC. It was routine practice to consult the Board before filming started in order to avoid shooting any scenes that would be considered prohibitive by the censors and would end up being cut. The Secretary of the BBFC, Arthur Watkins, told the company:

> We have now read the screenplay of *The Quatermass Experiment* which was enclosed with your letter of the 27th August. I must warn you at this stage that, while we accept this story in principle for the 'X' category, we could not certificate, even in that category, a film treatment in which the horrific element was so exaggerated

as to be nauseating and revolting to adult audiences. Nor can we
pass uncut, even in the 'X' category, sequences in which physical
agony and screams of pain or terror are unnecessarily exaggerated
or prolonged.[20]

Watkins then listed a series of specific objections, including close-ups of
Carroon's 'knotted hands' and 'gruesome' shots of dead bodies. In particular,
the censor disliked a sequence where Carroon is kidnapped from hospital
by three crooks, who are then killed in a burning car: 'Ramsay's screams
should not be unnecessarily prolonged; there should be no shot of him
on fire and the statement that the driver has been burned alive should be
omitted.' Hammer was compliant with the censor's demands: the offending
scene was removed.

The Quatermass Experiment wore its 'X' certificate with pride: Hammer
released the film as *The Quatermass Xperiment* (a later reissue restored the
'E'). The critical response was, by and large, positive. The film was praised
for Guest's brisk direction, and in particular for the performance of Richard
Wordsworth as the tragic astronaut Victor Carroon. It was regarded as much
as a horror film as science fiction, and its British origin was often emphasized.
Paul Dehn, film critic of the *News Chronicle* and himself an Academy Award-
winning screenwriter for *Seven Days to Noon* (1950), thought it 'is the best
and nastiest horror film that I have seen since the war. How jolly that it is
also British.'[21] The *Manchester Guardian* found it 'a lively piece of science
fiction' that 'quite neatly combines the horrific and the factual'.[22] William
Whitebait in the *New Statesman* thought it 'a better film than either *The
War of the Worlds* or *Them*'.[23] Even *The Times* conceded that 'Mr Val Guest,
the director, certainly knows his business when it comes to providing the
more horrid brand of thrills.'[24] *The Quatermass Experiment* was released on
a double bill with *Rififi*: the unusual combination of British exploitation
fare and polished French thriller was voted the best double feature of 1955
on the ABC circuit.[25] In the United States, where it was released by United
Artists, it was retitled *The Creeping Unknown* and paired with a horror film
called *The Black Sleep*.[26]

The Quatermass Experiment was no less a landmark for British cinema than
it had been for television. It was the first full-blown British entry in the cycle
of alien invasion and monster movies that had started with *The Thing from
Another World* (1951). Its success can be attributed partly to the exploitation
value of the 'X' certificate – Hammer had an uncanny knack for judging
the market – but also in large measure to its difference from other British
films of the time. The 1950s have often (if unfairly) been characterized as the
'doldrums era' of British cinema when the major genres – war, comedies,
domestic dramas – all adhered to a dominant realist aesthetic that privileged

sober narratives and emotional restraint. In contrast, however, David Pirie contends that the opening of *The Quatermass Experiment* --where the returning Quatermass rocket crashes in the countryside, rudely interrupting the amorous activities of a courting couple – 'seems to record the *intrusion* of Hammer into the cosy middle-class domesticity of the British cinema'.[27] *The Quatermass Experiment* represents everything that 'quality' British cinema was not: sensational, melodramatic, fantastic. It is also an extremely visceral film for its time: its images of bodily corruption, as Carroon's body is progressively infested by the alien parasite, anticipate by several decades the 'body horror' of films such as *Alien* and the remake of *The Fly*.[28]

Yet *The Quatermass Experiment* was also very much a film of its time. It is replete with visual references that locate it historically in 1950s Britain, including a bomb-damaged London that still bears the scars of the Blitz, and indicators of the post-war Welfare State ('Get Your National Health Prescription Here' declares a poster on the wall of a chemist's shop). It also provides a complex and peculiarly British commentary on the politics of the Cold War. On the one hand it can be located in the lineage of 1950s SF cinema that equates the alien invader with an external threat. That Carroon's body and mind have been absorbed by the extra-terrestrial organism that infiltrated the Quatermass rocket might be understood as a metaphor for the brainwashing scares of the Korean War: the returning hero (Carroon is an ex-RAF pilot) turns out to be under enemy control. On the other hand, however, the sympathetic characterization of Carroon as a victim, rather than a faceless menace, makes a reductive reading of the alien as representing a foreign and/or communist threat extremely difficult. In some respects, indeed, Quatermass is represented as more of a monster than Carroon: he seems indifferent to Carroon's fate ('There's no room for personal feelings in science') and is more concerned about the success of his experiment ('I launched it and I brought it back. That's quite an achievement, I think').

The Quatermass Experiment can also be read in the context of other issues affecting Britain at the time. In particular, it rehearses anxieties around the decline of British power and dependency on US protection. It is significant in this regard that the alien creature is hunted down and eventually destroyed by the uneasy and unequal Anglo-American alliance of Chief Inspector Lomax and Quatermass. Lomax's comment 'Nobody wins a cold war' refers not to superpower relations but to his edgy relationship with Quatermass. (Some critics noted that the film does not explain what Quatermass's position is: according to the script he is Director of the British-American Rocket Group.) The motif of Britain threatened by an alien menace from 'out there' also irresistibly brings to mind the response to immigration in the post-war period. The threat posed by the alien is its reproductive capacity: it is dispersing spores at an exponential rate. Is it too far-fetched to suggest

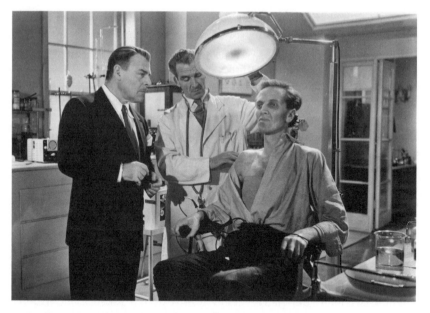

7. Professor Quatermass (Brian Donlevy) and Victor Carroon
(Richard Wordsworth) in *The Quatermass Experiment* (1955)
(Source: British Film Institute).

that this could be read as an expression of anxieties around the growth
of the immigrant population in Britain? The decade following the British
Nationality Act of 1948 saw around 180,000 Commonwealth immigrants
arrive in Britain, largely from the West Indies, India and Pakistan.[29] While
there is no evidence to suggest that such meanings were intended by the
film's producers, there is no denying the symbolism of the climax taking
place in Westminster Abbey. There is something quite subversive about the
idea of an alien creature seeding itself at the site of the Coronation of Queen
Elizabeth II only two years before. Whether this was intentional or not, *The
Quatermass Experiment* nevertheless suggests a sense of acute anxiety about
the tensions underlying British society that is markedly different from most
films of the time.

The Enemy Within: *Quatermass 2* (1957)

The success of *The Quatermass Experiment* made Hammer keen to produce
a sequel – and quickly. Hammer's production manager Jimmy Sangster

was pressed into service as writer of what would become *X – The Unknown* (another title that exploited its 'X' certificate status).[30] This was originally intended as a new Quatermass story, but when Nigel Kneale refused to allow the use of his character, the protagonist became Dr Adam Royston (Dean Jagger). It was to have been directed by one Joe Walton, who was replaced at the last minute by Leslie Norman.[31] 'Joe Walton' was in fact a pseudonym for the blacklisted Joseph Losey, who was removed from the picture at the insistence of its American star Dean Jagger.[32]

Quatermass 2 became possible when Hammer invited Kneale to adapt his television scripts for the big screen in collaboration with Val Guest.[33] The sequel's budget of £92,000 was double the first film's and was made possible by pre-selling the world distribution rights to United Artists. It also allowed for more location shooting: the film used the same location as the television serial, the Shell Haven oil refinery on the Thames estuary, to stand in for the mysterious government installation at Wynderden Flats. Kneale condensed the narrative and changed the ending: while on television Quatermass had taken a rocket into space to confront the alien invaders on their asteroid home, in the film an unmanned rocket is fired to destroy the asteroid. Kneale was unhappy that Brian Donlevy returned to play Quatermass again: 'Mr Donlevy had had another two years of soaking up a lot of Scotch every lunchtime. By the afternoon he couldn't remember what the story was, so it had to change to deal with that, which pretty well sank it as far as I was concerned.'[34] According to Guest, however, the biggest problem was Donlevy's toupee which blew off in the wind: 'I had to spend the rest of the day shooting scenes with his hat on tight.'[35]

Again the producers had to negotiate with the BBFC over the content of the film. The screenplay was submitted for pre-production scrutiny on 27 April 1956. An internal report by examiner Audrey Field provides an insight into the cultural prejudices of the BBFC:

> What nonsense! Sillier than *Quatermass I*, or the recent effusion from Hammer Films on the same lines [*X – The Unknown*]. However, it is the sort of nonsense which aims at an 'X' certificate and is quite disgusting, if not frightening enough, to get it. I think I am right in saying that *Quatermass II* on television was preceded by the customary caution about children and nervous people; and the only part I saw (which involved engulfing people with slime) was quite sickening enough to be kept away from the very young or the moderately squeamish. For 'X', there should be the customary general caution that the sky is not the limit, either in sights or sounds. But I think most of what is in the script could be done in a way which is not prohibitive.[36]

Arthur Watkins duly issued the 'customary general caution', telling Hammer that 'everything will depend upon reasonable discretion of treatment. Even for "X", the sights and sounds indicating terror and agony, and the portrayal of what is horrific and nauseating, can go too far.'[37]

The most problematic scene for the censors was one where a family, picnicking on a beach, are murdered by zombie-like paramilitary guards, and their bodies are driven back to the base. Watkins cautioned: 'The presence of dead bodies in the car should be very discreetly suggested and the shot of the little boy's blood-stained arm hanging out of the car should be omitted.'[38] The massacre of the family – a shocking scene that had featured in the television serial – was left out of the finished film. It was rather unusual that a scene considered suitable for television – even in a post-watershed slot – was deemed inappropriate for cinema. Watkins also highlighted several other specific points, including two scenes where a character is clubbed with a rifle butt, and 'the horrible death of Broadhead'. Broadhead's death – he is covered in poisonous black slime – did make it into the finished film and again demonstrates the highly visceral nature of the Hammer films. To this extent *The Quatermass Experiment* and *Quatermass 2* anticipate the visual excesses of the studio's Gothic horror films.

Quatermass 2 did not quite match the success of *The Quatermass Experiment*. Its reception was mixed. 'Inferior science fiction with occasional moments of genuine menace', was the verdict of the *Evening Standard*.[39] The *Financial Times* described it as 'science fiction which mixes schoolboyish innocence and zest with a sometimes genuinely creepy inventiveness'.[40] The *Monthly Film Bulletin* felt that 'this film has necessarily lost much of the quality of the original' in reducing the six-episode serial to an 85-minute feature. 'Nor is it helped by inexpert handling of unskilful actors.'[41] *Quatermass 2* formed half of one of cinema history's most incongruous double bills with *And God Created Woman*.[42] Unfortunately there is no evidence to indicate what audiences made of the combination of a pouting young Brigitte Bardot and exploding seed pods from outer space. In America, where *Quatermass 2* was released under the blandly generic title *Enemy from Space*, the reception was also mixed. The *Hollywood Reporter* found it 'a well-made British production – superior for its type', but *Variety* declared that 'British producers, when they turn to science-fiction, generally are vague in approach and this import does little to dispel the impression.'[43]

Quatermass 2 has often been seen as a British *Invasion of the Body Snatchers*: Pirie even calls it 'the greatest British anxiety movie of all'.[44] *Invasion of the Body Snatchers* (1956) has been understood as a statement about the paranoia that gripped America during the McCarthy witch hunts of the early 1950s.[45] There are certainly close parallels between the two films: both feature alien 'pods' taking over people's minds and bodies while the protagonist tries to raise the alarm. The films rehearse the tension between ideological conformity and individual free thought that was a feature of Cold War culture. It should be pointed out, however, that while *Quatermass 2* (film) came after *Invasion of the Body Snatchers*, Kneale had written the television serial before Don Siegel's film was released. And there are also some important differences. In *Quatermass 2*, for example, it is implied that the British state has already been taken over: no less a figure than the Commissioner of Metropolitan Police is revealed to be under alien control. The idea that an enemy is able to hide behind the mask of officialdom can surely be read – especially in the aftermath of the Suez Crisis (1956) – as a warning against complacency. To this extent the Quatermass films serve a very different ideological function to other British genres of the 1950s, such as war films or the Ealing comedies, which offered a reassuring image of national self-reliance.

Like its predecessor, *Quatermass 2* was responding to current issues in British society and politics. However, the issues themselves are different. *Quatermass 2* is more explicitly political: it can be read as a commentary on the rise of the secret state in Cold War Britain. The narrative revolves around an isolated government installation protected by sinister armed

8. The secret state: Quatermass (Brian Donlevy) is manhandled by sinister armed guards in *Quatermass 2* (1957) (Source: British Film Institute).

guards and surrounded by roads that lead nowhere. Kneale said this aspect was 'a conscious theme. It was a period when a lot of mysterious radar establishments and places of that sort had been built across the counties, and if anything it was done with even greater secrecy than it would be now, because there was a great nervousness in the country.'[46] Kneale probably had in mind installations like the Atomic Weapons Research Establishment at Aldermaston, Berkshire. The presence of the state in *Quatermass 2* is authoritarian and sinister: it forcibly breaks up communities by dislocating workers to new housing estates. Peter Hutchings reads the film as a statement about 'the changing role of the state in British life, the introduction of new technology ... and an associated sense that particular traditional values and social structures are being eroded'.[47] Again *Quatermass 2* explores the tensions and anxieties that lurk beneath the surface of social normality: people and institutions are not what they seem.

The social politics of *Quatermass 2* are nothing if not radical. Its resolution sees the breakdown of the consensual values that have traditionally been seen as a force for stability in British society and had been such an essential feature of the social and historical discourses of the Second World War. Here the suggestion is that old social structures and community ties are breaking down in the face of modernity – a modernity represented by the soulless estate in which the workers from the mysterious food processing plant are housed. The film climaxes in what amounts to a workers' uprising as they take up arms against their (alien) bosses. This can be understood as a fairly obvious metaphor for industrial unrest and class warfare. These were subjects that, even in the 1950s, the BBFC actively discouraged. Accordingly, most British films still promoted an ideology of consensus in which social differences were resolved. To this extent *Quatermass 2* demonstrates the potential of science fiction for exploring themes and anxieties that were largely overlooked in British cinema of the 1950s.

The Enemy Below:
Quatermass and the Pit (1967)

Val Guest would follow *Quatermass 2* with *The Abominable Snowman* (1957), a superior horror-thriller which Kneale adapted from his television play *The Creature*, but it would be a whole decade before the next Quatermass film, even though *Quatermass and the Pit* was produced for television in 1958. One reason for the delay was that Kneale wanted assurance that Donlevy would not be cast in the film of *Quatermass and the Pit*.[48] Another was that Hammer radically revised its production strategy following the box office success of *The Curse of Frankenstein* (1957) and *Dracula* (1958). These films inaugurated the cycle of Gothic horrors that would come to define the Hammer style. James Carreras gave another reason for the studio's move away from SF: 'Science fiction films are not easy to make. They call for lots of trick photography which sends the budget soaring and the faking has got to be good.'[49] Guest went on to direct another superior SF film, for British Lion, *The Day the Earth Caught Fire* (1961), notable for its semi-documentary style, and which won a British Film Academy Award for Best Screenplay for Guest and Wolf Mankowitz.

Although Kneale had written a screenplay for *Quatermass and the Pit* in 1961, the film was shelved for several years. It was revived in 1967 at a time when Hammer was looking once again to diversify its output in response to the saturation of the horror market. The studio attempted some more expensive productions including the fantasy adventure *One Million Years BC* (1966) and the SF film *Moon Zero Two* (1969). *Quatermass and the Pit* was shot at MGM's British studio at Borehamwood with a budget of £180,000. Its director was Roy Ward Baker, whose experience of making *A Night to Remember* (1958), about the sinking of the *Titanic*, was seen as evidence that he could handle the visual effects. The screenplay was by Kneale, who nevertheless felt the film 'suffered from shrinkage ... I don't think it was as good as the BBC's version.'[50] Baker, however, thought that Kneale's script 'was taut, exciting and an intriguing story with excellent narrative drive. It needed no work at all. All one had to do was cast it and shoot it.'[51] Hammer stalwart Andrew Keir played Quatermass – the studio's commercial success meant it was no longer subject to the casting whims of US distributors – and his performance was much closer to Kneale's concept of the character as a tweedy academic. It was released in Britain by Associated British Pathé and in America, entitled *Five Million Years to Earth*, by 20th Century-Fox.

Quatermass and the Pit seems not to have troubled the censors to any great degree – the limits of permissible horror had been gradually eroded in the decade since *Quatermass 2* – and it was passed uncut for an 'X' certificate. The critical response was broadly favourable. Dilys Powell in the *Sunday Times* wrote that it 'is produced and directed with dash – and an absolutely straight face ... Of its kind, *Quatermass and the Pit* is pretty smart.'[52] Penelope Mortimer in the *Observer* felt that 'this nonsense makes quite a good film, well put together, competently photographed, on the whole sturdily performed'.[53] John Russell Taylor wrote in *The Times*: 'It was always the most interesting of the series, because the least mechanistic, and the extra possibilities of the big screen are for once all beneficial to the story.'[54] And Cecil Wilson in the *Daily Mail* thought it was told 'with that deadly, dedicated seriousness so essential to these Quatermass nightmares'.[55] However, Margaret Hinxman in the *Sunday Telegraph* felt that 'Roy Baker's direction is rather prosaic and one misses the sharp edge of reason that gave the TV "Quatermasses" their special quality'.[56] The *Monthly Film Bulletin* agreed: 'It is a shame that this, the most interesting of Nigel Kneale's Quatermass parables, should prove the least satisfactory as a film.' [57]

Quatermass and the Pit is the closest of all the films to the television serial: it is also the most intellectually ambitious. It revolves around the discovery of a mysterious capsule – at first assumed to be an unexploded bomb – during the redevelopment of an underground railway station. This places *Quatermass and the Pit* in a tradition of film and television that represents the London Underground as a site of horror.[58] It also invokes the memory of the Second World War in its references to the Blitz. Quatermass and Dr Roney (James Donald) deduce that the capsule is of alien origin and that it crashed on Earth millions of years ago. Rather more disturbing, however, is their realization that the skeletal remains of pre-human 'ape men' have been preserved *inside* the capsule. Quatermass theorizes that 5 million years ago the Earth was colonized by Martians escaping their own planet as it died and who altered the course of evolution on Earth by experimenting on the indigenous inhabitants. This explanation is unpalatable to the government ('You are implying that we owe our human condition to the intervention of insects!?') and to the military (who prefer to believe the capsule is a Nazi propaganda weapon). It transpires that the 'race memory' of the Martians has been implanted into the human subconscious. Quatermass and Roney employ a telepathic device called a 'spectral oscillator' to work out that the Martians engaged in 'ritual slaughter to preserve a fixed society and rid it of mutations'. It seems reasonable to assume that even in 1967 this would have been understood as a reference to Nazi racial genocide.

Like its predecessors *Quatermass and the Pit* refers to a range of contemporary social and political issues. The Cold War background is once again prominent. As the film opens, the British Rocket Group is about to be taken over for military purposes in order to establish ballistic missile bases on the Moon. The film therefore rehearses a tension between the scientific establishment and the military. Keir's Quatermass is much more of a 'dove' than the more aggressive Donlevy version. He is an idealist who believes that space exploration represents 'a great chance to leave our vices behind – war first of all – not to go out there dragging our hatreds and our frontiers along with us'. This is contrasted with Colonel Breen (Julian Glover) who can barely conceal his contempt for Quatermass and Roney. The climax of the film features an outbreak of mass hysteria and communal violence in the streets of London as the Martian capsule draws energy from television equipment and the embedded 'race memory' of the population is awakened. Again the film challenges the idea of social cohesion: the suggestion here

9. 'We're the Martians now': Quatermass (Andrew Keir) and Dr Roney (James Donald) with a putrefied Martian in *Quatermass and the Pit* (1967) (Source: British Film Institute).

is that the potential for unrest and violence lurks beneath the surface of society and may erupt without warning. In the television serial this had been understood as a reference to the Notting Hill race riots in the summer of 1958 but the message remained timely in the film: 1967 saw the formation of the National Front and a spate of attacks on Asian immigrants in Bradford, Leeds, Leicester and Luton.

Quatermass and the Pit can also be understood as an allegory of colonialism. Like *The War of the Worlds* it invokes a parallel between alien invasion and colonization – with the British cast in the unfamiliar role of colonized rather than colonizers. The difference here is that the invasion has already taken place some 5 million years ago. The colonizers have died out but have left their racial and genetic imprint embedded in the human unconscious. As Roney's assistant Barbara Judd (Barbara Shelley) remarks: 'We're the Martians now.'[59] It is a profoundly disturbing conclusion that once again highlights the subversive nature of these films. While in previous films Quatermass had succeeded in overcoming the alien invasions, here he is shown ultimately to be powerless to prevent the infiltration as it has already taken place. To this extent *Quatermass and the Pit* can be read as a commentary on the decline of British power and a statement of Britain's strategic impotence by the late 1960s.

Quatermass Redux

Quatermass and the Pit would not be the last appearance of the doughty professor in British popular culture. A fourth television serial, written by Kneale, was announced in 1973.[60] In the event the BBC declined the project, but it was picked up by Euston Films, a subsidiary of Thames Television, who produced a four-part serial, entitled simply *Quatermass*, in 1979.[61] *Quatermass* – also released theatrically overseas as *The Quatermass Conclusion* – is set approximately in the year 2000 and posits a future in which social order has collapsed and Britain has become a spectator in the space race between the United States and Soviet Union. It is a thoroughly pessimistic vision of the future: cities have degenerated into lawlessness, the police force has been privatized, and there appears to be little effective central authority. Quatermass (played by John Mills), now retired, is an old man and his concern is to find his granddaughter who has become involved with a cult known as the Planet People. It transpires that the young are being 'harvested' by aliens: in a gloomily apocalyptic climax, Quatermass sets a trap for the aliens, primed with an atom bomb, and sacrifices his own life in the process. While it is consistent with the dystopian tone of much 1970s science fiction, *Quatermass* failed to make the impact of its predecessors. Its fate was not helped by a technicians' strike that took the ITV network off the air for several weeks during its initial broadcast.

In 1996 Radio 4 broadcast *The Quatermass Memoirs*, narrated by Andrew Keir as Quatermass, here reflecting on the scientific and ethical implications of his actions. (In the internal time line the memoirs are after the events of *Quatermass and the Pit* and before *Quatermass*.) In 2005 the digital channel BBC4 broadcast a feature-length remake of *The Quatermass Experiment* as an experiment in live drama. It starred Jason Flemyng as Quatermass and a pre-*Doctor Who* David Tennant as Dr Briscoe.[62] This was updated to the present day, deleting the Cold War references and bringing it into line with modern scientific and political developments: for example the Quatermass spaceship is now backed by private enterprise rather than a government project. In a neat symmetry, therefore, for what seems likely to be his final appearance, Quatermass returned to his origins in live television.[63]

Notes

1   See Sue Harper and Vincent Porter, *British Cinema of the 1950s: The Decline of Deference* (Oxford: Oxford University Press, 2003), pp.137–52; Wayne Kinsey, *Hammer Films:*

The Bray Studios Years (London: Reynolds & Hearn, 2002); Tom Johnson and Deborah Del Vecchio, *Hammer Films: An Exhaustive Filmography* (Jefferson NC: McFarland, 1996); and Sinclair McKay, *A Thing of Unspeakable Terror: The History of Hammer Films* (London: Aurum Press, 2007). On the Quatermass films see Peter Hutchings, ' "We're the Martians now": British sf invasion fantasies of the 1950s and 1960s', in I. Q. Hunter (ed.), *British Science Fiction Cinema* (London: Routledge, 1999), pp.33–47, and Dave Rolinson and Nick Cooper, ' "Bring Something Back": The Strange Career of Professor Bernard Quatermass', *Journal of Popular Film and Television*, 30: 3 (2002), pp.158–65.

[2] Viewing figures for each serial are collated by Andrew Pixley in the 'Viewing Notes' for the DVD *The Quatermass Collection* (BBCDVD1478), pp.44–7. On the television serials, see James Chapman, 'Quatermass and the origins of British television sf', in John R. Cook and Peter Wright (eds), *British Science Fiction Television: A Hitch Hiker's Guide* (London: I.B.Tauris, 2005), pp.21–51.

[3] BBC Written Archives Centre, Caversham, Reading (hereafter BBC WAC) T5/418: Viewer Research Report VR/43/421, 2 September 1953.

[4] BBC WAC T5/2540: Audience Research Report VR/55/529, 9 November 1955.

[5] BBC WAC T5/2302: Audience Research Report VR/58/706, 7 January 1959.

[6] Quoted in Lynda Miller and Julian Petley, 'Rudolph Cartier', *Sight & Sound*, 59: 2 (1990), pp.127–8.

[7] Paul Wells, 'Apocalypse Then! An Interview with Nigel Kneale', in Hunter (ed.), *British Science Fiction Cinema*, p.50.

[8] BBC WAC T5/2540: Kneale to Cecil McGivern, 5 November 1955.

[9] Charles Barr, 'Broadcasting and Cinema 2: Screens Within Screens', in Barr (ed.), *All Our Yesterdays: 90 Years of British Cinema* (London: British Film Institute, 1986), pp.206–224; Jason Jacobs, *The Intimate Screen: Early British Television Drama* (Oxford: Clarendon Press, 2000), pp.109–55; Catherine Johnson, 'Exploiting the Intimate Screen: *The Quatermass Experiment*, Fantasy and the Aesthetic Potential of Early Television Drama', in Janet Thumin (ed.), *Small Screens, Big Ideas: Television in the 1950s* (London: I.B.Tauris, 2002), pp.181–94.

[10] *The Quatermass Experiment* cost a total of £3,502 for six episodes, *Quatermass II*, £7,552 and *Quatermass and the Pit*, £17,578.

[11] BBC WAC T5/148: Cartier to C. Moodie, 12 June 1953.

[12] Ibid: Cartier to Richard Greenough (designer), 5 June 1953. *Planet of the Dragons* features a 'Space Lieutenant' and his 'Space Girl' battling monsters on a distant planet. It sounds not unlike the British-made *kitsch* classic *Fire Maidens from Outer Space* (Eros Films, dir. Cy Roth, 1956).

[13] For example, the climax of *The Quatermass Experiment* (film) interrupts a live television broadcast from Westminster Abbey. 'Kill transmission!' the director orders when cameras see the quivering monster. This can be read as a reminder that a technical fault had affected the last episode of *The Quatermass Experiment* on television.

[14] Nigel Kneale, 'Not Quite So Intimate', *Sight & Sound*, 28: 2 (1959), p.88.

[15] BBC WAC T5/418: G. M. Turner to Michael Barry (Head of Drama), 24 August 1953.

[16] Val Guest, *So You Want to Be in Pictures* (London: Reynolds & Hearn, 2001), p.131.

[17] BFI Unpublished Scripts Collection S2995: *The Quatermass Experiment*. Screenplay by Richard Landau and Val Guest, n.d.

[18] Guest, *So You Want to Be in Pictures*, p.131.

[19] Tony Aldgate, '*Women of Twilight*, *Cosh Boy* and the advent of the "X" certificate', *Journal of Popular British Cinema*, 3 (2000), pp.59–68.

20   BBFC file on *The Quatermass Experiment*: Arthur Watkins to Tommy Lyndon-Haynes, 10 September 1954.

21   *News Chronicle*, 26 August 1955.

22   *Manchester Guardian*, 27 August 1955.

23   *New Statesman*, 27 August 1955.

24   *The Times*, 29 August 1955.

25   *Kinematograph Weekly*, 15 December 1955, p.5.

26   'Horror Bill Starts Run', *Los Angeles Times*, 28 July 1956, p.32.

27   David Pirie, *A Heritage of Horror: The English Gothic Cinema, 1946–1972* (London: Gordon Fraser, 1973), p.29.

28   *Alien* (20th Century-Fox, dir. Ridley Scott, 1979); *The Fly* (20th Century-Fox, dir. David Cronenberg, 1986).

29   Kenneth O. Morgan, *The People's Peace: British History 1945–1990* (Oxford: Oxford University Press, 1992), p.202.

30   Jimmy Sangster, *Inside Hammer* (London: Reynolds & Hearn, 2001), pp.21–5.

31   *Kinematograph Weekly*, 16 January 1956, p.11.

32   Losey would later direct *The Damned* (1963) for Hammer.

33   The film uses the number '2', the television serial, the Roman numeral 'II'.

34   Wells, 'Apocalypse Then!', p.53.

35   Guest, *So You Want to Be in Pictures*, p.132.

36   BBFC file *Quatermass 2*: Script Reader's Report by Audrey Field, 2 May 1956.

37   Ibid: Arthur Watkins to Anthony Hinds, 11 May 1956.

38   Ibid.

39   *Evening Standard*, 23 May 1957.

40   *Financial Times*, 27 May 1957.

41   *Monthly Film Bulletin*, 24: 281 (June 1957), p.150.

42   *Kinematograph Weekly*, 11 July 1957, p.10.

43   *Hollywood Reporter*, 28 August 1957; *Variety*, 28 August 1957.

44   Pirie, *A Heritage of Horror*, p.31.

45   Peter Biskind, *Seeing Is Believing: How Hollywood Taught Us to Stop Worrying and Love the Fifties* (London: Pluto Press, 1984), pp.137–44; Stuart Samuels, 'The Age of Conspiracy and Conformity: *Invasion of the Body Snatchers*', in John E. O'Connor and Martin A. Jackson (eds), *American History/American Film* (New York: Ungar, 1979), pp.203–17.

46   Wells, 'Apocalypse Then!', p.53.

47   Peter Hutchings, 'Uncanny Landscapes in British Film and Television', *Visual Culture in Britain*, 5: 2 (2004), p.31.

48   *StarBurst*, 58 (June 1983), p.40.

49   Quoted in Johnson and Del Vecchio, *Hammer Films*, p.286.

50   Wells, 'Apocalypse Then!', p.54.

51   Roy Ward Baker, *The Director's Cut* (London: Reynolds & Hearn, 2000), p.124.

52   *Sunday Times*, 5 November 1967.

53   'Horrors of the city', *Observer*, 5 November 1967.

54   'A menace from Mars', *The Times*, 2 November 1967.

55   'A touch of terror on the Tube', *Daily Mail*, 2 November 1967.

56   *Sunday Telegraph*, 5 November 1967.

57   *Monthly Film Bulletin*, 34: 406 (November 1967), p.177.

58   Other examples of this trope include the *Doctor Who* story 'The Web of Fear' (1968) and the film *Death Line* (Rank, dir. Gary Sherman, 1972).

59   On television this line belongs to Quatermass: the change reflects a more significant role for Barbara Judd in the film.

60   'Quatermass and the Horrors of the Earth', *Daily Telegraph*, 3 September 1973.

61 *Quatermass* was directed by Piers Haggard, whose credits included the horror film *Blood on Satan's Claw* (1970) and the BBC's Dennis Potter serial *Pennies from Heaven* (1978).

62 *The Quatermass Experiment* (BBC4, sc: Richard Fell, dir. Sam Miller, tx 02.04.2005).

63 Nigel Kneale, who had a hand in all the Quatermass productions other than the film of *The Quatermass Experiment* – he acted as a special advisor for the BBC4 production – died in 2006 at the age of 84.

5

SEX AND THE SINGLE ROBOT: *FORBIDDEN PLANET* (1956)

In 1952 the head of production at MGM, Dore Schary, had no shortage of worries. Each day's mail brought a fresh set of concerns ranging from major scares to minor gripes. In April he received a report that certain people were asking around in New York City about his liberal playwriting in the 1930s.[1] More typical was the steady stream of notes from people seeking to redirect the studio's output in one way or the other. In the autumn of 1952 Schary received a note of this type from a colleague at the studio's New York office. The writer – Dan Terrell – noted that he was a father of two sons (aged 10 and 14) and that both boys were disappointed with MGM's present output. Their chief concern was the failure of the studio to apply itself to their favourite genre: science fiction. Terrell noted in a letter of 30 September:

> The boys point out that MGM is alleged to be the leading producer of motion pictures, but that another studio made that modern classic *The Day the Earth Stood Still*. They note that MGM employs a pretty good-looking girl named Esther Williams who swims, but that we let somebody else enjoy the services of George Pal, who floats about in outer space. They have gone so far as to insinuate that MGM would not hire a man from Mars if he landed his saucer right in the middle of Culver City.[2]

Though he didn't reply until November, Schary – a father to two budding critics himself – took the Terrell boys' concerns seriously enough to comment. 'In answer to their questions, you should point out that the Fox picture *The Day the Earth Stood Still* was a failure despite its good production. Also tell them that we keep looking desperately for a good story about the outer space regions, but we just haven't been able to find one.'[3]

Within a few weeks one of his producers was reviewing a story treatment that had the potential to become exactly the sort of high-profile SF story the Terrell boys had in mind. Good as his word, Schary embraced the project, which became *Forbidden Planet*. *Forbidden Planet* was a milestone in SF cinema. Its distinctions for audiences included its spectacular widescreen realization of an alien world, its depiction of far future space exploration and the first of what would be a long line of scene-stealing cinematic robots. As will be seen, even as it ventured into the unknown of outer space it also sought to probe the hardly less understood inner space of the human psyche and hinted at the dark realms of sexual taboo.

Forbidden Planet began with a story – *The Fatal Planet* – written by a one-time theatre producer, public relations executive, and aspiring SF novelist called Allen Adler and a painter (a veteran of the New Deal-era Works Project Administration mural projects) named Irving Block who was then working in studio special effects.[4] Their story told of a manned space mission by the space vessel *Emerald Star* to the planet Venus in the year 1976. The hero, John Grant, encountered the sole survivors of a previous Earth mission twenty years early (implausibly requiring interplanetary flight by 1956), a mysterious scientist named Adams and his beautiful daughter, Dorianne. They live in the ruins of a lost civilization. The father is initially hostile, attempting to warn the *Emerald Star* away, but the ship lands anyway. The new arrivals are drawn to Dorianne, and she to them, seeing young men for the first time in her life. Then tragedy strikes. Crewmen begin to die mysteriously. Grant deduces that an invisible monster is at large and succeeds in photographing the creature using an infrared camera. Adams joins forces with Grant to build a 'visabeam' device to render the creature visible. The humans destroy the creature and Dorianne and her father both opt to return to Earth with the *Emerald Star*.[5]

The story had the basic elements of the final film. Block later claimed that its central idea of a father and daughter shipwrecked in space was lifted from his favourite play, William Shakespeare's *The Tempest* in which Prospero, marooned magician and rightful Duke of Milan, raising his daughter Miranda on an island with the help of a magical servant, is challenged by the arrival of shipwrecked outsiders. Like the final film, Adler and Block's outline proposed characterizing the newcomers as stock naval types: wise-cracking enlisted men, a couple of heroic officers and a ship's doctor as a voice of reason. But there were major differences from the final film too, not least the undivided emphasis on the invisible monster. As far as Adler and Block were concerned, that idea alone was sufficient to carry the movie, which as first sketched could just as well have been called 'Attack of the Invisible Beast' and billed as a horror movie set in space. The draft story unfolded as a litany of the monster's doings: various thinly sketched characters perish at its hands. The creature is positioned as a sexual threat to the daughter, sneaking into her bedroom at one point. 'We can hear the SOUND of lustful breathing coming ever closer to the girl.'[6] While the story makes no explicit mention of any deeper meaning in the script, it is just possible that the writers had some thought of a political allegory on their minds (with the invisible monster as McCarthy). Why set the story in the year 1976 with its inconvenient need for the scientist to leave Earth in 1956 unless one wished to comment on the future of America as it hit the bicentennial of the Declaration of Independence?

The writers expected that their story would appeal to a minor studio in search of a B-picture, and planned to approach Allied Artists. Their agent suggested that they aim higher and arranged for them to pitch to MGM. The studio reader liked their treatment, commenting: 'Though quite undeveloped, there is an idea here for a science-fiction horror picture that should prove hair-raising.'[7] Adler and Block accordingly found MGM producer, Nicholas Nayfack, receptive, if concerned over the practicalities of exactly how an invisible monster could be represented on the screen. In later years Block recalled acting out scenes around Nayfack's office, speaking enthusiastically about sound effects and mysteriously appearing footprints. Nayfack bought the idea and was especially drawn to Block's remark that an invisible monster would cost him nothing. Nayfack bought the treatment. The production process had begun.[8]

It is an indication of Nayfack's hopes for the picture that he immediately passed the project to one of the most accomplished writers on MGM's payroll: Cyril Hume. Hume was what was known at the time as 'a class act'. Born in New Rochelle, New York in 1900, Hume attended Yale University after service in the Great War. He turned his experience into a novel *The Wife of the Centaur*, about the college career of a young and prematurely married writer. The novel became the publishing sensation of 1923 running to five editions in just a few months. Reviewers immediately compared Hume to F. Scott Fitzgerald. Though detractors wondered what he 'had to say' of enduring value, his marketability was beyond dispute. It came as no surprise when Metro snapped up the rights to *The Wife of the Centaur* for $25,000, and hired King Vidor to direct the adaptation.[9] His second novel, *Cruel Fellowship* (1925), also attracted positive attention, with the *Los Angeles Times* hailing it as 'an unquestioned artistic masterpiece'.[10] His third novel, *The Golden Dancer* (1926) was yet another coming of age story. Though praised by some for its 'realism and spirit of poetry', his star seemed to be setting. The *New York Times* rebuked Hume for seeming too interested in his own Hollywood adaptation noting: 'Many contemporary novelists are under suspicion of writing their novels with one eye or maybe both upon the silver screen. Mr. Hume … seems to be the first who has written his own continuity.'[11] The criticism was perceptive as Hume was increasingly drawn to Hollywood. While the fiction kept coming in 1929 he relocated to California and began a parallel career as a studio writer, married an actress (Helen Chandler) and surfaced at MGM writing the dialogue for the 1930 musical *New Moon*. Hume swiftly found a niche reworking stories set in exotic locations, including *Trader Horn* (1931) and *Flying Down to Rio* (1933), becoming a key writer in MGM's Tarzan cycle. He penned much of *Tarzan the Ape Man* (1932) and many other films in the series. He also helped cast the cycle's star, spotting Johnny Weismuller during a workout at the Hollywood athletic club, and persuading him to test for the title role.[12] Hume wrote two further books – *My Sister, My Bride* (1932) and *Myself and the Young Bowman and other Fantasies* (1932) – but from Tarzan onwards he became a safe pair of hands at MGM. He was never in the Academy Award limelight, though sometimes in the gossip columns as a couple of marriages went awry.[13] He mentored younger writer Richard Maibaum (now best known for his work on the James Bond films). Their nine joint projects included the adaptation of Fitzgerald's *The Great Gatsby* (1949). While working on *Forbidden Planet*, he and Maibaum won an Emmy for their controversial teleplay *Fearful Decision* (1954) about a kidnapping, which became the feature film *Ransom!* (1956).[14] Nayfack could expect that Hume would bring style and professionalism to the adaptation of the Adler/Block story. He would not be disappointed.

The brilliance of *Forbidden Planet* arrived with Cyril Hume. He developed Adler and Block's allusion to *The Tempest* and ran with the idea, updating Prospero's spirit servant Ariel into Robby the Robot.[15] More than this, Hume opened out the screenplay into much more than a monster story. He filled in the backstory of the creators of the ruins – a lost race that he named the Krell – and provided a coherent explanation for both their demise and the appearance of the mysterious creature. Under Hume's hand the project became a meditation on the nature of technology, on human ambition and frailty, on the destiny of civilizations, power and fatherhood, all told with finely-tuned dialogue.

As early as his first treatment Hume shifted the details of the story to the distant future and a planet, Altair IV, far away. He imagined a world in orbit around the star Altair, sixteen light years from Earth (and familiar to any amateur astronomer as one of the brightest stars in the American summer sky).[16] Hume was familiar with the contemporaneous literature of SF and space travel. His screenplay bristled with the requisite references to blasters, starships and hyper-drives. Hume identified the problem of insulating the crew during the deceleration from light speed and initially imagined their resorting to cushioned cocoons. In the final film the crew is kept safe inside columns of light. Hume's most significant borrowing from published SF was the robot Robby. Robby was every nut and bolt an extension of the fiction involving robots that was pioneered by Isaac Asimov in the 1940s, as anthologized in the seminal 1950 collection *I, Robot*, the first story of which concerns a robot servant also called Robby. Hume's Robby is bound by Asimov's three laws of robotics – the first stating that a robot may not harm a human.[17] It is Robby's inability to attack the invisible alien which tips off the hero that the creature might in fact be in some sense human too. The copying of Robby's name and the use of the three laws of robotics indicates not only that Hume knew Asimov's work, but also suggests that in choosing Robby's name he might even have been cracking an 'in joke' that his character Morbius had read the book too.

During the writing process Hume developed a political allegory within the story: he fastened on the theme of warning against dictatorship, and the story became a variation of the 'all power corrupts' idea, made especially interesting in the first flush of the nuclear age by the corrupted character being a scientist. This would be emphasized by the final speech of the film, but it was also embedded in one small, but eloquent, change. In the final drafts of the screenplay Hume altered the name of the vessel that had crashed on Altair IV from *Chronian* (an allusion to Chronos, Greek god of time) to *Bellerophon*. While to those schooled in Greek mythology the name would seem ironic – Bellerophon being the hero who killed the monster Chimera – to scholars of the nineteenth century the name would strike as redolent of themes of exile and the hubris of humanity. The British warship HMS *Bellerophon* achieved fame as the vessel which took Napoleon Bonaparte into exile. The name marked his Prospero as a potential dictator in Napoleonic mould.[18]

But even stronger than the political commentary was the hefty dose of Freud. The 1950s was a time when the theories of Freud were gaining traction, and underpinning the emergence of a culture in which the realization of the 'self' was placed in the foreground. Under Hume's hand *Forbidden Planet* became one the most fully realized of Hollywood's excursions into the universe of psychoanalysis: a stablemate of Alfred Hitchcock's *Spellbound* (1945) and Vincente Minnelli's *The Cobweb* (1955). One scholar has called Hume's script 'the most overtly Freudian screen play [*sic*] ever written'.[19] Hume used his knowledge of psychoanalytic theory to propel his drama. His protagonists, Morbius and Altaira (Alta for short), are father and daughter, living isolated from the world of human sexuality. Alta is unaware of her womanhood or the power she can exert over the opposite sex until the Earth ship arrives. Her meeting with the crew awakens her feelings, but it also rouses her father's jealousy. The invisible monster that attacks the newcomers is revealed to be a projection of his enraged Id (the inner animal, posited by Freud as a component of the personality) now rendered palpable by the mind expanding machinery left behind by the Krell civilization. Morbius sees what is happening and also realizes

that his Id monster was responsible for the death of the *Bellerophon*'s crew –
enraged by their suggestion that they should return home – and that the
unrestrained Ids of the Krell had wiped out that civilization in centuries
past. Full of remorse, Morbius sets the Krell's machinery to self-destruct
and allows his daughter and the surviving humans to escape. It was a
neat resolution with the classic Oedipal twist of a protagonist realizing
that the fault lay within themselves. During writing, the title of the
screenplay shifted from *Fatal Planet* to *Forbidden Planet*. It is possible that
the very notion of a 'forbidden planet' had a double meaning – both the
planet in the story and the taboo realms of unrestrained violence, self-
assertion and incest.

Besides the obsession of Morbius, Hume's treatment of the story included
other allusions to the subject of sexuality. Alta's awakening awareness of
desire and her desirability called for alluring costumes and a skinny dipping
scene. Hume planned an elaborate metaphor for her virginity, giving her
a mysterious power over the Earth wild animals that they brought to the
planet. Once her sexual desire has been awakened, she loses this power
and Commander Adams has to rescue her from a previously docile tiger.
The final cut of the film omitted a sequence in which the doctor explained
a mediaeval myth in which a virgin has power to tame a unicorn. There
was also some humour in the screenplay which turned on a sexual theme.
The comic cook, frustrated after many months in space, is shown prevailing
on Robby the Robot to bring whisky and female company. The clueless
robot arrives with a female chimp. But Hume's willingness to foreground
sexual issues ran somewhat ahead of Hollywood at that time. The sexual
dimension of the story immediately excited the interest of the guardians of
taste and decency: the Production Code Administration.

In the spring of 1953 Dore Schary's office submitted Hume's draft
screenplay to the PCA. Breen wrote back on 8 May and expressed concerns
about issues of sex and the representation of Alta and Robby. Breen
cautioned: 'The best taste should be exercised in selecting Alta's costume',
and she should not be pictured swimming in the nude or participate in
'unduly lustful kissing'. In the case of Robby, Breen was alarmed by a line
where the Doctor asks about Robby's sex: 'Please avoid a full-length shot
of Robby when Doc questions it, whether it is male or female.' His sole
request for outright deletion was the gag in which the cook asked Robby
for female companionship: 'We cannot approve the suggestion that Cook
is asking Robby to get him a girl for sex purposes...If the chimp is to be
brought into the story, it must be for some other reason than that which is
now used.' Hume was apparently reluctant to drop the gag as a year and
a half later, after reading the revised script, Breen was still concerned by
the implication that Robby was offering the cook a chimp for sex. At this

point Hume dropped the scene. In the final review of the script in February 1955 Geoffrey Shurlock of the PCA once again raised objections to Alta and Adams bathing together in the nude and, to the 'curious staring' at Robby's pelvic region to determine his sex. In April 1955 the PCA approved a film version with tactful handling of Robby's gender and a tasteful depiction of Altaira bathing in the nude.[20]

As though to counterbalance the sexuality, Hume's screenplay included multiple allusions to religion and projected a Christian norm into the future. When the crew sees the alien planet of Altair 4 for the first time, one exclaims: 'The Lord sure makes some beautiful worlds.' The Earth crew practise Christian ritual. When Chief Quinn is killed, the crew members hold a traditional Christian burial, and with Bible in hand, their commander speaks of 'ashes to ashes'. Hume's initial treatment for the studio even ponders the fusion of his SF projection with Christian lore musing: 'What journeys home certain of our descendants will be obliged to make on judgment day [sic].'[21] Religion is invoked as a barrier against the unbridled destructive force of the Id. In the initial draft the hero, Commander Adams, warns of 'the secret devil of every soul' and tells Morbius: 'We are all part monsters in our subconscious and so we have laws and religion.'[22] Until the last phase of production the film ended with the Commander's wedding to Alta, complete with the bosun intoning words from the standard Protestant wedding service: 'Dearly beloved, we are gathered together here in the sight of God and in the presence of this company.' The scene was thought significant enough to be written up in publicity as a 'wedding among the stars', and stills included a shot of the wedding party with the cook in the background carrying a wedding cake.[23] The final film omitted this scene – which would have played as rather too light hearted – and ended instead with an earlier speech in which Adams comforts his bride to be, saying that her father will be remembered. The context is, however, the drawing of a line between humanity and the divine. As the first draft put it:

> Alta, nothing is ever really lost. There's a ladder that reaches from the primeval slime up to the stars, and beyond them. In about a million years our team will have climbed up to that rung where the Krell stood in their moment of triumph and disaster. And then your father's name will stand like a milestone in the galaxy – warning Man to remember that he is not a god.

The twenty-first-century viewer may well ask what is going on here. The offhand religiosity is certainly consistent with US culture in the 1950s, and Hume's parenthetical remark about Judgement Day seems to reflect a willingness to indulge this. Yet the surface religiosity masks the real implications of the story and challenge that the actual discovery of an extraterrestrial civilization would pose to Earth-bound faiths. The 'god' affirmed in the closing speech is not an active Christian God but a metaphoric divinity: '*a* god' who stands as a symbol of the absolute and unchecked power that no human should ever possess. For Hume the reality or unreality of religion is not the point – its value lies in its ability to hold the darker nature of humanity in check. The final speech, with its evolutionary language and metaphoric gods, is just a little more subversive than the wedding ending would have been, and gives the film a humanist spin that would also be seen in the work of the inheritors of its influence, principally Gene Roddenberry.

The film's approach to technology is also worthy of comment. Hume was obviously keen to show a technologically advanced future for humanity with faster than light travel and then to trump it with glimpses of an even more technologically advanced alien civilization: the Krell. His humans are little marked by the technology around them. They are essentially stereotypes from military dramas of the previous decade. Their familiarity is one of the cords that connects the film to its mid-century audience and permits emotional identification. Their matter-of-fact use of the technology around them 'sells' their future world all the more convincingly to the audience. It was a bold move for the time to set the film entirely in the depths of space. The future Earth of *Forbidden Planet* is all the more impressive for being left to the audience's imagination.

The production of the film began in the spring of 1955. Schary brought in a reliable studio director, Fred M. Wilcox, best known for *Lassie Come Home* (1943) and other family films, to realize the project. For the key role of Professor Morbius the studio secured veteran actor Walter Pidgeon and for his daughter, newcomer Anne Francis. Lantern-jawed, Canadian-born Leslie Nielsen was cast as Commander Adams. As the project gathered momentum, Nayfack commissioned increasingly elaborate sets and impressive special effects, including the robot Robby. One executive managing the project, Joseph Cohen, alerted Schary to the ballooning budget but found Schary himself was bitten by the emerging vision of the film when he visited the set: 'I was fascinated by what they were doing', Schary recalled in later years, 'just fascinated'. Suddenly the upper ceiling on the budget shifted: 'I remember on that picture I just said: "Oh, come on, we've got something very good, just give the money, transfer funds."' Schary took to simply watching the construction of the sets, as the world of the future took shape on his own sound stage. The project swallowed just short of $2 million.[24] As the studio realized what it had in the making, it closed the sets to all outside observers. The secrecy gave an added frisson to the production.[25]

10. Futuristic spacecraft and an alien world to be realized in widescreen
and Technicolor: concept design for *Forbidden Planet* (1956)
(Source: British Film Institute).

As the end of 1955 came, the film was still not quite finished. The creation
of the Id monster required the loan of one of Disney's best artists, Joshua
Lawrence Meador. The final element of the production was an electronic
soundscape created by Louis and Bebe Barron, avant-garde musicians
whom Dore Schary himself discovered at a night club in Greenwich Village
and immediately recognized them as a perfect fit for the film. Their final
screen credit for 'electronic tonalities' rather than music was a sleight of
hand to avoid trouble with the musicians' union.[26]

As the film neared completion, the studio embarked on its promotional
campaign. Dore Schary intended the film to appeal to the widest possible
audience. Writing to an educator, he cited it alongside *Seven Brides for Seven
Brothers* (1954) as an example of wholesome MGM films 'that were designed
to reach the entire family'.[27] The film's marketing, however, shamelessly
pledged sex and traded on the sexuality of Alta as a major selling point
of the film. The US trailer for *Forbidden Planet* included a clip of a skinny
dipping Alta innocently asking Adams from the water: 'What's a bathing
suit?'[28] Most bizarrely perhaps the poster for the film re-interpreted the
mild-mannered Robby the Robot as a sexual predator. He was depicted

11. Sex on his positronic circuits: Robby the Robot is pictured carrying off
Altaira (Anne Francis) in a poster for *Forbidden Planet* (1956)
(Source: British Film Institute).

holding the limp and voluptuous body of Alta in a way that implies that he
had sex on his positronic circuits.

Forbidden Planet opened in March 1956 to generally enthusiastic
reviews. Jack Moffit in the *Hollywood Reporter* applauded both the element
of reputable science underpinning the fiction and the 'power corrupts'
theme. He was also impressed by Anne Francis' wardrobe, observing: 'The
costumes of the 23rd century are so revealing as to make any man now
living seek to prolong his life span ...'[29] *Variety* saw the film as a re-working
of themes familiar from low budget serials and television dramas like ABC's
recently axed *Space Patrol* (1950–5), noting: 'This is *Space Patrol* for adults
but the kiddies will be there too ...'[30] The film did not impress the Earth-
bound reviewers in New York City: Wanda Hale of the *New York Daily News*
called the film 'a shameful waste of electricity' and the reviewer of the *New
Yorker* dismissed it as 'a pleasant spoof of all the moonstruck nonsense the
movies have been dishing up about what goes on amongst our neighbors in
inter-stellar space.' The *New Yorker* spotted the debt to Freud but missed the
Shakespeare connection all together.[31] In fact the film's relationship to *The
Tempest* passed utterly unremarked until British reviewers saw the film later

that summer. The parallels were first set out by Alan Brien in his review for London's *Evening Standard*, and alluded to by C. A. Lejeune in *The Observer* the following weekend.[32] That reading of the film has since become central to critical interpretations and even newspaper listings of the film.[33] It strengthened the hand of those seeking to argue that science fiction should be taken seriously, and was also embraced by generations of literature teachers seeking to show that classic literature could be 'cool'. The link was such that when, in the 1980s, the British theatre director Bob Carlton created a musical version of the film, *Return to the Forbidden Planet*, using classic rock and roll numbers, he incorporated whole chunks of Shakespeare's dialogue and used the names of the Shakespearean characters: Prospero, Miranda and Ariel for the father, daughter and robot. The commander became 'Captain Tempest.' *Return to the Forbidden Planet* enjoyed an award-winning run, first at the Tricycle in Brent and then at the Cambridge Theatre in London's West End, before playing venues around the world, and has been successfully revived in the past decade.

Despite the critical acclaim, the film was not an unqualified box office success. *Variety* ranked it 61st for the year. Its earnings were insufficient to challenge the received wisdom that science fiction was more trouble than it was worth as a genre. With that lesson in mind, few of those involved with the film prospered. Of the original writers Allen Adler went on to co-write a story for an Allied Artists monster film with the redundant title *The Giant Behemoth (1959)* and to pen a dreary SF novel, *Mach 1: A Story of Planet Ionius*. Neither was a great success. He died in 1964.[34] Block continued as a special effects artist working on *Kronos* (1957), *The Atomic Submarine* (1959), *The Giant Behemoth* (1959) and other, now forgotten, B-pictures. He moved to a second career in academia, becoming a Professor of Art at California State University, Northridge. He was happy to speak about his role in *Forbidden Planet* and allowed the tale of his role to grow in the telling. He died in 1986.[35] Cyril Hume continued to write for film and television until his death in 1966. None of his later works attained especial prominence. His obituaries were terse. His first career as a novelist is now forgotten.[36] Nicholas Nayfack became rather stuck in the groove of robot pictures. He commissioned Hume to write a second film starring Robby, *The Invisible Boy* (1957), which never escaped the B-picture category. He died in 1958, aged just 49. Dore Schary's career at MGM did not long survive the modest success of *Forbidden Planet*. Schary and MGM parted company and the producer turned his attentions to Broadway. He died in 1980. Of the cast, Leslie Nielsen eventually found a career, though only in late middle age as a spoof of the Hollywood leading man he had embodied in 1956. Robby the Robot was periodically recycled for guest spots in other films and TV shows, including a couple of episodes of *Lost in Space*. He now resides in a private memorabilia collection. Such disappointing ends stand in contrast to the golden reputation of the film they collectively wrought.

For Schary the cult status of *Forbidden Planet* was a complete surprise. 'Candidly,' he noted in his memoirs, 'I did not expect it would have the interest it has maintained, which has increased in the years since it was made.'[37] But increase it did. *Forbidden Planet* became one of the most influential of all SF films. Its devotees range from John Carpenter, who was captivated by the vision of an alien landscape,[38] to Gene Roddenberry, who borrowed the idea of a navy-type story transported to space in the concept of *Star Trek* and paid homage to the film in certain stories within the original series.[39] Robby is plainly a forbear of George Lucas's C3PO, who echoes Robby's fluency in 187 languages when he claims to be 'fluent in over 6 million forms of communication'. The immense interiors of the Krell civilization also anticipate the limitless vistas inside the Death Star in *Star Wars*. That influence shows no signs of abating. At the time of writing, a *Forbidden Planet* prequel is projected. The prominence of the genre and its ability to generate the legendary grosses of *Star Wars*, *Avatar* and their ilk suggest that Schary's gamble was not so wide of the mark. One hopes that somewhere, the sons of Dan Terrell who nagged their dad to nag his boss back in 1952 are sitting back and enjoying the show.

Notes

1. Wisconsin Center for Film and Theatre Research, Madison, Wisconsin, Dore Schary papers (hereafter WCFTR Schary), Box 4: Correspondence: Victor Lasky to Schary n.d., *c.*April 1952.
2. Ibid: Dan Terrell (MGM, NYC) to Schary, 30 September 1952.
3. Ibid: Schary to Terrell, 17 November 1952.
4. For biographical details see Margaret Herrick Library, Academy of Motion Picture Arts and Sciences (hereafter AMPAS) Core Collection, biographical file: Allen Adler, obituary, *Variety*, 30 January 1964; biographical file: Irving Block, obituary, 'Special effects artist Irving Block, 73', *Chicago Tribune*, 9 May 1986. Block's credits included *Rocketship XM* (1950) and *Unknown World* (1951), which he also produced.
5. The original story is preserved in the USC MGM Script Collection, *Forbidden Planet*, file 8: Vault copy of *Fatal Planet*, copied 24-12-1952. Most accounts of the making of *Forbidden Planet* use only the synopsis available at the Herrick Library.
6. USC MGM Script Collection, *Forbidden Planet*, file 8: Vault copy of *Fatal Planet*.
7. AMPAS Turner/MGM Scripts f.F-607: *Forbidden Planet*. Report by Bill Cole on story *Fatal Planet* by Irving Block and Allen Adler, 11 November 1952 from Bernard Feins agency.
8. This paragraph is based on Block's interview with Steve Rubin, 'Retrospect: *Forbidden Planet*' *Cinefantastique*, 4: 1 (1976), pp.5–12. Block's memory is unreliable. He misdates his initial pitch to the spring of 1954, whereas the MGM archives indicate that the story was received in December 1952. He also criticizes Nayfack for making the monster visible at the end of the film, forgetting that this was part of his own story.

9   Wilson Follett, 'Six months of Fictioneering: June to December in the flow of novels', *New York Times*, 23 December 1923, p.5 (book review section); 'Metro buys "Wife of the Centaur"', *Baltimore Sun*, 16 December 1923, p.6; Fanny Butcher, 'Young Mr Hume has little to say but says it nicely', *Chicago Tribune*, 1 March 1924, p.11; Edwin Schallert, 'Playdom: Not Hume Book...' *Los Angeles Times*, 8 December 1924, p.A7.

10   Lillian C. Ford, 'A Tale Keyed to Low Tragedy', *Los Angeles Times*, 16 August 1925, p.26.

11   'The Time of Man... and four other novels', *Hartford Courant*, 12 September 1926, p.D6; and 'Mr. Benfield's stories and other works of fiction', *New York Times*, 29 August 1926, p.6. (book review section) Hume's next project was a volume of stories: *Street of the Malcontents, and other stories* (New York: Doubleday, Doran and company, 1927) and a novel: *A Dish for the Gods* (New York: George H. Doran company, 1929).

12   Johnny Weissmuller, Jr., *Tarzan: My Father* (Toronto: ECW Press, 2002), pp.55–7.

13   AMPAS Core Collection, biographical file: Cyril Hume. Hume's first marriage to Jan Barbara Alexander ended with her death in 1925. In 1926 he married Charlotte Dickinson, and in 1930, Helen Chandler (now best remembered as Mina, the object of Bela Lugosi's appetites in *Dracula*, in 1931). After their divorce in 1935 Hume swiftly married one Maxine Gagnon, who divorced him in a matter of months. His final marriage to Dorothy Wallace lasted until his death. For Hume in the gossip columns see 'Wife divorced screen writer, Cyril Hume', *Los Angeles Herald*, 27 April 1936.

14   On Maibaum see Patrick McGilligan, *Backstory: Interviews with Screenwriters of Hollywood's Golden Age* (Berkeley: University of California Press, 1986), pp.266–89.

15   Several critics have noted that Robby also doubles for Shakespeare's Caliban in some scenes, most obviously the comic scenes with the cook. See Bill Warren, *Keep Watching the Skies! American Science Fiction Movies of the Fifties: the 21st century edition* (Jefferson, NC: McFarland, 2010), p.299.

16   Altair is part of the constellation of Aqila (the eagle), and one of the three stars to make up the 'Summer Triangle' (with Vega and Deneb) visible in the USA and Europe during the summer months.

17   Isaac Asimov, *I, Robot* (New York: Gnome Press, 1950). The laws in full are: '1) A robot may not injure a human being or, through inaction, allow a human being to come to harm. 2) A robot must obey the orders given to it by human beings, except where such orders would conflict with the First Law. 3) A robot must protect its own existence as long as such protection does not conflict with the First or Second Laws.'

18   The memory of the role of HMS *Bellerophon* in Napoleon's demise was perpetuated in the sea shanty 'Boney was a warrior', and in 'Napoleon on the Bellerophon' as a subject for historical paintings dwelling on thwarted ambition, including two famous examples by Sir Charles Eastlake and Sir William Orchardson. For a recent study of the ship see David Cordingly, *The Billy Ruffian: The Bellerophon and the Downfall of Napoleon* (London: Bloomsbury, 2003).

19   William Indick, *Movies and the Mind: Theories of the Great Psychoanalysts Applied to Film* (Jefferson, NC: McFarland, 2004), p.33.

20   AMPAS Motion Picture Producers Association: Production Code Administration files: *Forbidden Planet*: Breen to Schary, 8 May 1953; Breen to Schary, 15 September 1954; Shurlock to Schary, 24 February 1955; Shurlock to Schary, 14 April 1955.

21   AMPAS Turner/MGM Scripts f.F-607: *Fatal Planet*. A screen-play treatment from Cyril Hume, 23 February 1953.

22   Ibid.

23   AMPAS Core Collection, publicity microfiche for *Forbidden Planet*. The wedding scene was still in the version of the script of March 1955 (Turner/MGM Scripts, f.F-615: *Forbidden Planet*: Script of 10 March 1955) and presumably (given the existence of stills of the scene), was filmed before being dropped. It is not among the deleted scenes now available on DVD releases of the film, however.

[24] *Cinefantastique*, vol. 8, no. 2 and 3, 1979 special issue on *Forbidden Planet* p.29.

[25] 'Metro veils in secrecy forbidden planet sets', *Variety*, 15 March 1955.

[26] Dore Schary, *Heyday: An Autobiography* (Boston: Little, Brown, 1979), p.290.

[27] WCFTR Schary Box 9: Schary to Lucy Baca (California Congress Parents and Teachers Association), 29 May 1956.

[28] AMPAS Turner/MGM Scripts f. F-617: *Forbidden Planet*. Trailer script, 21 March 1956.

[29] Jack Moffit, '*Forbidden Planet*: class A science fiction picture', *Hollywood Reporter*, 12 March 1956.

[30] *Variety*, 14 March 1956.

[31] *New Yorker*, 12 May 1956.

[32] Alan Brien, 'Shakespeare takes a journey into space', *Evening Standard*, 7 June 1956, p.7; C.A. Lejeune, 'At the films: Space Monster', *Observer*, 10 June 1956. The absence of contemporary recognition of the parallel has led Judith Buchanan to suggest that the association is entirely 'retrospective association'. See Judith Buchanan, '*Forbidden Planet* and the Retrospective Attribution of Intentions', in Deborah Cartmell, I. Q. Hunter and Imelda Whelehan (eds), *Retrovisions: Reinterpreting the Past in Fiction and Film* (London: Pluto Press, 2001), pp.148–62.

[33] Kenneth Von Gunden and Stuart H. Stock, *Twenty All-Time Great Science Fiction Films* (New York: Arlington House, 1982), pp.122–135; John Baxter, *Science Fiction in the Cinema* (London: Zwemmer, 1970), p.113.

[34] AMPAS Core Collection, biographical file: Allen Adler. *Giant Behemoth* (1959) was one of the films for which the Writers Guild of America issued revised credits to reinstate the work of a blacklisted author. See www.wga.org/subpage_writersresources. aspx?id=1958 Last accessed: 7 June 2012. Adler was not himself blacklisted.

[35] AMPAS Core Collection, biographical file: Irving Block. Block's artistic papers are held by the Smithsonian Institution: see www.aaa.si.edu/collections/collection/blocirvi. htm. Last accessed; 7 June 2012. Block's account of the making of the film, as given to Steve Rubin in 1976, includes claims of responsibility for elements of the film that the archival evidence suggests did not enter the script until Cyril Hume's drafts, which introduced the robot and Alta's mysterious relationship with animals. Block justifies his claim by his own interest in myth, and knowledge of the mediaeval legend of the unicorn. As the scene in which Doc Ostrow outlines the legend of the unicorn was deleted from the final cut, it is possible that Block had some sort of input into Hume's script. Alternatively he may have been recalling the novelization of the film or have been prompted by his interviewer, Rubin. See Steve Rubin, 'Retrospect: Forbidden Planet', *CineFantastique*, 4: 1 (1976), pp.5–13.

[36] For obituaries see *Film Daily*, 30 March 1966; and *Hollywood Reporter*, 26 March 1966.

[37] Schary, *Heyday: An Autobiography*, p.291.

[38] Mark Monahan, 'John Carpenter on Fred McLeod Wilcox's Forbidden Planet (1956)', *Daily Telegraph*, 11 August 2002, p.10.

[39] The influence of *Forbidden Planet* on *Star Trek* is most evident in the episode 'Requiem for Methuselah' (1969) by Jerome Bixby, but echoes are also detectable in the pilot 'The Cage' (1965) by Roddenberry; 'What Are Little Girls Made Of?' (1966) by Robert Bloch and 'The Enemy Within' (1966) by Richard Matheson.

6

THE WATERSHED:
2001: A SPACE ODYSSEY (1968)

Following the boom of the 1950s, the early 1960s were a fallow period for science fiction, the only films of note being George Pal's *The Time Machine* (1960), several British adaptations of John Wyndham – *Village of the Damned* (1960), *Children of the Damned* (1963) and *The Day of the Triffids* (1963) – and occasional forays into the genre by European *auteur* directors such as Jean-Luc Godard (*Alphaville*, 1965) and François Truffaut (*Fahrenheit 451*, 1966). To some extent the genre's decline in the cinema can be attributed to its shift to television, where series like *Voyage to the Bottom of the Sea* (1964–8), *The Time Tunnel* (1966–7), *Lost in Space* (1966–8) and *Star Trek* (1966–9) were nothing if not throwbacks to the *Buck Rogers* and *Flash Gordon* serials of the 1930s. At the same time, the acceleration of the Space Race had made space travel the stuff of fact rather than fantasy. On 12 April 1961 Yuri Gagarin of the Soviet Union became the first man to travel into Earth orbit in Vostok 1. Six weeks later – following the first American manned space flight by Alan Shepard on 5 May – President John F. Kennedy declared to Congress that 'this nation should commit itself to achieving the goal, before this decade is out, of landing a man on the Moon and returning him safely to Earth'.[1] It was against this background that Stanley Kubrick wrote to Arthur C. Clarke in March 1964 to sound him out about 'the possibility of doing the proverbial "really good" science-fiction movie' and inviting him to New York 'to determine whether an idea might exist or arise which would sufficiently interest both of us to want to collaborate on a screenplay'.[2]

Kubrick was one of a new generation of American filmmaking – others included Robert Aldrich, Samuel Fuller and Nicholas Ray – whose emergence in the 1950s coincided with the decline of the studio system. This was a period of major structural change in the film industry as the studios adapted to new conditions brought about following the Paramount

Decree of 1948 (the Supreme Court ruling that the studios must relinquish their ownership of movie theatres) and responded to the decline in cinema admissions. The trend throughout the 1950s was to release stars and other personnel from long-term contracts and to provide studio facilities and distribution for the growing number of independent producers and directors. These conditions allowed greater scope for directors to develop their own individual styles. From the start of his career Kubrick could be considered an *auteur*: for his early features, *Fear and Desire* (1953) and *Killer's Kiss* (1955), for example, he combined the roles of writer, director, cameraman and editor. He came to critical attention with *The Killing* (1956), a tense *film noir*, followed by the powerful anti-war drama *Paths of Glory* (1957). Kirk Douglas, the star of *Paths of Glory*, chose Kubrick to replace Anthony Mann as director of the historical epic *Spartacus* (1960). *Spartacus* returned $14.6 million at the US box office: Kubrick was now a hot ticket. He followed it with the controversial *Lolita* (1962) and the satirical *Dr Strangelove; or How I Learned to Stop Worrying and Love the Bomb* (1964): both films were critically acclaimed and performed well at the box office. The production of *2001* would reveal how much leeway a major studio (MGM) was prepared to allow him.[3]

From an auteurist point of view, *2001* has generally been seen as the middle part of a triptych of SF films with *Dr Strangelove* and Kubrick's adaptation of Anthony Burgess's *A Clockwork Orange* (1971). Philip French, for example, describes the films as 'a trilogy of admonitory fables set in a bleak, dehumanised future'.[4] This fits the dominant critical view of Kubrick's 'underlying pessimism and his bleak view of the essential nature of man'.[5] *Dr Strangelove* – like Sidney Lumet's contemporaneous *Fail Safe* (1964) – was a warning against the possibility of an accidental nuclear war, made in the wake of the Cuban Missiles Crisis of October 1962. It is a black comedy in which a mad US general launches an atomic attack on Russia: it ends with the triggering of a 'doomsday' device that will destroy the whole world.[6] However, the archival evidence would suggest that Kubrick had a rather different vision for his next film. His letter to Clarke identified three themes that interested him:

1. The reasons for believing in the existence of intelligent extraterrestrial life.
2. The impact (and perhaps even lack of impact in some quarters) such discovery would have on Earth in the near future.
3. A space-probe with a landing and exploration of the Moon and Mars.[7]

Following the bleak pessimism of *Dr Strangelove*, it seems that what Kubrick had in mind was an existential exploration of humanity's place in the cosmos. This was a matter of serious philosophical and scientific discussion at a time when human beings were making their first tentative steps into space. In any event *2001* cannot be seen simply as part of a dystopian trilogy with *Dr Strangelove* and *A Clockwork Orange*.

The choice of Arthur C. Clarke as his collaborator is further evidence to suggest that Kubrick wanted the film to have something positive to say about the future. Clarke's brand of science fiction was essentially optimistic in outlook and demonstrated his faith in social and technological progress. This is most evident in his novel *Childhood's End* (1953), which posits a benign extraterrestrial intervention in guiding human affairs. Clarke was also a passionate advocate of scientific education. He had been a founding member of the British Interplanetary Society in the 1930s and his work included much non-fiction. It was Clarke who had laid the theoretical foundations of the communications satellite in a paper entitled 'ExtraTerrestrial Relays' in 1945 – an idea that was becoming reality by the early 1960s with satellites such as Intelstat and Telstar. [8] Kubrick, too, was interested in the technology of space travel: his research notes for *2001* included hundreds of articles and clippings from scientific journals. It was also while researching *2001* that Kubrick came across an article that aroused his interest in the subject of Artificial Intelligence.[9]

Clarke responded enthusiastically to Kubrick's invitation. 'I also feel,' he replied, 'as you obviously do, that the "really good" science-fiction movie is a great many years overdue.' 'The only ones that came anywhere near qualifying for this,' he went on, 'were *The Day The Earth Stood Still*, *The Forbidden Planet* [sic] and, of course, those classic documentaries *Destination Moon* and *Things To Come*.'[10] He enclosed a copy of a letter he had written to the *Scientific American* speculating about the possibility of extraterrestrial life. The next day Clarke wrote again to tell Kubrick that 'I have thought of a nice opening for a space movie which might give you some ideas.' This came from his short story 'The Sentinel' (published in 1951), in which an expedition to the Moon triggers an 'alarm' placed there long ago by an advanced extraterrestrial civilization.[11] Clarke developed the premise thus:

> The situation described in *The Sentinel* then develops. Briefly, the explorers discover a strange mechanism like a giant crystal. The coating of meteor dust indicates that it has been on this isolated mountain ledge for millions of years. When investigated, it quietly destroys itself. But it has done its job: some of the scientists in the resulting debate decide, correctly, that it can only be a monitor – the equivalent of a celestial fire-alarm, set up long before life emerged on Earth. Perhaps most of the promising worlds in the

Galaxy have been seeded with such automatic watchmen. Now
one of them has signalled: 'Spacefaring intelligence observed,
Satellite 1, Planet 3, Sun 387649082X ...'[12]

This was the premise from which *2001* developed: the motif of 'first contact'
between human beings and an extraterrestrial life form. However, it would
take four years, and many rewrites, before the film would finally reach
the screen.

Kubrick and Clarke met in New York in April 1964 and began work on
a film story. They agreed from the outset that they would write a treatment
to pitch to a studio, which they would then use as the basis for a screenplay,
while Clarke would turn the screenplay into a novel to be published to
coincide with the release of the film. The treatment developed from a first
draft entitled *Project Space*, to a typescript in novel form entitled *Across the
Sea of Stars*. This is set in 1987 'when the colonisation of the Moon is starting
and the manned exploration of the Solar System is just getting under way'.[13]
By the end of 1964 Kubrick and Clarke had completed their 'film story', now
entitled *Journey Beyond the Stars*, which is recognisable as the basis of the
film. *Journey Beyond the Stars* is in two parts. Part I is set in prehistoric Africa
where a tribe of man-apes 'on the long, pathetic road to racial extinction'
discover a mysterious transparent cube that emits a low drumming sound.
This episode was partly based on Clarke's story 'Encounter in the Dawn'
in which extraterrestrials arrive on Earth some 100,000 years ago and are
witnessed by a primitive human who believes they are gods.[14] Part II begins
on 5 October 2001: Presidential Scientific Adviser Dr Heywood Floyd takes a
shuttle to an orbiting space station where he attends a high-level summit to
discuss the discovery of a mysterious pyramid of alien origin on the Moon. It
is transmitting radio signals towards Jupiter. It is decided to send a mission
'to search for any evidence tending to prove or disprove the connection
between the Pyramid and Jupiter'. Following a long voyage, bedevilled by
various accidents and a malfunctioning on-board computer, the spaceship
Discovery, commanded by David H. Bowman, arrives in orbit around
Jupiter. A mysterious 'hole' is detected above the fifth moon. Bowman pilots
a pod into the hole and is transported to another solar system where he sees
hundreds of spaceships in 'a gigantic orbital parking lot' and a vast city of
towering skyscrapers inhabited by eight-feet tall humanoids. Bowman is
guided to a hotel suite, which he finds strangely familiar. At this point he
realizes that 'his hosts had based their ideas of terrestrial living upon TV
programs. His feeling that he was inside a movie set was almost literally
true.' A telephone rings and Bowman is assured that 'you will be returned
to your world without any ill effects'. A door opens where he sees the same
cube that had appeared in the prologue. At this point the narrative ends.[15]

This was the treatment that Kubrick and Clarke pitched to MGM. In February 1965 the studio announced that Kubrick was to film *Journey Beyond the Stars* in Cinerama for release in late 1966.[16] Peter Krämer has argued that MGM's decision to back the film was 'firmly grounded in recent trends in Hollywood entertainment'.[17] The studio evidently saw it as a major event film: the press release declared that it 'will transform our civilization, as the voyages of the Renaissance brought about the end of the Dark Ages'. To this extent the film was being placed in the lineage of widescreen spectaculars that had been the dominant box office attractions of recent times. MGM had reaped vast rewards with historical epics such as *Ben-Hur* (1959) and *Doctor Zhivago* (1965). The decision to release the film in Cinerama, the widest of widescreen formats, was consistent with the studio's strategy during the 1960s: other MGM-Cinerama releases were *How the West Was Won* (1962), *The Wonderful World of the Brothers Grimm* (1963), *Grand Prix* (1966) and *Ice Station Zebra* (1968).[18] In this reading it was the epic and visual qualities of the film that the studio believed would appeal to cinema-goers as much as its science fictional elements. At the same time, however, there is reason to believe that the studio also saw the collaboration of Kubrick and Clarke as a marketable element. Kubrick had directed *Lolita* for MGM, which brought considerable critical kudos, while in 1965 MGM had also been considering a film of *Childhood's End* to be produced by George Pal from a script by Howard Koch. This project seems to have stalled shortly after the studio committed to *Journey Beyond the Stars*.[19]

The contractual arrangements for *2001* demonstrate the byzantine political economy of the film industry in the post-studio period. Since 1962 Kubrick had been under contract to the New York-based Polaris Productions to whom he had rendered 'exclusive services ... as a producer and director of theatrical motion pictures'.[20] MGM contracted Polaris to produce a film 'now tentatively entitled *2001: A Space Odyssey* based on an unpublished novel to be written by Stanley Kubrick and Arthur Clarke'. MGM agreed a budget of up to $5 million and retained the right to approve the three principal cast members.[21] It also imposed some peculiar conditions. One was that the screenplay 'shall be of at least as high quality as the screenplays prepared by Mr Kubrick for the motion pictures *Lolita* and *Dr Strangelove*'. It is difficult to see how this quality requirement could have been assessed: Kubrick has written 'What does this mean?' on the draft contract. MGM also insisted that the film should be produced and directed by one of four named individuals: Alfred Hitchcock, David Lean, Billy Wilder or Stanley Kubrick. In truth there was never any suggestion that anyone other than Kubrick would direct *2001*, but it is an intriguing insight into which directors the studio considered bankable. The final requirement was 'that the Photoplay shall qualify as a British film and shall be eligible for participation in the Fund operated by the British Film Fund Agency'.[22] The British Film Production Fund (also known as the Eady Levy) had been set up in 1951 to incentivize investment in the ailing British production sector. It paid a subsidy to producers and distributors of eligible films based on a percentage of ticket sales: in order to qualify, a film had to be produced by a nominally British production company using British studio facilities and British personnel.[23] Polaris therefore set up a British-based subsidiary, Hawk Films, to undertake the production at MGM's British studio at Borehamwood.

Kubrick and Clarke now set to work turning their film story into a screenplay. It was a long distance collaboration. Following the first draft, written in New York in spring 1965, Kubrick moved to London to start pre-production work on the film while Clarke returned to his home in Ceylon.[24] The production history of 2001 was unusual in that there was never a definitive shooting script: the screenplay was continuously being revised not only before and during principal photography (which began on 17 December 1965 and lasted for seven months) but afterwards. At the same time as collaborating on the screenplay, Clarke was also writing the novel based on the screenplay. Krämer describes the production of 2001 as a 'constantly evolving' process. He writes: 'This evolution can be understood in terms of two overlapping movements of, on the one hand, narrative and thematic elaboration (predominant in the early stages and applying to both novel and film), and, on the other, formal contraction, accelerating towards the end of the production process, but only with regard to the film.'[25] The production records also reveal differences emerging between Clarke, who emphasized the importance of narrative and exposition, and Kubrick, who attached less significance to narrative comprehension than he did to the formal properties of the film.

The first full screenplay of 2001, known as the 'Athena Screenplay', was completed in July 1965.[26] It follows the broad trajectory of the *Journey Beyond the Stars* treatment with the addition of an extensive voice-over narration, which is used to link sequences and provide background information. This includes the information that in 2001 there are 'twenty-seven nations in the nuclear club' and that the Soviet Union, United States, France and China all have 1000-megaton bombs in orbit 'capable of incinerating the entire Earth's surface from an altitude of 100 miles'. The anti-nuclear theme – which would not make it into the finished film – was the most direct thematic link between 2001 and *Dr Strangelove*. There are several other major differences from the final film. In this version the *Discovery* crew are cognizant of the purpose of their mission, and the mishaps they encounter on the journey to Jupiter are accidents caused by a malfunctioning computer (called Athena). One astronaut (Poole) is lost when his transport pod detaches from the ship and he is set adrift in space; the rest of the crew are successfully revived from suspended animation. However, Clarke was not happy with the ending. In August 1965 he wrote to Kubrick: 'The weakness of our ending was that we never explained what happened to Bowman, but left it entirely to the imagination. Well, we can't explain it – but we can symbolise it perfectly in a way that will push all sorts of subconscious and even Freudian buttons.' Clarke suggested that Bowman should return to Earth having gained knowledge of extraterrestrial science. Clarke evidently saw the ending of the film in a positive light: Bowman's acquisition of alien technology 'symbolises all the new wisdom of the stars'. Clarke also explained the link between the opening prehistoric sequence and the ending in terms of an extraterrestrial influence in human evolution: 'The ship is man's new tool – the equivalent of Moonwatcher's weapons ... Both in the novel and in the movie, this can have a hell of a punch, and I'm sure it solves all our problems.'[27]

A revised screenplay was prepared by the time shooting commenced in December 1965.[28] By this time a number of significant changes had been made. These mostly involved the addition of more conflict and drama on the voyage to Saturn (it changed back to Jupiter in a later draft). So now the crew of the *Discovery* have not been told the purpose of their mission, which has been held back from them. There is an assumption 'that the intentions of this alien world are potentially dangerous to us' and so the mission is veiled in secrecy. Only the ship's computer, now called Hal 9000, knows the true purpose of the mission. Hal malfunctions and causes Poole's death while he is repairing a malfunctioning antenna. Bowman wants to revive the hibernating astronauts but is prevented from doing so by Hal. When Hal turns off the life-support system, killing the other crewmembers, Bowman disconnects him. Mission Control now reveals the purpose of the mission and explains that Hal's malfunction was due to programming that compelled him to conceal information from the crew: 'We believe his truth programming and the instructions to lie, gradually resulted in an incompatible conflict, and faced with this dilemma, he developed, for want of a better description, neurotic symptoms.' The ending was still not finalized. This draft merely includes a statement to the effect that: 'The intention here is to present a breathtakingly beautiful and comprehensive sense of different extraterrestrial worlds. The narration will suggest images and situations as you read it.' This is the first indication that the climax of the film would be conceived purely as a visual and sensory experience.

The screenplay continued to evolve even as the film was on the studio floor. Kubrick became particularly concerned with the role of Hal and the explanation for his 'nervous breakdown': indeed he seems to have been more interested in the characterization of the computer than the human beings in the film. The 'Other Hal Screenplay' of February 1966 is credited to Kubrick and Clarke but appears to have been Kubrick's work alone. It introduced the idea that Hal suffers a sort of schizophrenic crisis and splits into two personalities. It is 'Other Hal' who reveals the purpose of the mission to Bowman and explains what has caused his namesake's breakdown: 'Hal is not just a machine. He's a highly specialised brain. He may be a complex of micro-electronic circuitry, but mentally and emotionally he is a conscious being, capable of pain and pleasure.'[29] Clarke, who evidently was not consulted, was sceptical about the change: 'The sudden emergence of Hal 2 is quite unexplained and unbelievable. If we are to do it this way, we must prepare the ground much more carefully. I agree it's an interesting idea – better than a pre-taped message which happens to pop up.'[30] Kubrick dropped the idea but continued to revise the scenes featuring Hal:

> I think a great improvement in the story would be for all the present explanation about Hal and the reason he breaks down to take place as poetic narration during the sequence where Bowman is outside the ship recovering Poole, and Hal is finally alone and in complete control of the ship. This would replace the present scene where Other Hal explains to Bowman what the problem has been. The scene would still remain where Hal begs for his life. The same general reasons for Hal's breakdown will be given, but in a more poetic way.[31]

The correspondence suggests that by this stage in the production Kubrick was driving the changes, while Clarke was becoming sidelined.

There is also evidence of some tension regarding the preparation of the novel. Clarke was keen to press ahead because he needed the advance to pay his outstanding tax bill to the Government of Ceylon.[32] Kubrick, however, was now too preoccupied with filming to give any attention to the novel – though he insisted it could not be published without his approval. In July 1966 Kubrick wrote a terse letter reprimanding Clarke for showing the manuscript to potential publishers and asserting his own moral rights over the matter:

> I trust that you appreciate the spirit in which this offering is being made, since, though I regret the problem, I nevertheless feel completely self-righteous about the present situation. No-one can know more than yourself how my obligations and responsibilities during the preparation and actual filming have

completely absorbed every day, seven days a week, and under these circumstances I have obviously had no opportunity at all to do my share of the revisions to the book. It is my right to do this and I have repeatedly expressed to you how important I believe the revisions to be.

When you went to New York you promised not to show the manuscript to anyone. Instead of which you allowed Scott [Scott Meredith, Clarke's agent] to submit it to two publishers and Playboy magazine. [33]

Kubrick offered Clarke his share of the advance, to be repaid from the royalties, on condition 'that you will persuade Scott Meredith not to further submit the manuscript of the novel without both our consents'. In the event publication of the novel would be delayed by several months. It is difficult to avoid the impression that Kubrick delayed the publication of the novel so that it would be his version of *2001* rather than Clarke's that the public saw first.

The issue over the novel was an indication of the control that Kubrick exercised over all aspects of the production. At times this bordered on the obsessive. Kubrick was infamous for the secrecy that surrounded the making of his films. He would not allow journalists on the set, and insisted on personally approving all press and interviews. On one occasion he cabled publicity manager Roger Caras in the United States: 'Okay Hollis Alpert if you really believe he is on our side.'[34] This secrecy even extended to the studio backing the film. He ordered that all confidential telegrams should be sent to his London home rather than Borehamwood: 'The reason for not using Hawkfilms is the occasional routing of cables, etc, through the MGM operating office.'[35] It was not long before MGM was becoming concerned about the project. The studio baulked when Kubrick wanted to announce the start of production in *Le Figaro* and *Der Stern* as well as the usual trade papers. Caras told Kubrick: 'They're not very happy about all of this, Stan, and I feel that they are doing this simply to make you happy.'[36]

Nevertheless, the publicity strategy succeeded in generating much interest in the film. The production discourse of *2001* emphasized two aspects. The first was its seriousness. As Caras put it: 'There are no monsters in the film, Mickey Mouse and Buck Rogers have been eliminated, there are no terrible Russian lady astronauts. This will, in fact, be the world's first science fiction film worthy of the name, in that it will be a logical extension of today's techniques and technologies.'[37] The second, consistent with MGM's interest in the film, was its spectacle. As one internal memo put it: 'All publicity released concerning *2001: A Space Odyssey* should sell its great *size*, great *scope*, great *adventure*, great *excitement*, and absolute *authenticity* of the film. It should stress as well the *wonder, beauty,* and awe-inspiring qualities of the film and space.'[38]

The production of *2001* depended upon the assistance of numerous external agencies. The overriding imperative was authenticity. Early in the production Roger Caras wrote to the National Aeronautics and Space Administration to request their cooperation: '*2001: A Space Odyssey* will present an effective, dramatic and honest story of the space age as it is now opening up before us. It presents NASA, and what is about to come as a result of NASA's efforts, in the best possible context.'[39] The film was an early pioneer of product placement as companies such as American Express and Pan American allowed the use of their brands in return for promotional tie-ins. One of the product partners was IBM Computers, which was, however, concerned about the representation of the malfunctioning computer in the film. Caras evidently had to smooth some ruffled corporate feathers: 'Sometime ago I explained to IBM at great length the change in the script as it effects HAL ... I made it very clear, and this is completely true to the best of my knowledge, that the name IBM is never associated with equipment failure but that it is obviously not an IBM machine.'[40] Kubrick was evidently at pains to ensure that the technological hardware depicted in the film would be accurate: 'We are badly in need of a mad computer expert who can be around and advise on dialogue and jargon ... It should be someone who has his eyes on the future of computers, and not just a "stick-in-the-mud" type.'[41] But the film's claim to authenticity did not persuade all experts. Professor Harold Urey of the University of California San Diego – one of several astronomers approached to be interviewed for a prologue – was sceptical in the extreme: 'It would seem to me most improbable that one would find an artifact on the moon of extraterrestrial intelligence and I would not like to introduce a film that presents this point of view.'[42]

Principal photography of *2001* was completed in July 1966, but Kubrick spent longer over the post-production of the film than had ever been anticipated. This was not merely a matter of perfecting the complex visual effects: it was also the result of ongoing uncertainty over the formal structure of the film. The idea of the 'talking heads' prologue was abandoned – though not until after several interviews had been shot, including Sir Bernard Lovell at the Jodrell Bank Observatory, that would be used in publicity for the film.[43] Kubrick continued to revise the narration throughout 1967. By this time Clarke was evidently becoming frustrated with the process. When Clarke asked for payment for the additional work he was being asked to do beyond the screenplay, Kubrick told him: 'I hope you can understand there is a kind of psychological barrier to any payment like this coming at this time after a film has gone so considerably over budget and after a very sizeable sum has been paid for a screenplay as well as the ancillary payments for other writing services.'[44]

The most important change to the film in post-production was the decision to dispense with voice-over narration. This was a late decision. In September 1967 Kubrick was still testing narrators and seems to have settled on Douglas Rain: 'I think he's perfect, he's got just the right amount of Winston Hibbler [sic], the intelligent friend next door quality, with a great deal of sincerity, and yet, I think, an arresting quality.'[45] But in November 1967 he cabled Clarke: 'As more film cut together it became apparent narration was not needed.'[46] Rain would be used instead as the voice of Hal 9000. Another late change concerned the music. An original score had been commissioned from composer Alex North, who was writing music for the film until early in 1968 when he was peremptorily informed that his work was surplus to requirements. In late January 1968 North wrote to Kubrick: 'I'm sorry it all had to end this way without some discussion in connection with the music I had written, and was prepared to do my best to comply with your wishes, and believe me I did my best under the awkward situation of having to use as models the tracks you were accustomed to listening to ...'[47] At the last moment Kubrick had decided to use classical music extracts, particularly Richard Strauss's *Thus Spoke Zarathustra* for the opening titles and Johann Strauss's waltz *The Blue Danube* for scenes of space vehicles in orbit. Yet there is evidence to suggest he had this in mind from earlier in the process. In August 1967, for example, he wrote to the BBC to request a recording of a piece he had heard on the radio: 'On Friday, 18th August I heard a very interesting piece of music called "Requiem" by a composer named Ligeti. I believe this composition might be of use to me in my film, *2001: A Space Odyssey*, which is now in the completion stage.'[48] Ligeti's *Requiem* is used in the film to accompany the appearances of the alien monolith.

These changes radically transformed the style and formal structure of the film. The effect of dropping the narration was to remove the explanatory framework of the narrative. This decision has typically been understood as a consequence of Kubrick's desire to shift the film away from the classical Hollywood narrative towards something closer to 'the enigmatic symbolism of European art cinema'.[49] The open-ended and ambiguous narrative was a characteristic of European *auteur* directors such as Michelangelo Antonioni (*L'avventura*, 1960), Federico Fellini (*8½*, 1963) and Luis Buñuel (*Belle de Jour*, 1967). In particular the long scenes of daily routine on board the *Discovery* are reminiscent of the slowness of art cinema. This was also consistent with Kubrick's views on film style. In 1965 he had said: 'Most film cutting seems to me rather compulsive ... There is usually little purpose to the cut

12. The space wheel demonstrates how Stanley Kubrick wanted to represent a technologically realistic future in *2001: A Space Odyssey* (1968) (Source: British Film Institute).

and each purposeless cut you make simply lessens the effect of the first purposeful cut that might come along.'[50] *2001* includes one of the most famous 'purposeful' cuts in film history: from a bone thrown into the air by the ape 'Moonwatcher' to a space vessel in orbit.[51]

The extended post-production period meant that *2001* was not ready for release until April 1968. Its world première was in Washington DC on 2 April, followed by premières in New York, Los Angeles, Boston, Detroit, Houston, London, Johannesburg, Tokyo, Osaka and Sydney.[52] Following the first US screenings Kubrick cut 19 minutes from the film.[53] *2001* was released initially in 70-millimetre as a 'roadshow' attraction in selected cinemas equipped with the curved screens necessary for Cinerama presentation. It was a box office sensation. After five weeks it had grossed over $1 million 'in only eight reserved-seat engagements'.[54] After eleven weeks it passed $3 million in 35 engagements.[55] *2001* was recognized with an Academy Award for its special effects: this was collected by Kubrick, who was credited for special effects alongside Wally Veevers (a veteran of Korda's *Things to Come*), Douglas Trumbull, Con Pederson and Tom Howard. A general release in 35-millimetre followed in 1969 and returned a further $6 million.[56] This coincided with the climax of the US space programme: in July 1969 the Apollo 11 mission fulfilled Kennedy's aim of landing astronauts on the Moon and returning them safely to Earth. This evidently benefited the film: the distributors noticed a 'sharp increase in business since man landed on the moon'.[57] By 1978 – when it was reissued following the success of *Star Wars* and *Close Encounters of the Third Kind* – *2001* had grossed around $26 million.[58]

For all its popular success, however, the critical reception of *2001* was mixed. The major New York critics were somewhat underwhelmed by a film they recognized as a major technical achievement but felt was over-long and too ambiguous. Renata Adler of the *New York Times*, for example, thought that 'it is somewhere between hypnotic and immensely boring' and complained that 'the uncompromising slowness of the movie makes it hard to sit through without talking'.[59] A recurring complaint was that Kubrick seemed more interested in technological hardware than plotting and characterization. Hollis Alpert in the *Saturday Review* felt that 'for all the beautiful models, the marvelous constructions, the sensational perspectives, the effort to equate scientific accuracy with imaginative predictions, there's a gnawing lack of some genuinely human contact with the participants in the adventure'.[60] The most negative response came from Andrew Sarris in *Village Voice*, who condemned it as 'a thoroughly uninteresting failure and the most damning demonstration yet of Stanley Kubrick's inability to tell a story coherently and with a consistent point of view'.[61]

However, the aspects of the film that the New York critics disliked were precisely the qualities that were championed by reviewers in the new cinephile magazines of the 1960s. It was in the pages of these magazines – whose readership comprised younger and progressive readers – that the cult of *2001* began to emerge. *Film Comment*, for example, felt that '*2001* is one of the most entertaining as well as insightful films ever to have appeared on screen'.[62] *Cineaste* devoted several articles to the film. H. Mark Gasser believed that it was 'light years ahead of the average film in terms of content and presentation' and compared Kubrick with some of the greats of film history: 'In his flair for experimentation and restless progressivism, Kubrick reminds one of Godard, Chaplin, and Antonioni; in his unstinting drive for perfection, of Lang; in his passion for the exciting, the difficult, the complex, of Welles and Griffith.'[63] Cliff Barker argued that the reason for the negative reactions of the New York critics was 'because it did not fit into their vocabulary of film criticism. It did not adhere to standard dramatic technique; but it was defenseless to the conventional weapons of cleverness and searing witticisms.'[64] And Gary Crowdus suggested that 'a significant factor' in determining the response to *2001* 'seems to be which side of 30 you're on'. He felt that 'the older generation ... seem unable to comprehend the purely visual narrative, or appreciate the visually abstract, sequences of the film'.[65] This point was echoed by Saul Bass, the celebrated animator and graphic artist who designed the posters for the film. He wrote to Kubrick: 'I saw your film and just wanted you to know how beautiful and exciting I found it. Apparently most everybody else does too, even those few who worry about your ending. For me it was a fascinating, breathtaking experience.'[66]

Other sources also attest to the particular appeal of *2001* for younger audiences. The *Daily Express* journalist Victor Davis told Kubrick: 'I think I detect signs also that the film is developing as something of a cult. Its meanings are certainly much discussed among young people, and I see that both John Lennon and Mick Jagger are your unwavering admirers.'[67] It has become something of a received wisdom that the concluding sequence of *2001* – in which Bowman travels through a kaleidoscopic time-warp (referred to in the script and novel as the 'Stargate') – was understood as a drug-induced 'trip'. This reading was suggested by several contemporaries. Hollis Alpert, for example, wrote: 'What happens next might cause some moviegoers to wonder if a solution of LSD had been wafted through the air-conditioning system, for the astronaut now, presumably, enters unknown dimensions of time and space not unlike a psychedelic tunnel in the heavens.' The British critic Nina Hibbin described it as 'a breathtaking psychedelic Cinerama ride to – I know not where'.[68] The 70-millimetre reissue of *2001* in 1970 was advertised with the tag line: 'The Ultimate Trip'.[69]

2001: A Space Odyssey marks a watershed in the history of SF cinema. It was a landmark for several reasons. It was the first SF film to be a genuine blockbuster and proved that what had sometimes been regarded in the industry as a marginal genre could be major box office. Its success prompted a cycle of big-budget SF films from the major studios. These included *Marooned* (1969), *The Forbin Project* (1969), *The Andromeda Strain* (1970), *Silent Running* (1971) and *The Omega Man* (1971).[70] *2001* was particularly influential on two student filmmaking who made their breakthrough in the 1970s. Warner Bros. backed George Lucas's *THX 1138* (1970), a dystopian film indebted to Aldous Huxley's *Brave New World*, while John Carpenter's *Dark Star* (1974) was a 'spaced out' low-budget comedy intended as an irreverent antidote to what some saw as the pretentiousness of Kubrick's film. And the Russian director Andrei Tarkovsky made *Solaris* (1971), from a novel by Stanislaw Lem, whose slow narrative and philosophical complexity prompted some western critics to claim it as a Soviet response to *2001*. While none of these films matched the success of *2001*, they demonstrated an interest in exploring the philosophical and scientific themes inherent within SF cinema. *2001* also set a new benchmark for special effects that has been surpassed only by George Lucas's *Star Wars* (1977) and James Cameron's *Avatar* (2009). Cameron had already acknowledged the impact of *2001* in recruiting members of its production team, including editor Ray Lovejoy, for *Aliens* (1986). Other films to demonstrate the influence of *2001* include its official sequel, *2010* (1984), based on Clarke's novel *2010: Odyssey Two*, *The Abyss* (1989), *Contact* (1997) and *Mission to Mars* (2000).[71] During the making of *Contact*, director Robert Zemeckis had the entire crew watch *2001* 'for inspiration'.[72]

13. An iconic close-up of Bowman (Keir Dullea) entering the 'Stargate' in *2001: A Space Odyssey* (1968) (Source: British Film Institute).

The importance of *2001* is also evident in the range of critical interpretations the film has prompted. It is the *Citizen Kane* of SF cinema: critics search for the meaning of its closing scenes – in which Bowman apparently sees himself in the future, dying of old age before he is reborn as the 'Starchild' – as if, like *Kane*'s 'Rosebud', it will unlock the secrets of the film. There have been many metaphysical readings of *2001*. This early appreciation from the *Christian Century* is fairly representative: 'I think it has to do with how man's reach is automatically invented, how by reaching beyond himself man can hope to reach into himself – and how by reaching in he goes beyond.'[73] In such readings the ambiguity of the film is surpassed by that of the critic. Other critics have applied structuralist analysis to the film, concluding that it maps the 'odyssey of man': in this reading the 'Dawn of Man' sequence 'signifies man's liberation from the animal condition', while the Stargate sequence 'signifies the transcendence of the human condition'.[74] Such is the lack of consensus on the meaning of *2001* that it has even been described as 'an uninterpretable film'.[75]

Perhaps the key to understanding *2001* is not to search for meaning like some Holy Grail but rather to appreciate it on the level that Kubrick intended: as a sensory rather than a narrative experience. The production history reveals how Clarke's thematic and existential concept of the film was overtaken by Kubrick's visual and formal concept. The production and post-production process saw the stripping away of extraneous elements, including the narration and most of the references to the Cold War, while at the same time transforming the film stylistically. The popular success of *2001* within the cinephile culture made it the first (and to date perhaps the only) art-house blockbuster. It also demonstrates, as did *Things to Come* before it, the essential difference between SF literature, concerned as it with ideas and philosophy, and SF cinema, in which visual spectacle is paramount. In this context *2001* can be seen not only as the film that influenced all that came afterwards, but also as the culmination of a process that began with the early 'trick' films of Méliès: a celebration of the medium's capacity for spectacle and illusion.

Notes

1   Quoted in William E. Burrows, *This New Ocean: The Story of the First Space Age* (New York: Modern Library, 1999), p.330.

2   Archive and Special Collections Centre, University of the Arts, London, SK/12/8/1/12: Stanley Kubrick to Arthur C. Clarke, 31 March 1964.

3   The critical literature on Kubrick is surprisingly limited: it is to be hoped the opening of the Stanley Kubrick Archive will facilitate more critical and historical studies. In the meantime see: Mario Falsetto, *Stanley Kubrick: A Narrative and Stylistic Analysis* (Westport CT: McFarland, 2001); Norman Kagan, *The Cinema of Stanley Kubrick* (Oxford: Roundhouse, rev. edn 1995); Robert Kolker, *A Cinema of Loneliness: Penn, Stone, Kubrick, Scorsese, Spielberg, Altman* (Oxford: Oxford University Press, 2000). On *2001*, see Michel Chion, *Kubrick's Cinema Odyssey* (London: British Film Institute, 2001); Robert Kolker (ed.), *Stanley Kubrick's 2001: A Space Odyssey – New Essays* (Oxford: Oxford University Press, 2006); and Peter Krämer, *2001: A Space Odyssey* (London: Palgrave/British Film Institute, 2010). Krämer is the only previous commentator to have made use of the extensive holdings of the Stanley Kubrick Archive.

4   Philip French, '*A Clockwork Orange*', *Sight & Sound*, 59: 2 (1990), p.86.

5   Ephraim Katz, *The Macmillan International Film Encyclopedia* (London: Macmillan, 1996), p.768.

6   See Charles Maland, '*Dr Strangelove* (1964): Nightmare Comedy and the Ideology of Liberal Consensus', in Peter C. Rollins (ed.), *Hollywood as Historian: American Film in a Cultural Context* (Lexington: University Press of Kentucky, rev. edn 1998), pp.190–210; and Jonathan Kirshner, 'Subverting the Cold War in the 1960s: *Dr Strangelove*, *The Manchurian Candidate*, and *The* [sic] *Planet of the Apes*', *Film and History*, 31: 2 (2001), pp.40–44.

7   SK/12/8/1/12: Kubrick to Clarke, 31 March 1964.

8   See Robin Anne Reid, *Arthur C. Clarke: A Critical Companion* (Westport CT: Greenwood Press, 1997). Clarke's own *Astounding Days: A Science Fictional Autobiography* (New York: Bantam Dell, 1990) is rather more interesting than the bland authorized biography by Neil McAleer, *Arthur C. Clarke: The Authorized Biography* (London: Contemporary Books, 1992).

9   Marvin Minsky, 'Steps Toward Artificial Intelligence', *Proceedings of the IRE*, 49: 1 (January 1961). Minsky was head of the Artificial Intelligence Project at the Massachusetts Institute of Technology: Kubrick arranged to meet him in London in 1965 (SK/12/8/1/34). Kubrick worked on a film project known as *A.I.* intermittently from the 1970s but felt that special effects technology was not yet sufficiently advanced to make it possible. The project was handed to Steven Spielberg in the mid-1990s and was finally realized as *A.I.: Artificial Intelligence* (DreamWorks, dir. Steven Spielberg, 2001).

10   SK/12/8/1/12: Arthur C. Clarke to Kubrick, 8 April 1964.

11   Arthur C. Clarke, 'The Sentinel', *The Collected Stories* (London: Gollancz, 2001), pp.301–8. The story was first published as 'Sentinel of Eternity' in *10 Story Fantasy* in spring 1951.

12 SK/12/8/1/12: Clarke to Kubrick, 9 April 1964.

13 SK12/1/1/1: 'Project: Space – First Draft Outline', n.d., and 'Novel First Draft – Across the Sea of Stars', 4 June 1964.

14 Arthur C. Clarke, 'Encounter in the Dawn', *The Collected Stories*, pp.460–9. The story was first published in *Amazing*, June/July 1953.

15 SK/12/1/1/2: 'Journey Beyond the Stars: A Film Story' by Stanley Kubrick and Arthur C. Clarke, 280 pp, n.d.

16 BFI Library microfiche for *2001*: 'Stanley Kubrick to Film *Journey Beyond the Stars* in Cinerama for MGM', 23 February 1965. In a letter to his friend Alexander Walker, film critic of the *Evening Standard*, Kubrick wrote: 'Would you be a dear sport and let me know the date that you receive a release from the London office of MGM announcing my new project. I won't explain why I want to know and I would appreciate it if you would regard this inquiry as confidential' (SK 12/8/1/87: Kubrick to Walker, 2 March 1965).

17 Krämer, *2001: A Space Odyssey*, p.40.

18 Cinerama originally used three cameras and three projectors with a giant curved screen that filled the field of vision. It was used initially for travelogues such as *This Is Cinerama* (1952). *How the West Was Won* was the first fiction film shot in the process. Later films abandoned the three-camera system and replaced it with a single 70-millimetre camera. *2001* was actually shot in Ultra-Panavision (65-millimetre anamorphic) and released in Cinerama.

19 UCLA George Pal Collection Box 8 f.10 contains readers' reports both on the novel *Childhood's End* (23 July 1953) and on the screenplay by Howard Koch (2 April 1965). Box 8 f.8 includes a handwritten note by Koch in regard to his own work: 'The screenplay, as I re-read it, seems somewhat sparse in certain areas. Economy in film treatment is a virtue up to a point, but I believe on this occasion I overdid it.' There is also evidence that John Frankenheimer was interested in the book. Clarke told Kubrick 'that Frankenheimer has bought, or wants to buy, *Childhood's End*' (SK 12/8/1/12: Clarke to Kubrick, 30 June 1967).

20 SK/12/2/5: Louis C. Blau to Kubrick, n.d. (*c.*January 1965).

21 An annex to the contract suggests that Keir Dullea was already confirmed in the role of 'First Astronaut'. Other possible casting suggestions included John Gavin, Rod Taylor, Hugh O'Brian, George Hamilton or James Coburn for the 'Second Astronaut' (the role went to Gary Lockwood, who was also on the shortlist for 'Moonwatcher'), Robert Montgomery, Jose Ferrer, Joseph Cotten, Robert Ryan, Henry Fonda or George C. Scott for Dr Heywood Floyd (William Sylvester, who played the part, is not on the list), and Robert Shaw, Toshiro Mifune, Albert Finney and (again) Jose Ferrer for 'Moonwatcher'.

22 Ibid: Letter of agreement between MGM and Polaris Productions, 22 May 1965.

23 Margaret Dickinson and Sarah Street, *Cinema and State: The Film Industry and the British Government 1927–84* (London: British Film Institute, 1985), pp.225–47.

24 Communications were problematic. In a letter of 13 September 1966 Clarke gave Kubrick the telex address of the Sheeraez Hotel in Colombo with the warning: 'The instrument is at the HQ of the Ceylon Mafia, and I hope I don't get caught in any cross-fire' (SK/12/8/1/12).

25 Krämer, *2001: A Space Odyssey*, p.43.

26 SK/12/1/2/2: *2001: A Space Odyssey* ('Athena Screenplay'). Screenplay by Stanley Kubrick and Arthur C. Clarke, 6 July 1965.

27 SK/12/8/1/12: Clarke to Kubrick, 25 August 1965.

28 SK/12//1/2/2: *2001: A Space Odyssey*. Screenplay by Stanley Kubrick and Arthur C. Clarke, n.d. but including individual pages dated between 4 October and 7 December 1965.

[29] SK/12/1/2/3: *2001: A Space Odyssey* ('Other Hal Screenplay'). Screenplay by Stanley Kubrick and Arthur C. Clarke, n.d. but including pages dated between 19 November 1965 and 16 February 1966.

[30] SK/12/8/1/12: Clarke to Kubrick, 3 March 1966.

[31] Ibid: Kubrick to Clarke, 7 March 1966.

[32] Clarke's back taxes are mentioned several times in his correspondence with Kubrick. His travel from his home in Colombo was severely curtailed due to the money he owed.

[33] Ibid: Kubrick to Clarke, 12 July 1966.

[34] SK/12/8/1/1: Kubrick to Roger Caras, 15 September 1965.

[35] SK/12/8/3/29: Ray Lovejoy to Roger Caras, 10 August 1965.

[36] SK/12/8/1/1: Caras to Kubrick, 26 October 1965. MGM felt that the cost of placing an advertisement in *Le Figaro* ($4,684) could be better used in promoting the finished film.

[37] Ibid: Caras to Ross Garrett (The 3M Company), 29 June 1965.

[38] Ibid: 'Criteria for Publicity for *2001: A Space Odyssey*', n.d.

[39] Ibid: Roger Caras to Julian Scheer (NASA Office of Public Affairs), 1 July 1965.

[40] Ibid: Caras to Kubrick, 13 September 1966.

[41] Ibid: Kubrick to Caras, 22 September 1965.

[42] Ibid: Harold C. Urey to Caras, 7 February 1966.

[43] Ibid: Sir Bernard Lovell to Caras, 7 February 1966.

[44] SK/ 12/8/1/12: Kubrick to Clarke, 27 December 1967.

[45] SK/12/8/1/5: Kubrick to Floyd Peterson, 25 September 1967.

[46] Ibid: Kubrick to Clarke, 23 November 1967.

[47] SK/12/8/1/53: Alex North to Kubrick, 29 January 1968. North's letter suggests that he had been asked to score the film without seeing all of it: 'All the best to you on the film ... wish I had seen more of it ... what I saw is pretty sensational ... so good luck man!!!!'

[48] SK/12/8/1/44: Kubrick to Eric Roseberry, 24 August 1967.

[49] Kristin Thompson and David Bordwell, *Film History: An Introduction* (New York: McGraw-Hill, 1994), p.708.

[50] SK/12/8/1/29: *Herald Tribune* notes, 23 November 1965.

[51] *A Canterbury Tale* (Rank/The Archers, dir. Michael Powell, 1944) features a similar device with a cut from a medieval falcon to a Spitfire in flight. Most commentators have understood the cut in *2001* as a brilliant temporal ellipsis. However, there is a thematic link that is evident only from the unpublished script. The bone is a weapon: the ape known as 'Moonwatcher' has just used it to kill another ape. The space vessel is also a weapon: the narration dropped from the film establishes that it is an orbiting nuclear weapons platform.

[52] '"Odyssey" on time', *Film and Television Daily*, 27 March 1968, p.1.

[53] 'Kubrick trims "2001" by 19 mins', *Variety*, 17 April 1968.

[54] SK/12/5/2/3: MGM press release, 9 May 1968.

[55] Ibid: MGM press release, 19 June 1968.

[56] 'All-time boxoffice champs', *Variety*, 7 January 1970, p.25.

[57] SK/12/5/5: William A. Madden to 'All Branch and Division Managers', 25 July 1969.

[58] 'All-time film rental champs', *Variety*, 10 May 1993, pp.C76–106.

[59] *New York Times*, 4 April 1968, p.58.

[60] *Saturday Review*, 20 April 1968, p.18.

[61] *Village Voice*, 11 April 1968, p.45.

[62] Elie Flatto, 'The Eternal Renewal', *Film Comment* 5: 4 (Winter 1969), p.8.

[63] H. Mark Glasser, '2001: A Space Odyssey', *Cineaste* 2:1 (Summer 1968), p.11.

[64] Cliff Barker, 'Is *2001* Worth Seeing Twice?', *Cineaste* 2: 1 (Summer 1968), p.15.

65 Gary Crowdus, 'A Tentative for the Viewing of *2001*', *Cineaste* 2: 1 (Summer 1968), p.12.

66 SK/12/8/1/3: Saul Bass to Kubrick, 25 April 1968.

67 SK/12/8/1/19: Victor Davis to Kubrick, 1 July 1968.

68 *Morning Star*, 1 May 1968.

69 Krämer, *2001: A Space Odyssey*, p.92.

70 *Marooned* (Columbia, dir. John Sturges, 1969); *The Forbin Project* (aka *Colossus: The Forbin Project*, Universal, dir. Joseph Sargent, 1970); *The Andromeda Strain* (Universal, dir. Robert Wise, 1970), *Silent Running* (Universal, dir. Douglas Trumbull, 1971); *The Omega Man* (Warner Bros., dir. Boris Segal, 1971).

71 *2010* (MGM, dir. Peter Hyams, 1984); *The Abyss* (Lightstorm/20th Century-Fox, dir. James Cameron, 1989); *Contact* (Warner Bros., dir. Robert Zemeckis, 1997); *Mission to Mars* (Touchstone Pictures, dir. Brian De Palma, 2000).

72 Norman Kagan, *The Cinema of Robert Zemeckis* (Lanham MA: Taylor Trade Publishing, 2003), pp.159–81.

73 Fred Myers, 'Sci-Fi Triumph', *The Christian Century*, 26 June 1968.

74 J. P. Dumont and J. Monod, 'Beyond the Infinite: A Structural Analysis of *2001: A Space Odyssey*', *Quarterly Review of Film Studies* 3: 3 (1978), p.315.

75 David Boyd, 'Mode and Meaning in *2001*', *Journal of Popular Film* 6: 3 (1978), p.202.

7

MONKEY BUSINESS:
PLANET OF THE APES (1968)

Pierre Boulle is best known to the Anglophone world as author of *The Bridge on the River Kwai*, turned into an Academy Award-winning film by David Lean in 1957. In one of the great ironies of cinema history Boulle received an Academy Award for Best Screenplay even though he had nothing to do with writing the film: his screen credit disguised the fact that the screenplay was the work of two Hollywood blacklistees, Carl Foreman and Michael Wilson.[1] In addition to *Kwai* Boulle wrote another two dozen novels and numerous short stories. *La planète des singes* – published in 1963 and translated into English as *Monkey Planet* – is a satirical fantasy in the tradition of *Gulliver's Travels*. It concerns an astronaut who finds himself on a planet similar to Earth but where evolution has taken a different course and intelligent, talking apes are the dominant species. Boulle said that he was inspired 'by a visit to the zoo where I watched the gorillas. I was impressed by their human-like expressions. It led me to dwell upon and imagine relationships between humans and apes.' However, he did not think it would work as a film: 'I never thought it could be made into a film. It seemed to me too difficult, and there was the chance that it would appear ridiculous.'[2]

Monkey Planet begins with a couple who, while holidaying on an interstellar cruise liner, discover (literally) a message in a bottle. It turns out to be a manuscript written by one Ulysse Mérou and cast into space in the hope of 'averting the appalling scourge which is menacing the human race'.[3] Ulysse is a friend of Professor Antelle, who has invented a spaceship capable of travelling at the speed of light. They travel to the solar system of the star Betelgeuse, where they find a planet similar to Earth, which they name Soror ('Sister') and where they encounter a group of primitive, mute humans. The humans are ambushed by a hunting party of gorillas, wearing clothes and armed with guns. Ulysse is captured and taken with other captives to the apes' city where he proves his intelligence in a series of experiments. When the apes discover Ulysse is able to speak, he is released from captivity. He is adopted by Zira, a female chimpanzee, and her fiancé Cornelius who teach him about ape society and customs. Ulysse selects an indigenous female, Nova, as a mate. Meanwhile, an archæological expedition uncovers evidence of a human civilization on the planet that existed before the apes. Experiments in reclaiming the memories of indigenous humans reveal that the apes were once domestic pets and servants who took over as their human masters sank into moral degeneracy. The orangutan scientist Dr Zaius fears that Ulysse 'might found a new race on this planet'.[4] Zira and Cornelius help Ulysse escape with Nova, who is pregnant. The novel ends with a double twist. Ulysse travels back to Earth, 700 years after he had left, only to find it is ruled by apes. At this point Ulysse's manuscript ends. The couple who have found it dismiss it as a practical joke because they do not believe any man could be so intelligent: at this point it is revealed that they themselves are chimpanzees.

While Boulle was sceptical that the book could be made into a film, producer Arthur P. Jacobs saw potential in the story. Jacobs, formerly a publicist for MGM and Warner Bros., exemplified the new generation of independent producers who emerged following the break-up of the Hollywood studio system. The practice now was for the producer to put together a package of script, star and director, which they would offer to one of the majors. Jacobs, who wanted to make a fantasy adventure movie in the tradition of *King Kong*, averred that 'I spent about three and a half years of everyone refusing to make the movie.'[5] He commissioned a set of concept sketches which he showed to Charlton Heston. Heston was one of the biggest box office stars in Hollywood but was looking for a part to break the run of historical 'great man' roles he had played in films such as *Ben-Hur*, *El Cid*, *55 Days at Peking*, *The Agony and the Ecstasy*, *The War Lord* and *Khartoum*. In his autobiography Heston recalled:

> The novel was singularly uncinematic; there wasn't even a treatment outlining an effective script. Still, I smelled a good film in it. All Arthur had was the rights to the novel and a portfolio of paintings depicting possible scenes ... He spent the next year and a half in Development Hell, trudging from studio to studio with the paintings and being laughed at.[6]

Heston suggested director Franklin J. Schaffner, who had made *The War Lord* and who 'liked it enough to commit as director'. The next stage was to develop a suitable script.

Jacobs turned to Rod Serling, the television dramatist who had scripted the acclaimed live play *Requiem for a Heavyweight* and who was well versed in science fiction as executive producer, writer-in-chief and narrator of the anthology series *The Twilight Zone* (1959–64). Serling had also written for motion pictures, including the film of *Requiem for a Heavyweight* (1962), the suspense thriller *Yellow Canary* (1964) and the political melodrama *Seven Days in May* (1964). Serling, whose work demonstrates a consistent interest in progressive social causes, later told a newspaper that in his view 'the singular evil of our time is prejudice. In almost everything I have written, there is a thread of this: man's seemingly palpable need to dislike someone other than himself.'[7] This theme would manifest itself in *Planet of the Apes*, which Serling adapted freely from the novel. In the process Boulle's evolutionary fable was transformed into a commentary on contemporary American society.

Serling wrote several drafts of *Planet of the Apes*, all of which differ in significant ways from both the novel and the finished film. He abandoned Boulle's framing device, and instead opened the screenplay with a spacecraft from Earth landing on an unknown planet, and with three astronauts awakening from suspended animation (a fourth, female, astronaut has died due to the failure of her life-support unit). He followed Boulle in representing the apes' society as monotheistic and technologically advanced – they use telephones, cars and helicopters – and developed an idea alluded to only briefly in the book, that the entire ape culture and science was derived from the human civilization that had existed before:

> *Thomas:* You don't have a culture, Mr Cornelius. Or a science. Or an industry. The houses you live in, the buildings you occupy, the clothes you wear, the things you believe, the books you read, the very God you worship – that all came from Man! Five hundred – a thousand years ago – but not from an ape mind. Or an ape will. Or the logic, the reason, or the rationale of an ape. You're imitators. *You've been mimicking the creature Man, who was there ahead of you!*[8]

It transpires that Dr Zaius (whose role is much enhanced from the book) already knew of the existence of a human civilization. Zaius is afraid of Thomas, not because he might reproduce, as in the book, but because his existence undermines the apes' entire belief system.

Serling also introduced several ideas not present in the book. The theme of mankind's treatment of other species became a comment on supremacist attitudes towards supposedly inferior races. This was a theme that had particular resonance in 1960s America through the Civil Rights movement, though Serling was also following precedents from popular culture. In particular there are strong echoes of Richard Connell's classic story 'The Most Dangerous Game', in which a shipwrecked big-game hunter finds himself the prey in a manhunt led by a deranged Russian aristocrat on a Caribbean island. The twist here is that the apes are the hunters and man is the prey. Serling describes a hunting party of apes 'dressed immaculately in the white garb and pith helmets of British hunters ... all dressed as members of a safari carrying guns of different calibre'. Thomas also learns that the apes carry out culls of the indigenous humans. Zira justifies this as a form of pest control: 'This is not from choice, Mr Thomas. We try to keep them isolated but they reproduce quickly. Very often they'll travel in bands and steal food.' This causes Thomas to reflect on his own attitude towards animals: 'I swear to God ... if I ever get another chance, I won't even set a mouse trap!'[9]

The other major theme that Serling introduced into *Planet of the Apes* was the spectre of nuclear war. This addition locates the film within a trend of post-war apocalyptic fiction: other films predicting a nuclear holocaust included *On the Beach* (1959), from the novel by Neville Shute, the satirical *Dr Strangelove; Or, How I Leaned to Stop Worrying and Love the Bomb* (1964), and *The War Game* (1965), a harrowing documentary-drama produced for British television but released theatrically in the United States.[10] Serling had also contributed to this genre in the *Twilight Zone* episode 'Time Enough at Last', in which a meek bank clerk is the only survivor of an atomic attack. Serling wrote several references to nuclear war into *Planet of the Apes*. In one scene Thomas explains the atomic bomb to ape scientists in order to demonstrate the scientific advances made by humans on his own planet. He is taken aback by their shocked response: 'Forgive us, Mr Thomas. But to use a bomb as you describe even *once* – suggests to us, who have never even had a war – that you are scientifically advanced ... but there remains a question as to *how* civilized?'[11] This theme is further developed when archæological evidence reveals that the humans who once inhabited the planet died in a nuclear holocaust (they discover the skeletons of a family in an underground shelter, killed by radiation and thermal burns). The revelation sets up a key exchange between Thomas and Dr Zaius concerning mankind's propensity for violence and self-destruction:

> *Dr Zaius:* Man has always been a menace. His wisdom must walk hand in hand with his idiocy. His emotions conquer his logic. Deep down he's a belligerent animal who must give battle to everything around him. And in the process, he will always destroy himself.
>   (A pause)

This is the truth we've dug out of a hole, Mr Thomas. It's the truth you've told us about in describing the history of your own planet.

(Another pause)

We apes have no death wish, Mr Thomas.

Thomas: Does it occur to you, Dr Zaius, that on earth Man has finally become civilized? I'm proof of that. I'm proof that he has reached out for the stars – and gathered them in. And that for the first time in the history of my race – perhaps the history of the universe – he has ceased to be the destroyer.[12]

This was Serling's addition – there is no equivalent scene in the book – though Thomas's faith in scientific progress and moral regeneration is a characteristic shared with Ulysse Mérou.

However, Serling's most radical departure from the novel was the denouement, where it is revealed that the planet of the apes is in fact Earth in the distant future. There have been hints of this throughout, in the familiar star patterns and a map of the ape lands that resembles North America. It turns out that Thomas has travelled through a space-time warp and has arrived back at his point of origin two millennia later. It was Serling's idea that the last shot of the film should be the remains of the Statue of Liberty – a brilliantly visual way of showing the audience that this is Earth – though he struggled to incorporate the idea dramatically. In one early draft, for example, Thomas flies over the statue in a helicopter. The script describes a 'PAN DOWN from it to see what Thomas has already seen ... But this time it is caught in the blaze of the morning sun revealing it as what it is – the top part of the Statue of Liberty.'[13] In a later script, shown to Charlton Heston in March 1965, Thomas is shot dead at the foot of the statue, while the apes are left wondering what his last words ('I'm afraid there's no place left to go') meant. The final image is as haunting on the page as it would prove on the screen:

SLOWLY THE CAMERA RISES and PULLS BACK – the sun is just rising and is now clearly illuminating the area.

As the CAMERA RISES and RISES HIGHER and HIGHER and FURTHER and FURTHER AWAY FROM the funeral procession, we see now for the first time what the metal 'arm' is.

Caught in the blaze of the morning sun, we see in what is the beginning of an excavation – the top part of the STATUE OF LIBERTY.

On a BLACK SCREEN – with NO MUSIC – the CREDITS slowly appear on a roll.[14]

There are conflicting accounts of how Pierre Boulle responded to the changes made to his story. According to Jacobs: 'I sent the finished script to Boulle, and he wrote back, saying he thought it was more inventive than his own ending, and wished that he had thought of it when he wrote the book.'[15] However, this is contradicted by Boulle himself: 'I disliked somewhat the ending that was used – the Statue of Liberty – which the critics seemed to like, but personally I prefer my own.'[16]

Jacobs now had a package – but still none of the studios would back the film. Warner Bros. baulked when it was estimated it would cost $10 million.[17] On 3 November 1965 Heston recorded in his diary: 'The Planet of the Apes project seems in limbo. Jacobs is now thinking of trying to sweat the budget down to two million, which seems ridiculous.'[18] Early in 1966, however, Richard Zanuck, son of Darryl F. Zanuck, and now production chief at his father's old studio, 20th Century-Fox, agreed to commission a screen test of the ape make-ups. On 7 March 1966 Heston 'went over to Fox for an hour to rehearse the test for The Planet of the Apes. I'm a little sorry I agreed to do it, on a film not even approved yet, but I did agree.'[19] The test sequence was the discussion between Thomas (Heston) and Dr Zaius (Edward G. Robinson). 'The Apes test looked good', Heston recorded a week later. 'If the question is whether or the not the ape makeup is laughable, the answer is no, it's very plausible.'[20] Zanuck had said that he would back the film if nobody laughed at the test, but it would still be another six months before the film finally got the go-ahead. 'There seem to be some stirrings from Fox on Planet of the Apes, which I thought had long since disappeared,' Heston noted on 23 September 1966.[21] Zanuck's caution over what was recognized as a risky project needs to be understood in the context of the problems at Fox during the 1960s. The studio had narrowly escaped bankruptcy following its expensive production of Cleopatra (1963), and, although it had recouped its losses with The Sound of Music (1965), Zanuck was understandably somewhat risk-averse. It seems that what finally persuaded him was not the screen test but the box office success of Fantastic Voyage (1966), another SF film backed by the studio. Planet of the Apes was green-lit on 26 September 1966.[22]

However, Fox would agree only to a budget of $5 million (in the event the production cost of the film was $5.8 million). It therefore became necessary to revise the screenplay with a view to reducing costs. Jacobs turned to Michael Wilson, an uncredited contributor to both The Bridge on the River Kwai and Lawrence of Arabia (1962), but who with the blacklist weakened following the end of the studio system, was once again able to work openly as a screenwriter. Wilson's solution for reducing the cost of the film was to present ape society as less technologically advanced, thus removing the need for futuristic sets, and to cut out props such as the vehicle the Earth astronauts use to explore the planet (they have to travel on foot instead). But he also made other changes that significantly altered the tone of the film. Taylor (as Thomas was now called) became a much more cynical character than in Serling's script. His sense of disillusionment is established in the opening scene where he records a log entry before joining his fellow astronauts in suspended animation ('I leave the twentieth century without regret'), he scoffs when one of his fellow astronauts plants the Stars and Stripes on the new planet, and his initial reaction upon encountering the indigenous humans is scornful in the extreme ('If that's the best there is around here, in six months we'll be running this planet'). Wilson maintained the ending at the Statue of Liberty, but rather than killing Taylor has him sink to his knees in despair while exclaiming: 'Ohhh, My God ... I'm back. It's home – all the time ... So they did it. They finally did it. YOU MANIACS!! You blew it all up! God damn you! GOD ... DAMN ... YOU ... ALL ... TO HELL!'[23] This recalls the end of *The Bridge on the River Kwai* where Clipton (James Donald) exclaims: 'Madness! Madness!'

Wilson made several other important changes. He replaced a scene where Thomas is invited to speak to the ape assembly with a much more adversarial scene, in which Taylor is brought before a tribunal to establish the truth of his claim to be from another planet. Taylor, however, is not allowed to speak: his protests are shouted down as 'heresy'. The motif of the tribunal or inquisition was a favourite device of blacklisted writers to comment on their own experience before the notorious House UnAmerican Activities Committee in the early 1950s. One draft even included a line where Zaius declares 'there is a conspiracy afoot to undermine the very cornerstone of our faith' – recalling the inflammatory rhetoric of Senator McCarthy – while to make the point even more explicit, Taylor remarks that 'back on Earth, in my time, men in power prized intelligence less than they feared it. And when intelligence threatened to expose their cherished myths they were compelled to suppress it.'[24] In the event these lines were cut from the shooting script: by the late 1960s other issues, particularly Civil Rights and Vietnam, had replaced McCarthyism as the rallying cry for the American left.

Wilson also inserted more references to religion, giving Zaius the title of Minister of Science and Chief Defender of the Faith ('There is no contradiction between faith and science') and developing ape theology by introducing the Sacred Scrolls ('Beware the beast man, for he is the devil's spawn. Alone among God's primates, he kills for sport'). And crucially, Wilson turned ape society into a caste system with a distinct hierarchy of species. This was understood as a means of asserting the film's credentials as a social commentary:

> Zira and Galen, as chimpanzees, are inferior in the simian social
> structure to Dr Zaius, their chieftain, who is an orangutan.
> The parallels to the social order on Earth begin to clarify, with
> the baboons as the lowest rung – and therefore restricted as to
> employment, civil rights and privilege – and the orangutans as the
> creme de la creme, the simian aristocracy.[25]

In the event the underclass of baboons – clearly intended as analogous to
African Americans – were cut from the shooting script. But scenes in earlier
drafts where baboons carry placards declaring 'Down with Discrimination'
and 'Freedom Now' would suggest that Wilson (a white left-liberal) saw
Planet of the Apes as a statement about Civil Rights.[26]

It had been planned to shoot the film in Britain in the spring of 1967.[27] The
rationale for this would have been to qualify for a subsidy from the Eady
Levy, a fund that provided an economic incentive for so-called 'runaway'
productions to be shot in British studios.[28] Early in 1967, however, Fox
decided to make the film in the United States. This was due to the choice of
locations. According to cinematographer Leon Shamroy: 'We were looking
for a landscape weird and "unearthly" enough to suggest the possible terrain
of another planet.'[29] The Colorado River in Utah and Arizona provided a
suitable location, while the ape village was built at the Fox ranch, north of
Los Angeles. But the change of location pushed up the cost. On 28 April
1967 Heston recorded:

> Fox, in a panic over the projected cost of Apes (brought on in part by
> their decision to shoot the film here instead of overseas), has now
> decided to bring the budget down a bit ... By cutting the shooting
> days from fifty-five to forty-five, they seem to save a great deal of
> money, but the film can't be *shot* in that time.[30]

The production of Planet of the Apes was not without its problems. A month
before location shooting was due to commence, the casting of several key
parts was still not decided. Edward G. Robinson had been pencilled in to
play Zaius, but, aged 74, he found the heavy make-up too arduous and
withdrew: the part went to Maurice Evans. Kim Hunter, similarly, was a
late replacement for Julie Harris as Zira. One of the most difficult parts was
Nova, who remains mute throughout the film. In the event the part went
to Linda Harrison, a model who then happened to be Richard Zanuck's
girlfriend. Heston felt she was not really up to the job: 'Linda H. has
problems, but Frank's keeping her nearly immobile in her scenes, which
works.'[31] It was a physically arduous shoot, especially for Heston, who
spent much of the film as a captive while wearing only a loincloth. One

entry in his diary records: 'It occurs to me that there's hardly been a scene in this bloody film in which I've not been dragged, choked, netted, chased, doused, whipped, poked, shot, gagged, stoned, leaped on, or generally mistreated.'[32] One anecdote from the filming is particularly interesting. Heston noticed that the ape caste system was reinforced by the behaviour of the performers:

> I noted a curious anomaly on the location shoots. At lunch, the ape actors lunched separately, since their makeups limited them to liquid foods taken through a straw. But beyond that, they self-segregated by species: gorillas at one table, chimps at another, and orangutans at still a third. I leave it to the anthropologists to figure this out.[33]

Heston himself was evidently closely involved in decisions on set and in rewriting some of his own dialogue. He contributed one of the most famous lines when Taylor, after being pursued around the ape village, speaks to his captors for the first time (he has been shot in the throat and has temporarily lost his voice). In the shooting script the line is rather tame: 'No! That's where I draw the line! I won't wear a muzzle!' Heston replaced this with: 'Take your dirty hands off me, you damned monkey!' In the finished film the line is: 'Take your stinking paws off me you damned dirty ape!'[34]

Planet of the Apes was released in February 1968 (it preceded *2001* by two months), and was generally well received by the critics, who thought it a superior example of the genre. Pauline Kael, film critic of the *New Yorker*, called it 'one of the best science-fiction fantasies ever'.[35] There was universal praise for the ape masks, which won a special Academy Award for make-up artist John Chambers. It was the public response that mattered most to the studio, however, and here Zanuck had every reason to be delighted as *Planet of the Apes* became a 'gargantuan box office hit'.[36] It would eventually gross over $32 million.[37] Within weeks of its release, Zanuck had commissioned a sequel. On 10 April executive producer Mort Abrahams wrote to Rod Serling:

> In a discussion of this project with the studio the other day, Arthur and I mentioned that we had a preliminary conversation with you, and Dick Zanuck and David Brown were delighted. They did tell us, and I think it only fair to tell you, that on their own they had their Paris office contact Pierre Boulle and had asked Boulle to come up with some ideas for a sequel. Although he was not very enthusiastic or optimistic, Boulle did promise to give it some thought.[38]

In the event Boulle and Serling both wrote treatments for the sequel, though neither of them was deemed satisfactory. Boulle's treatment, entitled *Planet of the Men*, had Taylor and Nova founding a new colony of humans who arm themselves for protection against the apes. Years later the apes launch a war of extermination against the humans in which Taylor, Zira and Cornelius are all killed.[39] Serling's treatment, entitled *The Dark Side of the Earth*, had Taylor finding a surviving colony of humans and helping them to rebuild their technology, when another spaceship arrives. The apes again start a war against the humans – this time in response to provocation – leading to a massacre in which most of the apes are killed. Taylor, escaping in the spaceship, deliberately crashes it into the village: 'Taylor knows what will happen in the new earth society. He's seen it happen. Already evidence of class ... groupings ... prejudice ... hatreds. A microcosm of the earth he remembers. Best, he decides, to let evolution begin again. Destroy everything – and let the deity try it all over again.'[40]

While aspects of both the Boulle and Serling treatments would turn up in the sequel, eventually entitled *Beneath the Planet of the Apes*, the final screenplay was the work of Paul Dehn. Dehn was a British writer and critic whose films included *Seven Days to Noon* (1950), for which he shared an Academy Award, the James Bond thriller *Goldfinger* (1964) and two John le Carré adaptations, *The Spy Who Came in from the Cold* (1965) and *The Deadly Affair* (1966). Dehn said he was attracted by the challenge of 'finding a follow-up to the marvellous last sequence with the head of the Statue of Liberty protruding through the sand on the shore. It gave me the idea of an underground civilisation.'[41] Dehn also had to work around Charlton Heston's insistence that he would make only a brief 'guest star' appearance and wanted to be killed off at the beginning of the film.[42] In the event Taylor disappears at the start of the film – which takes up immediately where *Planet of the Apes* finished – when he falls into a void in the Forbidden Zone. Another astronaut, Brent (James Franciscus), arrives in search of Taylor, is captured by the apes, escapes, and is pursued into the Forbidden Zone where he discovers a colony of mutant humans living in the remains of the New York subway and worshipping a huge 'doomsday bomb'. In a gloomily nihilistic climax Zaius, Brent and Taylor are all killed: Taylor's last act is to detonate the doomsday bomb. A sombre voice-over declares: 'In one of the countless billions of galaxies in the universe lies a medium-sized yellow star, and one of its satellites, a green and insignificant planet, is now dead.'

Beneath the Planet of the Apes (1970), directed by television journeyman Ted Post, had a lower budget than *Planet* ($3 million). It was a rule of thumb in the film industry that a sequel was likely to gross around forty per cent less than the first film. So it transpired with *Beneath the Planet of the Apes*, which grossed $19 million. According to his own account, Dehn received a telegram from the studio declaring: 'Apes exist – sequel required.'[43] In the event Dehn would script another three *Apes* movies. *Escape from the Planet of the Apes* (1971), directed by Don Taylor, revealed that three of the apes (Cornelius, Zira and Milo) escaped the Earth's destruction at the end of *Beneath* by salvaging Taylor's spaceship and travelling back in time to 1973. *Escape* inverts the narrative of Boulle's novel in that here it is the apes who find themselves in an unfamiliar world where they are a novelty, and humans are in the ascendancy. The talking apes are initially treated as celebrities, but when Dr Otto Hasslein (Eric Braeden), the US President's chief scientific adviser, discovers that apes will, in the future, become the dominant species on Earth, he recommends their destruction. Aided by two animal psychologists who have befriended them, Cornelius and Zira, who is pregnant, both escape. Zira gives birth to a son, whom she substitutes for a baby chimpanzee in a circus run by the sympathetic Armando (Ricardo Montalban). Cornelius and Zira are hunted down and killed. The film ends with their baby saying 'Mama! Mama!'

It was in *Escape* that the narrative focus of the *Apes* series switched from humans to the apes. This continued in the last two films, *Conquest of the Planet of the Apes* (1972) and *Battle for the Planet of the Apes* (1973), both directed by J. Lee Thompson, the British director best known for *The Guns of Navarone* (1961). *Conquest of the Planet of the Apes* completes the ideological realignment that had begun in *Escape*. In 1992 California has become a police state ruled by Governor Breck (Don Murray). Apes have been trained to perform menial tasks and are treated as slaves by their human masters. The son of Cornelius and Zira is now a young adult chimpanzee called Caesar (Roddy McDowall), who has been hidden in the circus by Armando. When Armando is arrested, following a run-in with the police, Breck suspects the truth and orders Caesar's destruction. Caesar, however, infiltrates the slave population where his superior intelligence establishes him as their leader. The apes arm themselves. Following Armando's death in police custody, Caesar leads the apes in an armed revolt that overthrows the regime. The film concludes with Caesar urging his fellow apes to 'cast out your anger! Tonight we have seen the birth of the planet of the apes!'[44]

Battle for the Planet of the Apes, with a script by John William and Joyce Hopper Corrington from a story by Dehn, concluded the film series. *Battle* is set a generation after the events of *Conquest* (the precise date is unclear) and takes place following an atomic war that has devastated North America. Caesar is again cast in the role of peacemaker as he tries to broker a peace settlement between apes and humans. He is opposed by belligerent gorilla

General Aldo (Claude Akins) and by a colony of revanchist humans living in the irradiated ruins of the Forbidden City. When the humans attack the ape settlement, they are defeated in a pitched battle: the apes and surviving humans agree to try to build a new society together. In a coda set in AD 2670, the Lawgiver (John Huston) tells a mixed group of ape and human children that Caesar's legacy has been 'apes and humans living in friendship, harmony and peace'.

If the sequels were subject to the law of diminishing returns – *Battle* is generally considered the weakest of the films and had the lowest gross revenues ($8.8 million) – the *Apes* series nevertheless represents both a major production achievement and a significant landmark in the history of SF cinema. One reviewer called the *Apes* series 'the first epic of filmed science fiction'.[45] It demonstrated the potential for the SF film series: a continuous narrative unfolding across a cycle of films. To this extent the *Apes* series can be seen as the forerunner of *Star Wars*, *Star Trek*, *Alien*, *Terminator* and other SF and fantasy franchises. It even highlighted the potential of spin-off merchandising, with *Planet of the Apes* toys, masks, comic books and film novelizations. The screening of the films on television found new fans and even prompted a television series, *Planet of the Apes*, which ran for 14 episodes in 1974. The television series returned to the idea of a semi-feudal world where humans have become the slaves of apes. It maintained continuity with the films by casting Roddy McDowall – who played Cornelius in *Planet* and *Escape*, and Caesar in *Conquest* and *Battle* – as a sympathetic chimpanzee called Galen who helps two human astronauts who arrive in the future.

Furthermore, the *Apes* series can be seen, quite explicitly, as a commentary on issues affecting American society and politics in the 1960s and early 1970s. The films coincided with a particularly troubled period in modern US history. *Planet* was released when America was reeling from the Tet Offensive, which marked the heaviest fighting of the Vietnam War, and was followed within months by the assassinations of Martin Luther King (4 April 1968) and Robert Kennedy (5 June 1968). *Beneath* includes what can only be read as an allegory of the divisions in American society caused by Vietnam as the belligerent General Ursus (James Gregory) launches a military expedition into the Forbidden Zone and his gorilla troops break up an anti-war demonstration by chimpanzees carrying placards declaring 'Unite in Peace'. The unsympathetic characterization of politicians in *Escape* and *Conquest* reflected growing public distrust of politics in the early 1970s, while *Conquest*, which climaxes in a full-scale revolt, bore some parallel with events such as the Kent State University shootings (4 May 1970) and the Attica prison riots in New York (6–13 September 1971). As Eric Greene argues in his study of the series: 'Although fiction, the *Apes* films were

14. Zira (Kim Hunter) and Cornelius (Roddy McDowall) encounter a talking human: Taylor (Charlton Heston) in *Planet of the Apes* (1968) (Source: British Film Institute).

successful, in part, because they related to the social and political realities, pressures, and crises of the time.'[46]

The recurring theme of all the films is race. The series as a whole is based around a continual power struggle between humans and apes, but this struggle is formulated differently in each film. The racial politics of *Planet* are somewhat ambiguous. Heston's star persona invites audience identification with Taylor, though the character, initially at least, is arrogant and unsympathetic. His revulsion at the gorillas ('Take your stinking paws off me you damned dirty ape!') might be construed as racism – invoking the idea of 'dirty' blacks – and the shooting script includes a more explicit reference when Taylor calls the gorilla Julius a 'black monster'. Taylor might be seen as analogous to a white supremacist faced with his worst nightmare: a world ruled by blacks. To this extent, *Planet* might be read as a cautionary tale for white Americans who feared the empowerment of African Americans.

Beneath similarly invites identification with the oppressed humans, while at the same time accentuating the inter-species differences within ape society that featured in *Planet*. The gorillas, who in *Planet* featured as brutal policemen or menial workers (the other apes regard them as lazy and stupid), play a more dominant role in *Beneath*, where they seem to have gained control of the ape council. In *Escape* and *Conquest*, however, the power relationship between apes and humans is entirely reversed. The audience is now invited to identify with the apes, while humans have become the oppressors. The inter-species differences between the apes that characterized the first two films are entirely absent – literally so in *Escape*, where the only apes are three chimpanzees – while the sympathetic human characters are a Hispanic (Armando) and an African American (MacDonald [Hari Rhodes], the assistant to Governor Breck, who helps Caesar escape his persecutors in *Conquest*). *Conquest* is the most explicit allegory of all the films, making direct parallels between the treatment of the apes and the institution of slavery. As Caesar remarks to MacDonald: 'You, above everyone else, should understand ... We cannot be free until we have power.'

Battle, in other respects the least interesting of the series, is arguably the most complex in its racial politics. It is structurally different from the other films in that it does not invite sole sympathy either for human (*Planet*, *Beneath*) or ape (*Escape*, *Conquest*). Caesar is still the principal protagonist but he is no longer an outsider but leader of a mixed community of apes and humans. The two groups co-exist uneasily: humans are free but do not enjoy equal rights even under Caesar's benevolent leadership. The inter-species differences between the apes re-emerge: General Aldo and the gorillas are a rival power base to the moderate Caesar. Is it entirely too fanciful to see Aldo, an advocate of violent action who wishes to kill all humans, as representing radical 'Black Power' activists such as Stokely Carmichael whose inflammatory rhetoric (Carmichael notoriously spoke of 'killing the honkies') fanned the flames of racial violence? It is Aldo who violates the sacred law of the apes ('Ape shall not kill ape') when he kills Caesar's son Cornelius. Caesar's recognition that apes are just as capable of violence as humans leads him to seek reconciliation with the surviving humans. *Battle* is essentially a narrative of conflict resolution: thus a series notable for its dystopian and apocalyptic vision of the future concluded on a note of optimism and hope.

There is ample evidence to suggest that contemporaries understood the *Apes* films as commentaries on American society. The *Hollywood Reporter* felt that *Planet* stood out from other adventure films 'in its relevance to the consuming issues of its time'.[47] The *New York Times* labelled it 'an anti-war film and a science-fiction liberal tract'.[48] These elements were, if anything, more pronounced in the first sequel. Penelope Gilliat in the *New Yorker* felt that the social comment was rather too heavy-handed: '*Beneath the Planet of the Apes* is the most left-wing ape picture I have ever seen ... I can think of no large subject on which it hasn't got an upright, worried, thunderingly platitudinous opinion to drop on your toes.'[49] British critic Alexander Walker also recognized that *'Beneath the Planet of the Apes* finds space to parody current American dilemmas.'[50] The racial politics of the films were also recognized. As *Time* magazine observed: 'All the pictures have had deliberate racial overtones that are far from flattering to whites; the oppression of the apes has been equated with the denial of civil rights to US blacks.'[51] Some British critics felt that *Conquest* was too insistent on the Civil Rights parallels: George Melly found it 'unexpectedly offensive' on account of 'a clumsy allegorical hysteria in which the apes are insultingly equated with Black Power'.[52] Mark Kermode later averred – albeit perhaps with tongue slightly in cheek – that 'the seeds of the adolescent Marxist/Leninist leanings which I displayed in the mid-eighties were actually sown in the early seventies during a double bill of *Beneath the Planet of the Apes* and *Conquest of the Planet of the Apes* at the ABC Turnpike Lane'.[53]

Planet of the Apes has remained a touchstone in American popular culture: it has been referenced in *Saturday Night Live* and *The Simpsons*, while Mel Brooks spoofed the Statue of Liberty scene in *Spaceballs* (1987). In 1994 gangsta rappers Da Lench Mob released an album entitled *Planet of da Apes* (a follow-up to their *Guerrillas in tha Mist*) that was promoted as 'the soundtrack to Armageddon'. There have been several abortive *Apes* film projects. In 1988 Fox announced *Return to the Planet of the Apes*, and in the early 1990s James Cameron and Oliver Stone were both linked with a remake of *Planet of the Apes* starring Arnold Schwarzenegger. The 2001 *Planet of the Apes*, directed by Tim Burton, was a 'revisioning' of the story that combined elements of Boulle's novel and the original film. Burton's film sets the action on another planet and adapts Boulle's ending so that astronaut Leo Donaldson (Mark Wahlberg) returns to Earth only to discover it is now ruled by gorilla General Thade (Tim Roth). At the same time there are references to the 1968 film in the casting of Charlton Heston as Thade's father and through the dialogue, with one of the apes declaring: 'Take your stinking hands off me you damned dirty human!' Heston also appears by proxy – through a clip of his film *The Agony and the Ecstasy* showing on television – in the latest reboot of the franchise, the 2011 *Rise of the Planet of the Apes*, directed by Rupert Wyatt. This film offered an alternative narrative for the events of *Conquest* in which intelligent apes, now the result of genetic experimentation, revolt against their oppressors. In a sign of the advances in special effects technology, the apes were now digitally created through the technique of motion capture rather than played by actors in latex masks. Again the film includes allusions to the original films, including Caesar (Andy Serkis) building a model of the Statue of Liberty, characters named after Arthur P. Jacobs, Rod Serling and Michael Wilson, and the reiteration of the famous line: 'Take your stinkin' paws off me you damn dirty ape!' It would seem that by the early twenty-first century what most preoccupied the filmmaking were not the social and political subtexts of the story but rather a postmodern awareness of its place in popular film culture.

Notes

1.   Kevin Brownlow, 'The Making of David Lean's Film of *The Bridge on the River Kwai*', *Cineaste*, 22: 2 (1996), pp.10–16. In 1992 Columbia Pictures reissued the film with an amended credit for Foreman and Wilson.

2.   'Pierre Boulle' [interview by Jean Claude Morlot], *Cinefantastique*, 2: 2 (1972), p.18.

3.   Pierre Boulle, *Monkey Planet*, trans. Xan Fielding (Harmondsworth: Penguin, 1966), p.11.

4.   Ibid: p.166.

5.   'Arthur P. Jacobs' [interview by Dale Winogura and Jack Hirshberg], *Cinefantastique*, 2: 2 (1972), p.19.

6.   Charlton Heston, *In the Arena: The Autobiography* (London: HarperCollins, 1995), p.373.

7.   Quoted in 'Serling in Creative Mainstream', *Los Angeles Times*, 25 June 1967.

8.   Margaret Herrick Library, Academy of Motion Picture Arts and Sciences (hereafter AMPAS), Charlton Heston Papers Box 12 f.129: *Planet of the Apes*. Screenplay by Rod Serling, 1 March 1965.

9.   Ibid.

10.   *On the Beach* (United Artists, dir. Stanley Kramer, 1959); *Dr Strangelove; or, How I Learned to Stop Worrying and Love the Bomb* (Columbia, dir. Stanley Kubrick, 1964); *The War Game* (BBC, dir. Peter Watkins, 1965).

11.   The scene is a precise parallel of Book II of *Gulliver's Travels* where Lemuel's proud explanation of the marvels of gunpowder prompts a response from the King of Brobdingnag: 'I cannot but conclude the Bulk of your Natives to be the most pernicious Race of little odious Vermin that Nature ever suffered to crawl upon the surface of the Earth.'

12.   Wisconsin Center for Film and Theater Research (WCFTR) US MSS 43 AN Serling Box 43 f.7: *Planet of the Apes*. Second Draft Screenplay by Rod Serling, 23 December 1964.

13.   Ibid.

14.   AMPAS Heston Box 12 f.129: *Planet of the Apes*. Screenplay by Rod Serling, 1 March 1965.

15.   'Arthur P. Jacobs', p.19.

16.   'Pierre Boulle', p.18.

17.   Eric Greene, *Planet of the Apes as American Myth: Race, Politics, and Popular Culture* (Middletown CT: Wesleyan University Press, 1998), p.2.

18.   Charlton Heston, *The Actor's Life: Journals 1956–1976*, ed. Hollis Alpert (New York: E. P. Dutton, 1978), p.237.

19.   Ibid: p.248.

20.   Ibid: p.249.

21.   Ibid: p.260.

22.   Ibid.

23 AMPAS Heston Box 12 f.130: *Planet of the Apes*. Screenplay by Michael Wilson. Shooting Script, 5 May 1967.

24 MHL Core Collection Scripts: *Planet of the Apes*. Screenplay by Michael Wilson, 17 January 1967.

25 AMPAS MPAA PCA file *Planet of the Apes*: Synopsis of 'Planet of the Apes' by James Denton, 15 May 1967.

26 Greene, *Planet of the Apes as American Myth*, p.30.

27 Heston, *The Actor's Life*, p.260.

28 Jonathan Stubbs, 'The Eady Levy: A Runaway Bribe? Hollywood Production and British Subsidy in the Early 1960s', *Journal of British Cinema and Television*, 6: 1 (2009), pp.1–20.

29 BFI Library microfiche on *Planet of the Apes*: National Film Theatre programme note by Terry Staples, entitled 'What If ...?', n.d.

30 Heston, *The Actor's Life*, p.271.

31 Ibid: p.274.

32 Ibid: p.276.

33 Heston, *In the Arena*, p.397.

34 AMPAS Heston Box 12 f.130: *Planet of the Apes*. Screenplay by Michael Wilson. Shooting Script, 5 May 1967.

35 *New Yorker*, 6 February 1968.

36 *The Hollywood Reporter*, 5 February 1968, p.5.

37 *The Hollywood Reporter*, 6 May 1971, p.4.

38 WCFTR USS MS 43 AN Serling Box 43 f.6: Mort Abrahams to Serling, 10 April 1968.

39 Greene, *Planet of the Apes as American Myth*, p.59.

40 WCFTR USS MS 43 AN Serling Box 43 f.6: 'The Dark Side of the Earth: A Sequel to Planet of the Apes', n.d.

41 'Planner of the Apes', *Film Review*, 22: 10 (October 1972), p.23.

42 Heston, *The Actor's Life*, p.398.

43 Greene, *Planet of the Apes as American Myth*, p.71.

44 A review of *Conquest* in *Cinefantastique* complained that the ending 'looks and sounds tacked-on' and that 'Caesar's transition from warlord to peacemaker, though essential, is not believable' (*Cinefantastique*, 3: 1 [1973], p.29). It was indeed tacked on: the ending of the film had been reshot following adverse reaction from test audiences. Initially the victorious apes had bludgeoned Governor Breck to death and Caesar had declared that humans would be treated as slaves. In the final cut Breck's life is spared and Caesar's speech adopts a more conciliatory tone. Greene, *Planet of the Apes as American Myth*, pp.108–10.

45 Frederick S. Clarke, 'Escape from the Planet of the Apes', *Cinefantastique* (1971), p.28.

46 Greene, *Planet of the Apes as American Myth*, p.9. For further commentary, see Jonathan Kirshner, 'Subverting the Cold War in the 1960s: *Dr Strangelove*, *The Manchurian Candidate*, and *The* [sic] *Planet of the Apes*', *Film and History*, 31: 2 (2009), pp.40–44; and Sheryl Vint, 'Simians, subjectivity and sociality: *2001: A Space Odyssey* and two versions of *Planet of the Apes*', *Science Fiction Film and Television*, 2: 2 (2009), pp.225–50.

47 *Hollywood Reporter*, 5 February 1968, p.3.

48 *New York Times*, 9 February 1968, p.55.

49 *New Yorker*, 20 June 1970.

50 *Evening Standard*, 28 May 1970.

51 'Onward and Apeward', *Time*, 5 June 1972.

52 *Observer*, 30 July 1972.

53 Mark Kermode, *It's Only a Movie: Reel Life Adventures of a Film Obsessive* (London: Arrow Books, 2010), p.17.

8

STRETCHING THE GENRE:
THE HELLSTROM CHRONICLE (1971)

1971 was already shaping up to be a vintage year for American SF cinema. The spring saw the release of George Lucas's debut feature *THX-1138* and the adaptation of Michael Crichton's novel *The Andromeda Strain*. The summer brought Charlton Heston in the post-apocalyptic *The Omega Man*, and something unexpected. He looked every inch the rumpled academic of popular imagination. He stared into the camera with a hunted look as he introduced himself:

> My name is Nils Hellstrom. If that rings a bell at all, it's probably in connection with words 'fanatic' – 'lunatic' – 'heretic'. Actually I'm a scientist, and these other descriptions have come as result of my dedication to my work…After nine years of concentrated work I've learned something that no one wants to hear. But unless someone does…we, as a species, might pass from existence without ever knowing why.

Here was the familiar scientist – Cassandra – with a message to deliver, but this time the warning was real. The world, he warned, would surely one day be overrun by 'an army that was here long before us and is ultimately better equipped to survive than we; battalions of mindless soldiers entering the contest with capabilities beyond our imagination.' He was talking about insects. He concluded: 'And if you in this theatre dare to think this is lunacy I invite you to remain in your seat. Draw your own conclusion, and learn the inevitable destiny of ignorance.' What followed was *The Hellstrom Chronicle*.

The realms of science fiction and documentary film have seldom intersected. Documentary is limited by an inherent requirement to represent what is. Science fiction represents what is not (or not yet). *The*

Hellstrom Chronicle bridged this divide. It stands as an intriguing blend of the SF genre and the nature documentary, and provides a clear indication of the strength and appeal of the genre by 1971. For all its liberties with the 'rules' of documentary, the result won both audience acclaim and the Academy Award for best documentary feature. Yet, as will be seen, the ultimate commitment to the genre-blending frame had come rather late to the project.

The *Hellstrom Chronicle* began in early 1969 as an ambitious plan for a wildlife film in the mind of the reigning king of American television documentary, David L. Wolper. Wolper had noted the untapped potential of insect footage in 1966 when making a National Geographic television special for CBS called *The Hidden World of Insects*. Wolper called the associate producer and photographer on that project and a regular director/producer of these specials – Walon Green – to see what he thought about building a feature-length documentary around insects. Green, who had just branched into screenwriting as the author of the western *The Wild Bunch* (1969), responded with enthusiasm and suggested an innovative angle for the film. Green recalled the rather shocking claims made by a Brazilian entomologist who he had encountered during the making of *The Hidden World of Insects* that the insects might actually be mankind's rivals as the ultimate dominant species on the planet. It was a bleak projection but Green felt that humanity was due for a wakeup call. As he recalled in later years:

> As a lifelong amateur ornithologist and dedicated nature buff, I felt very strongly about the accelerated destruction of the natural world. When the film was made, the peregrine falcon was down to 150 pairs nationwide, countless other birds were teetering, poisons were in our food, our water, and no one really cared. I was angry. I liked the idea that on Darwinian terms adaptation may outweigh intelligence as a selective advantage. It seemed the perfect comeuppance for our species. The insects may still be the proof of that.[1]

The outline for the documentary evolved around Green's concept of a Darwinian struggle for the future of the planet.

Initially titled *Project X*, the film swiftly metamorphosed into *The Insects*. Wolper's initial pitch for an insect documentary included a hint of what was to come. Although there was no suggestion of the radical fictional framing device used in the eventual movie, from the outset the producers used SF invasion metaphors and looked to deliver a visual experience as other-worldly as anything yet seen in outer space. The pitch opened with an epigram from the Belgian playwright and entomologist Maurice Maeterlinck that spoke of insects as invaders from another planet: 'Something in the insect seems alien to the habits, morals and psychology of this world, as if it had come from some other planet...more monstrous, more infernal than our own.' The theme reappeared in the body of the pitch, which promised:

> David L. Wolper will again create a revolution in viewing experience, uniting the actuality of the documentary with the visual drama of the wide screen to transport the audience into the incredible, *alien realm* of insects. In a filmic experience conceived for the mass audience, the drama of the *rival worlds* of insects and man will come to the big screen with the full impact of reality.[2]

When describing individual scenes, the producers used the same language. Promising to capture 35mm footage of a battle with locusts in Anatolia, the pitch promised: 'The filming will carry the impact of an attack by alien beings on the gentle wheat fields of Asia Minor ...' The document concluded that 'The magnificent and bizarre beauty...and the impending horror of the little known realm will bombard the senses of the cinema audience with a host of new sensations in David L. Wolper's forthcoming film on THE INSECTS.'[3]

The pitch immediately won a $6,000 fee for the television rights from ABC. Wolper duly assigned Walon Green to direct, and dispatched a camera crew around the world to capture the necessary footage. In the end it took nine months of filming spread over two years and travel to eleven countries, working with the latest macro lenses to complete the filming. The principal cinematographers were a German, Helmut Barth and two Americans, Ken Middleham (who provided the close-up footage from his basement in Riverside, California) and Green himself who worked both in the field and at a Wolper office on Wilshire Boulevard.[4]

The film presented plenty of technical challenges, from lighting the insects without accidentally frying them, to physically keeping them in front of the lens. In Africa the crew worked in bathing suits to avoid the problem of ants climbing into their clothes and employed locals to brush off the more intrepid creatures before they could bite. It took five weeks in the Ugandan bush and the opening of thirty-seven mounds to capture five minutes of footage. The climactic scene in which relentless driver ants build a bridge across a river by piling one on another was filmed by relocating an entire colony to an small island on the Galana river in Tsavo National Park in Kenya, a feat accomplished by dousing them with carbon dioxide and sucking them into a bag with a vacuum cleaner and carrying them by plane.[5]

With the privations of the field behind them, the next task was to generate a linking script. The task fell to a regular Wolper writer, David Seltzer. The early drafts followed a conventional wildlife documentary structure, though ideas from science fiction were never far below the surface. Although the team toyed with titles smacking at various genres, including the vaguely biblical title *The Last Plague*, the loosely sporting *Man v. Insect*,[6] and war film-ish. *The Silent Enemy* and *The Silent War*,[7] SF seemed to be the default setting. Wolper's files include a treatment entitled *The Aliens* and even a suggestion of an H.G. Wells tribute and calling the film *The War of the Worlds*.[8] Perhaps such was only to be expected, given the tradition of insect enemies in SF films like *Them!* (1954), *Tarantula* (1955) or *The Beginning of the End* (1957). More than this, the scripts all proposed an opening nicknamed 'the *Star Trek* sequence'. This was to have been an opening zoom through the cosmos from the ultimate wide shot of the galaxy, in through space with star fields on either side, and past planets to a full frame of the Earth. The commentary would run: 'Though a mere speck against the backdrop of infinity, the planet Earth is unique. Of its millions of neighboring stars it alone contains the mysterious force called "life" ...' Insects would be introduced as a branch of life at odds with humanity: 'Though coexisting on the same landscape, theirs is a world apart. It is alien, unemotional, and without mercy.'[9]

But Wolper had a problem. When he screened the first rough cut, the film simply did not work. It was no more than a succession of brilliant sequences of insect life (and death). Wolper recalled abandoning himself to rage and frustration when he saw what he had created at a screening party at his home. Equally frustrated his colleagues screamed back. Somehow in the frenzy the writer David Seltzer had a moment of clarity and proposed creating a human dimension for the film in the form of a rogue scientist who could embody the most disturbing notion that the production team had encountered during their research: the idea that insects might emerge as the dominant species on earth and outlive humanity. Science fiction had moved from being a visual influence and a key metaphor in the script to furnishing the organizing narrative logic of the film and providing one the genre's stock characters. Seltzer proposed that the film would keep cutting back to sequences featuring the mad scientist – initially called Haelstrom – and swiftly devised a distinctive voice for the character, a blend of science and an almost evangelical apocalypticism: 'In God's grotesque spawn of children,' Haelstrom began, 'the angriest of all would inherit the earth ...' The film would also need new sequences, including something dealing with the insects mounting resistance to the pesticide DDT, and a sequence examining bees (for this they used stock footage from a Japanese film called *Secret in the Hive*). It seemed a small price to pay for an ingenious solution.[10]

With Wolper's blessing, Seltzer set to work over the Christmas holiday of 1970, generating a revised script with feverish speed. Entitled *The Haelstrom Chronicle*, it seemed like a nod to the classic SF anthology: *The Martian Chronicles* (1950) by Ray Bradbury. The name Haelstrom/ Hellstrom was inspired. It evoked both hell and a maelstrom, and was an obscure term for a particular kind of charlatan: a psychic who 'read' for his clients by holding onto their forearm. The script called for an elaborate sequence to establish the Haelstrom character including 'newsreel' of the scientist making his way through an angry mob at one of his public lectures, vox pops of 'citizens' giving their opinion on his dismissal from his college, and an 'appearance' on Merv Griffin's talk show, in which the host subjected the scientist to some fairly obvious quips about the penchant of Black Widows for eating their mates after sex. Wolper's files contain a note to the producer dated 30 December: 'It is essential that you read this tonight as Seltzer is leaving this weekend for Hawaii and would like to get in at least a couple of days work on revisions before he goes.'[11] Wolper loved it. Most of the script would go forward essentially unchanged, though Seltzer found it was possible to introduce his protagonist with a single monologue rather than the fake actuality. By the end of January the script was approaching its final form, including the ultimate spelling of the name Hellstrom. Wolper duly engaged an actor Lawrence Pressman to portray Dr Hellstrom, and one of his regular directors – Ed Spiegel – to capture the necessary footage. Racing against the clock, they bolted the film back together around its new narrative skeleton and prayed that the public would buy it.[12]

The final element in the film came from the musical score. Seltzer's script called for music to unsettle the audience. A note in the margin suggested Stockhausen, but the task of providing appropriate music fell to the Argentine-born jazz composer Lalo Schifrin. Best-known for his theme music to *Mission: Impossible,* Schifrin had a distinguished track record of composing for documentaries. He reported: 'I attempted to create a fantasy of the insect world – a concatenation of earth sounds as I imagine they might seem to the insects themselves. Since I anticipated no protests from any hastily organized insect "lib" groups, I confess I took generous artistic license.'[13] Schifrin's instruments included plenty of percussion, including instruments from worlds alien to Americans – Africa and Japan – and the still new MOOG synthesizer, a sound already identified with notions of the alien and the future.

15. A fictional scientist with a factual message of doom: Nils Hellstrom (Lawrence Pressman) in the Oscar winning *The Hellstrom Chronicle* (1971) (Source: British Film Institute).

The finished film began with a claim to veracity: academic acknowledgements to bolster its credentials. Then it hit hard. As the screen erupts in images of lava, a voice is heard: 'The earth was created not with the gentle caress of love but with the brutal violence of rape.' It is a shocking challenge to the typical talk of benevolent 'mother nature' usually heard in nature films. As mysterious music plays we see clouds, then ice crystals forming, then cells dividing. Life is beginning. The voice returns: 'In evolution's greatest irony one of the first creatures to appear would be the last to remain for incubating in the darkened womb of pre-history was a seed of grotesque variation; a fetus with the capability to dominate all.' An insect wriggles free from its cocoon and stretches into a freeze frame as the title appears: '*The Hellstrom Chonicle* – in association with Nils Hellstrom'. The camera pans down to a beetle racing across a landscape in which blades of grass loom like poplars. Two beetles engage in brutal combat, the camera pulls back to a young human couple oblivious to the carnage just inches from their heads. Back again from the couple we find the figure of Hellstrom, who then launches into his introduction.

Hellstrom conducts the viewer though a succession of locations, including a nuclear testing ground in Rocky Valley, Nevada, where insects were first noticed to be immune to the effects of radiation; screening rooms where we see clips of films bearing out the innate human dread of insects, specifically the giant mutant ants of *Them!* (1954) and horror of a human engulfed in ants in *The Naked Jungle* (1954); labs where he examines enlarged sculptures of insect bodies and tiny specimens; the street where human reactions to insects are tested in candid camera confrontations; and the field where he directly encounters some of the more remarkable creatures. These linking scenes are intercut with astonishing footage of the life and death of insects: the single day of life that is the existence of a mayfly; combat between red and black ants; the 'royal chariot' of the driver ants in which thousands heave the bloated body of their queen in search of a new nest site; and the deadly mating of the Black Widow spider. Quite beside the unsettling implications of Hellstrom's thesis and the shock value of the scenes depicted, the films great achievement lay in its transformation of the microscopic world of the insect into a giant and surreal spectacle. The final image of the film – after Hellstrom had signed off saying there was nothing humanity could do to alter its fate – was more horror than science fiction: the silhouette of a beetle rampant against a rising moon.

Seltzer's script was deliciously overblown. Hellstrom proclaimed the variety of insects as 'limitless as the imagination of the insane'. He lurched from razor sharp Darwinism to a rhetorical religiosity in which he fantasized about viewing the ironic smile on the face of God when he decided that the insects would inherit the earth. He spun off into psychoanalysis: 'Psychiatrists tell me that from childhood nightmares to adult schizophrenia, the insect is a common fixation in the human mind. Partly because his face seems so evil... partly because he is so indestructible.' In amongst the metaphors and hyperbole there were allusions to the world of science fiction. Hellstrom compared an insect combat to 'a battle of gruesome robots'. But most of the narration was calculated to unnerve the audience by challenging complacent assumptions of the superiority and uniqueness of humanity. Hellstrom identified insect-analogues to agriculture, warehousing, nurseries, language, social order, strategy, camouflage, organization and even broadcasting (thanks to the ability of the Luna Moth to summon a mate by spreading its pheromone across a twenty-mile radius). He emphasized their strength, their endurance, their power of flight and astonishing ability to reproduce: 'In the time it takes a single human embryo to develop, this insect could reproduce four hundred and one billion, three hundred and sixty million of his kind.' Hellstrom's argument about the inevitable victory of insects had implications for its time. There is obvious comment on the nuclear jeopardy inherent in the Cold War. The opening scene at a Nevada nuclear test facility in which he predicts that insects would inherit a world made uninhabitable for humanity by nuclear war was an obvious argument for East-West détente. There are broadly anti-war statements as when images of ants fighting in the midst of their own body parts are matched with the pointed remark: 'Let it be said of the harvester ant that he displayed more than one similarity to man.' There was even an echo of the lessons of Vietnam in Hellstrom's remark that: 'It is the mistake of arrogance to equate size with significance, for the less visible an enemy the more powerful his threat.' There was a whiff of the paranoia at large in Nixon's America. The *New York Times* critic Peter Schjeldahl described Hellstrom as 'a Daniel Ellsberg-type figure of mingled self-righteousness and suffering humanity', referencing the Defense Department whistle-blower who defied the establishment and leaked the Pentagon Papers on the Vietnam War.[14] The ultimate target was American society: its unquestioning pursuit of modernity and orgy of consumption. Hellstrom declared:

> It is the need for individual luxury that creates the technology that destroys the planet making it uninhabitable for all but ONE. The insect. The industrial waste that poisons our air...the DDT that poisons our food source...the radiation that destroys our very flesh...are to the insect nothing more than a gentle perfume. In the toxins that are killing us and our fellow creatures, the insects live, reproduce, thrive...and gain strength by virtue of our growing weakness.

At the last moment of the film – before the end credits – a title explained that Hellstrom was a fictional creation, but insisted that the facts were real and his views reflected genuine scientific hypotheses. It only remained to see whether the public would accept the sleight of hand.

With the film complete, the Wolper organization readied their marketing, again blending the codes of SF and documentary. The poster/press ad featured the wing of a moth, photographed in such a way as to resemble an enormous face – the text ran 'Shocking. Beautiful. Brilliant. Sensual. Deadly...and in the end only *they* will survive. *The Hellstrom Chronicle*. Science fiction? No. Science Fact.'[15] The theatrical trailer proceeded in a similar vein with the journalist Chet Huntley, who had only recently retired from anchoring the evening news for NBC, adding his credibility to Hellstrom's prophesy of doom:

> This is Chet Huntley. If any living species is to inherit the earth, it will not be man. Long before the time that hydrogen bombs and

pollution have put an end to us, we will face competition for the earth itself... from a life form we arrogantly ignore. If this sounds like science fiction, let me assure you it is not. It is science-fact... set forth in a compelling and awesome motion picture entitled THE HELLSTROM CHRONICLE. For those of you who wonder just who will inherit the earth: THE HELLSTROM CHRONICLE holds the answer.[16]

The follow-up trailer focused instead on clips of the insects in battle spiced with SF metaphors: 'they prepare for war with the efficiency of unstoppable robots.'[17]

Despite its unusual format, *The Hellstrom Chronicle* was astonishingly well received. It premiered at the Cannes Film Festival in June 1971 and immediately won both a special award from the High Committee of Cinema Technique and a European distribution deal with Fox. Further awards followed from the San Sebastian Festival in Spain and the Venice Festival in Italy. High praise came from Moscow. In its American reviews, *Variety* was impressed, noting 'the excitement of science fiction in its factually scientific approach'. Its only two concerns were over the 'ultra somber vision of man's future' and the question of whether the film would reach its audience: 'Whether the film industry can market such a unique feature is another matter but rich rewards are in sight wherever distributors and exhibitors can rise to the occasion.[18] Further rave reviews helped build the necessary momentum. Jay Cocks in *Time* magazine praised the film:

> Not since *2001* has a movie so cannily inverted consciousness and altered audience perception as *The Hellstrom Chronicle*. It is a wry and scarifying cautionary tale... Like all good science fiction, *The Hellstrom Chronicle* suggests an alternate reality, then surrounds you with it, inducing a weird sense of disorientation ... [I]t is a trip much worth taking.[19]

Judith Crist in *The New Yorker* spoke of 'a stunner, totally absorbing'.[20] The syndicated columnist Bob Considine called it: 'The most remarkable motion picture ever made. Period.'[21] The SF specific reviewers were no less enthusiastic. Dale Winogura in *Cinefantastique* wrote: 'Science fact is the basis here, but its presentation is a cross-breed of official *cinéma-vérité*, factual exposition and beautiful, terrifying and amazing imagery that takes on a science fiction mystique... it's a cold sterile masterpiece.'[22] A press packet archived at the Lincoln Center has a telling line scrawled across the page in felt pen by an unknown reviewer: 'The most brilliant (and beautiful) horror film I have ever seen. Don't go alone. Go stoned.'[23]

Duly primed by the reviewers, as Wolper had hoped *The Hellstrom Chronicle* did terrific business for a documentary. The film broke the record for first week earnings on its opening screen in Los Angeles, grossing $36,949 in its first week at Loew's Crest in Westwood. Wolper had a small hand in breaking the record. When he heard that they were just a few tickets short of the record, he bought a block of tickets just to nudge his film over the line.[24] Over the next six months the film took enough, nationally, to make *Variety*'s list of 'Big Rental Films' for 1971 (ranking in the mid-seventies). Having cost $850,000, it took around $3 million in domestic release, yielding $1,500,000 to the screens and a similar sum to the producers.[25] The film did so well that it attracted that most American of compliments – the frivolous law suit. Marvin Weinstein, a butcher depicted with his permission in the candid camera sequence in which customers react to a giant bug on their meat, tried to sue Wolper for $250,000 for invasion of privacy, arguing that the film didn't properly reflect his professional performance. The case got nowhere.[26]

The film also had its detractors. The exterminator's trade journal *Pest Control*, viewing for those with a vested interest, deemed the film 'well worth seeing; especially for the pest control industry' but felt that the problems with DDT had been overstated.[27] More seriously, the *Hollywood Reporter* questioned the use of a fictional scientist as a frame and felt that Pressman's performance 'gave credence to his detractor's comments while at the same time casting doubt on the sincerity of the film makers'. They felt that 'The character could at least have been presented as a sane man, a careful caring and humorous man and the film would have had far more impact.'[28] In the *New York Times* Peter Schjeldahl tended to agree. He raided against the 'nursery level Darwinism' of the commentary and complained: 'Drenched in a kind of sickish extract of physical and moral disgust... here is a nature film that looks to have been calculated to make us hate nature.'[29] The *Catholic Chronicle* concluded 'David Wolper didn't really need an unethical gimmick to interest viewers in the magnificent footage ...'[30] Walon Green had already gone on the offensive, defending the need for artistic licence even in documentary, in an interview for *Motion Picture Daily*.[31] Wolper merely wished that the critics could have sat with him and endured the tedium of the original pre-Hellstrom rough cut.[32]

The film was widely released around the world, playing in France as *Des insectes et des hommes* (insects and men) and in Spain as *Los herederos de la tierra* (the inheritors of the earth). Other markets used a variant on the US title.[33] British reviewers sided with the American purists and were unanimous in their dislike of the Hellstrom character, holding that his rhetoric undermined the credibility of the whole. Fortunately, most agreed with Nina Hibbin in the *Morning Star* that 'the inanities of this studio-invented creature are well worth suffering for the sake of the pictorial record of the real creatures of the insect world'.[34] Derek Malcolm in *The Guardian* quipped that it dwarfed Disney's forays into natural history and 'Makes *The Living Desert* look dead.'[35] The *Daily Mail* doubted that the home of British scares 'Hammer could have created anything more horrific'.[36] George Melly in *The Observer* noted that here was a film 'for once justifying the string of emotive adjectives they're using on the posters', and hailed 'a multi-legged, many-eyed version of *100 Days of Sodom*'.[37] Further awards followed. The British Society of Film and Television (now BAFTA) awarded the film the Robert Flaherty award for documentary. Shortly thereafter it won the Academy Award for best documentary feature. The unusual format allowed for David Seltzer to be nominated for best script for a screen drama by the Writers Guild of America. He lost to Penelope Gilliatt's *Sunday Bloody Sunday*.[38]

The *Hellstrom Chronicle* had an impact within the SF genre under whose flag it had sailed. The film inspired the great SF novelist Frank Herbert (best known for his *Dune* cycle) to write a novel about a group of humans secretly attempting to live their lives according to insect principles. The novel was originally also to be titled *The Hellstrom Chronicle* but became *Hellstrom's Hive* and appeared in 1973.[39] Similarly, after viewing the film *The Hellstrom Chronicle*, Paul Radin, the producer behind the recent wildlife-related hits *Born Free* and *Living Free*, realized that rather than attempting a third film about lions, he should dramatize *The Hellstrom Chronicle*'s prophesy of a war between insects and humanity. He felt that, with humans in the drama and a dose of *2001* type mysticism, it 'can't miss'.[40] The plan became Paramount's *Phase IV* (1974), the first feature directed by Saul Bass. The film showed ants developing a collective intelligence in response to an evolutionary shove from an extraterrestrial source and mobilizing against a group of scientists. The crew included *Hellstrom Chronicle* wildlife photographer Ken Middleham, who finally left his basement to film the ant sequences in East Africa.[41]

The *Hellstrom* influence could also detected in the 1973 SF-horror-disaster novel by Thomas Page entitled *The Haephestus Plague* in which fire belching cockroaches emerge from an earthquake fault and are exploited by a mad scientist. Paramount doubled down on their bet on the commercial viability of Hellstrom-ism by adapting the novel as *Bug* (1975), the last film produced by the master of B-movie horror, William Castle. Once again Ken Middleham handled the insect photography.[42] Neither *Bug* nor *Phase IV* was a great commercial success, although *Phase IV* achieved a certain cult following. Both films were cited by critics as evidence of an SF boom.[43] 1977 saw mutant insects on the loose once more in a post-nuclear wasteland in Fox's

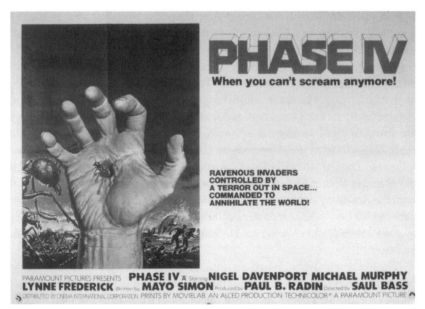

16. Inspired by Hellstrom: a poster for Saul Bass (dir.) *Phase IV* (1974)
(Source: British Film Institute).

risible *Damnation Alley*. Middleham provided the close-up photography yet
again. His final feature film credit would be in a decidedly un-SF work:
Terrence Malick's historical drama *Days of Heaven* (1979), which required a
locust swarm.[44]

The men behind *Hellstrom* prospered. David L. Wolper included insects
in his documentary about sex in the animal kingdom *Birds do it, Bees do
it* (1974) but found still greater success with the emerging genre of the
television mini-series. His *Roots* (1977) has been hailed as one of the
great milestones in American understanding of the African-American
experience. He died in 2010 as a legend of television production.
Walon Green ultimately found his forte as a writer and producer of
gritty television drama. He was part of the team behind *Law and Order*
(1990–2010) and its variants, and *ER* (1994–2009). The writer David Seltzer
achieved considerable success with his script for The *Omen* (1976) – an ideal
outlet for his apocalyptic turn of phrase – and later, mixed writing with
work as producer and director. Lawrence Pressman became increasingly
visible with a major role in *Shaft* (1971) and it became increasingly unlikely
that he could fool an audience that he was anything other than an actor.
He continued to be cast as scientists and became best known to the audiences

as the senior doctor in the medical comedy/drama *Doogie Howser, MD* (1989–93).

Insects remain a stock source for SF villains. More recent examples have included the giant bugs of *Starship Troopers* (1997) and insectoid 'Species 8472' in *Star Trek: Voyager*. The concern over mankind's negative impact on the environment implicit within *The Hellstrom Chronicle* endures as a significant theme in both SF and documentary film. Ironically, forty years on, the film's assumption that insects could survive every punishment humanity could throw in their direction now seems overly optimistic. Contemporary thinking emphasizes the interdependence of species. The rapid depletion of bee populations across the northern hemisphere raises the prospect of an agricultural crisis stemming from radically reduced rates of pollination. Humanity and insects may yet go down together.

What then does *The Hellstrom Chronicle* tell us about the development of the SF genre? The production materials reveal that the genre was strong enough by the early 1970s to provide elements that a canny producer like Wolper could exploit, to build a successful film in an unrelated field. *2001: A Space Odyssey* had demonstrated a public interest in astonishing and alien visuals. The other aspects of SF dropped into place behind that, including a host of script metaphors of alien realms, robots and warring worlds, elements in the music, clips from the genre, the title, and the stock character of the psychotic Dr Hellstrom. The film's SF credentials are strengthened by the fact that it inspired further SF: stoking a sub-genre in SF insect horror. While the film is only occasionally included in the roll call of 1970s SF films,[45] it is one instance of how an outlying example of a genre can illuminate the whole. Despite his eye rolling, the genre busting Dr Hellstrom and his amazing bugs deserve to be remembered.

Notes

[1]   Walon Green to Cull (author), 21 January 2011.
[2]   David L.Wolper papers, David L. Wolper Center for the Study of the Documentary at the University of Southern California (hereafter DLW), Box 208, f.003: Hellstrom story pitch (*c.* late 1969): '*David L. Wolper presents THE INSECTS*'.
[3]   DLW, Box 208, f.003: Hellstrom story pitch: '*David L. Wolper presents THE INSECTS*'.
[4]   David L. Wolper, *Producer* (New York: Scribner, 2003), p.175.
[5]   See press kits for *Hellstrom Chronicle* preserved at New York Public Library, Lincoln Center, Library for the Performing Arts, MFL + NC 2278 #6, and British Film Institute micro jacket.
[6]   DLW Box 067, f.019, 2 November 1970 outline for *The Last Plague* (with *Man Vs Insect* written in as title). 4 Ibid: November 1970 revised outline for *The Last Plague*.
[7]   DLW Box 067 f.020: Script for *The Silent Enemy*, 1 December 1970.
[8]   DLW Box 068, f.001: Treatment, *The Aliens*, n.d.

9   DLW Box 067 f.020: Script for *The Silent Enemy*, 1 December 1970.
10 DLW Box 068 f.002: Undated outline featuring Haelstrom character. Wolper, *Producer*, pp.177–8. *Secret in the Hive* is in DLW Box 067 f.009.
11 DWP Box 068 f.003: Script for *The Haelstrom Chronicle* and memo to Wolper, 30 December 1971. Other scenes proposed here but eventually deleted included a sustained sequence in which Haelstrom would give the audience a tour of a typical American home, revealing the typical infestations of bugs as he went.
12 DLW Box 068 f.005: Script dated 19 January 1971. See also Margaret Herrick Library, Academy of Motion Picture Arts and Sciences (AMPAS), Malcolm Leo papers, VF 469: Script for *Hellstrom Chronicle* labelled final draft, 24 February 1971. This version has minor differences from the film as completed. The 'rape' opening mentioned below is still not present, and there is still a scene set at Hellstrom's house in which he reveals the bug population.
13 DLW Box 208 f.006: Press kit for *Hellstrom Chronicle*, remarks by Lalo Schifrin.
14 Peter Schjeldahl, 'Suddenly one missed Walt Disney', *New York Times*, 22 August 1971.
15 DLW Box 208 f.008.
16 DLW Box 068 f.013: Script for trailer as shot 17 June 1971.
17 Ibid: Script for second trailer.
18 *Variety*, 16 June 1971.
19 Jay Cocks, 'Bug's eye view' *Time*, 16 July 1971.
20 These reviews were quoted in a centre spread ad in *Hollywood Reporter*, 2 August 1971.
21 Bob Considine, 'Awesome insects on view', *Los Angeles Herald-Examiner*, 19 July 1971.
22 Quoted in Craig W. Anderson, *Science Fiction Films of the Seventies*, McFarland, Jefferson NC, 1985, p.37.
23 New York Public Library, Lincoln Center: *Hellstrom Chronicle* press kit (preserved at MFL + NC 2278 #6).
24 'Crest Hellstrom Record', *Hollywood Reporter*, 30 July 1971. Wolper, *Producer*, p.179. The previous record holder had been *Five Easy Pieces*.
25 'Big rental films of '71', *Variety* anniversary issue, 5 January 1972, p.67. The budget was cited in 'Fresh box office success themes insects inherit world', *Variety*, 30 June 1971.
26 'Butcher bugged by *Hellstrom Chronicle* asking pride balm', *Variety*, 8 March 1972.
27 Stanley Rachesky (extension entomologist, University of Illinois), 'Lets Talk about Fundamentals', *Pest Control* (November 1971).
28 'Hellstrom Beautiful', *Hollywood Reporter*, 25 June 1971.
29 Peter Schjeldahl, 'Suddenly one missed Walt Disney', *New York Times*, 22 August 1971. For similar concerns over the Hellstrom frame, see William Paul, 'Dr Hellstrom is a bit buggy', *Village Voice*, 12 August 1971; Roy Pinney, 'The Hellstrom Chronicle', *Today's Film Maker*, May 1972, pp.65–6; DeWitt Robbeleth, 'The Hellstrom Chronicle', *Audience* # 39, September 1971.
30 James Arnold, 'Hellstrom didn't need semonizing', *Catholic Chronicle*, 19 November 1971.
31 Charles Aaronson, 'No "regulations" for documentaries', *Motion Picture Daily*, 7 July 1971.
32 Wolper, *Producer*, p.179.
33 Documentation relating to distribution is archived in DLW Box 208, f.001.
34 Nina Hibbin, 'Enthralling', *Morning Star*, 9 October 1971.
35 Derek Malcolm, 'The Hellstrom Chronicle', *Guardian*, 28 October 1971.
36 Cecil Wilson, 'When the ants come marching in', *Daily Mail*, 27 October 1971.
37 George Melly, 'The Hellstrom Chronicle', *The Observer*, 31 October 1971.

[38]   A selection of cuttings on these wins can be found in DLW Box 208, f.008.

[39]   DLW Box 067, f.014 includes a manuscript draft of Frank Herbert's novel then titled *The Hellstrom Chronicle* with a covering note from the MCA agency dated 4 August 1972. Frank Herbert, *Hellstrom's Hive* (New York: Doubleday, 1973).

[40]   Bart Mills, 'The Anty Hero', *The Guardian*, 10 February 1973, p.10, reprinted as Bart Mills, 'Ants take over the world in Phase I', *Los Angeles Times*, 18 February 1973, p.22.

[41]   For an analysis of this film see Craig W. Anderson, *Science Fiction Films of the Seventies*, (Jefferson NC: McFarland, 1985), pp.71–73. For background see AMPAS Saul Bass papers, *Phase IV* files, especially script # 1, legal # 21 and publicity, #35. For an interview with Middleham see Don Shay, '*Phase IV*: The Microcosmic world of Ken Middleham', *Cinefex*, 3 (1980).

[42]   Famous for his in-theatre gimmicks, Castle initially planned to install a special device in theatres to brush over patron's feet and terrify them during the marauding roach scenes. In the end he had to be content with merely ostentatiously taking out $1 million life insurance policy on his lead giant cockroach, Hercules, for the duration of their publicity tour. William Castle, *Step Right Up! I'm gonna scare the pants off America: The Memoirs of Hollywood's Master Showman* (New York: Putnam, 1976), pp.247–56. *Time*, 10 June 1974, p.68. Caste found Middleham through his executive assistant Marge Pinns, who had worked on *The Hellstrom Chronicle*.

[43]   Vincent Canby, 'Movies are more sci-fi than ever', *New York Times*, 17 March 1974; Arthur Herzog, 'Science fiction movies are catching on in a weary America', *New York Times*, 25 August 1974, S2, pp.1, 11. Reviews of *Bug* ranged from 'a clever blend of horror and science fiction' in 'Hot Horror', *Sunday Mirror* (London), 9 November 1975, to 'flaming rubbish' in Arthur Shirkell, 'Super bugs that can go to blazes', *Daily Mirror*, 7 November 1975.

[44]   Ken Middleham worked on Wolper's documentary survey of beastly sex, *Birds do it, Bees do it* (1974) and provided time-lapse effects for *The Mutations* (dir. Jack Cardiff, 1974).

[45]   Craig W. Anderson, *Science Fiction Films of the Seventies* (Jefferson, NC: McFarland, 1985), pp. 35–7, 73.

FUTURE IMPERFECT:
LOGAN'S RUN (1976)

Dystopian futures have been one of the recurring themes of SF literature: major examples of this tradition include H. G. Wells's *When the Sleeper Wakes*, Aldous Huxley's *Brave New World*, George Orwell's *Nineteen Eighty-Four*, Ray Bradbury's *Fahrenheit 451* and Anthony Burgess's *A Clockwork Orange*. *Logan's Run*, published in 1967 by two Californian writers, William F. Nolan and George Clayton Johnson, was a minor addition to this genre. *Logan's Run* is perhaps best described as a *Brave New World* for the sixties: in the world of AD 2116 citizens lead a life of hedonistic excess until they reach the age of 21, when a super-computer known as the Thinker enforces a policy of universal euthanasia. Like many SF writers Nolan and Johnson were using the genre to comment on contemporary social trends and attitudes. In *Logan's Run* it was the rise of youth culture in the 1960s. The book's opening makes this quite explicit: 'The seeds of the Little War were planted in a restless summer during the mid-1960s, with sit-ins and student demonstrations as youth tested its strength.'[1]

Nolan and Johnson, both former artists, were contemporaries of Richard Matheson, Ray Bradbury and Harlan Ellison. Nolan started out writing stories for SF magazines, while Johnson wrote several original teleplays for *The Twilight Zone* (1959–64) and an early *Star Trek* episode ('The Man-Trap'). *Logan's Run*, written in three weeks in the summer of 1965, was their first novel. It is a fast-paced, episodic story that privileges action and movement ahead of narrative plausibility or psychological realism. With its short scenes and spare prose, *Logan's Run* reads more like a screenplay than a novel. Johnson explained: 'We wrote the whole book almost as a scenario for a movie, because that was our goal, to sell the story as a book first, as a lever to get it made into a movie later.'[2]

Logan's Run is a compendium of genre themes and motifs. An indication of the many influences that informed the book can be found in the two pages of dedications 'to all the wild friends we grew up with – and who were with us when we wrote this book'. These include (in no particular order) *King Kong, The Most Dangerous Game, Frankenstein, Flash Gordon, Buck Rogers, Dick Tracy, Tarzan, The Wizard of Oz, The Man in the Iron Mask, Gunga Din, Batman, Superman, The Time Machine* and *Citizen Kane*. In particular *Logan's Run* drew upon pulp magazines such as *Astounding Science Fiction* and *Black Mask*. The most obvious manifestation of this is in its occasionally lurid details. At one point, for example, the heroine Jessica finds herself 'spread-eagled and helpless, pinned, naked, to a tilted slab. Her body was trembling with chill. Facing her was a steeply inclined slideway. Balanced delicately on the high lip of the slide was a massive ten-ton ice block.'[3]

At the same time as drawing upon all the clichés of pulp SF, however, *Logan's Run* was also very much a tract for its time. It is replete with references to the counter-culture and the permissive society. As in Huxley's *Brave New World*, the state encourages personal and sexual gratification in order to keep the population compliant: pleasure is a form of social control. *Logan's Run* pictures a society that embodies, in extreme form, the permissive values of the 1960s. There are references to recreational drug use ('hallucimills' offer narcotics such as Lysergic Foam – 'an extension of the old LSD formula developed more than a century and a half ago') and sexual promiscuity is rife (there is no marriage but citizens frequent 'love shops' for 'pair ups'). However, the protagonist, Logan, has started to be affected by a sense of ennui regarding the pleasure society, which ultimately causes him to reject its doctrines.

Logan's Run was published by Little Dial Press in 1967. The MGM Script Files at the Margaret Herrick Library reveal that the manuscript was submitted to the studio prior to the book's publication.[4] MGM, no doubt observing the success of 20th Century-Fox's *Fantastic Voyage* (1966), paid $100,000 for the film rights to *Logan's Run*.[5] Johnson and Nolan delivered two full screenplays, dated 7 December 1966 and 21 February 1967. It is no surprise that they stuck very closely to the book. Logan is a Sandman, one of an elite group of police enforcers whose job is to terminate 'runners' (those who refuse to enter a 'Sleepshop' when they reach 21 – indicated by a crystal embedded in their palm since birth turning black). Logan and fellow Sandman Francis pursue a runner called Doyle whose dying word is 'Sanctuary'. Sanctuary is rumoured to be a place at the end of an underground escape route run by someone called Ballard. Logan, having arrived at 'lastday', resolves to find Sanctuary by posing as a runner, in order to kill Ballard. He follows a lead from a key, found on Doyle's body, to a surgery where runners go to alter their facial appearance. Here he meets Jessica, a runner who mistakes him for Doyle. (In the book Jessica is

17. Logan (Michael York) and Jessica (Jenny Agutter) before their 'run' in *Logan's Run* (1976) (Source: British Film Institute).

Doyle's sister: in the screenplay she does not know what Doyle looks like.) The underground has given Jessica a key to a subterranean maze where high-speed cars can travel anywhere in the world within seconds. Logan and Jessica are transported to an undersea city where they narrowly escape death when it floods; to the North Pole where they find a prison colony run by an android called Box; to the Black Hills of Dakota where they encounter the sadistic Pleasure Gypsies; and finally to Washington DC where they find Ballard. When Logan does not kill Ballard as he intended, Ballard reveals his true identity: none other than Logan's erstwhile colleague Francis. Logan and Jessica leave Earth in a rocket ship bound for the off-world colony of Sanctuary.[6]

The Johnson-Nolan screenplay embodies the same themes as the book – and the same structural flaws. It is clear that the authors saw youth as a force for historical change. Writing against a background of growing social unrest – the first student-led protests against US involvement in Vietnam were organized in the spring of 1965 – Johnson and Nolan foretold a youth rebellion spreading across the United States. A 'narration done in a *March of Time* style' declares: 'Angry young people took over State capitols, county seats, city halls. Within two weeks the reins of power lay firmly in the hands of youth. The Little War had ended.' What follows is a technocratic dictatorship: 'The age of government by computer began. The first of the giant Sleepshops went into full operation in Chicago. A maximum age limit was imposed and the original DS [Deep Sleep] units were formed. Soon, all the world was young.' The future of *Logan's Run* – the screenplay dates the action as *c*.2072 – is a dystopia in which revolution has created a society built on ideological dogma.

It is not difficult to see why the Johnson-Nolan screenplay was deemed unsuitable for filming. Logan himself lacks clear psychological motivation – he sets out to find Sanctuary almost on a whim and his ideological conversion from Sandman to runner is unconvincing – and the screenplay is very episodic. The second half, in particular, betrays its origin in serials such as *Flash Gordon* and *Buck Rogers*, as Logan and Jessica proceed through a series of bizarre though unrelated adventures. There is also an unpleasant undercurrent of voyeurism and misogyny. A scene where the man-machine Box forces Logan and Jessica to pose naked while he creates an ice sculpture of them, for example, is a gratuitous excuse for a nude scene. The most perverse scene is the encounter with the Pleasure Gypsies, whose leader Rutago poisons the couple and makes Logan cut an ounce of flesh from Jessica's thigh for the antidote. The element of sadism suggested here reflects a trend towards physical cruelty in genre films during the mid-1960s such as Cornel Wilde's *The Naked Prey* (1966) and the Spaghetti Westerns of Sergio Leone. Johnson and Nolan's second draft reinserted a sequence from the book where Logan is required to have sexual intercourse with a group of gypsy girls, while Jessica 'has to surrender to Rutago'.[7] These scenes are entirely gratuitous: they seem to have been included purely for sensation rather than for any genuine plot reason.

It may be that MGM commissioned the screenplay of *Logan's Run* from Johnson and Nolan as a sop to the authors: in any event the studio discarded their script and brought in its own people to develop the project. George Pal, who had joined MGM from Paramount – his films for the studio included *The Time Machine* (1960), *The Wonderful World of the Brothers Grimm* (1962), *The 7 Faces of Dr Lao* (1964) and *The Power* (1967) – was to produce, while Richard Maibaum, an experienced screenwriter whose stock was high following the success of the James Bond films, was hired to write a new screenplay.[8] Maibaum approached it very much in the spirit of the Bond movies:

> *Logan's Run*, as I see it, is a send up of the science fiction film, a deadpan spoof which might appropriately be subtitled JAMES BOND IN TOMORROWLAND. The writers of the novel have assured me that this was their intention, too. Basically it's a wild, outrageous chase, with our protagonists encountering monsters and marvels, but it must always be played with complete seriousness. I believe audiences today find this approach entertaining.[9]

Maibaum seems to have envisaged the film in the style of *Barbarella* (1968), Roger Vadim's film of the SF comic strip by Jean-Claude Forest, notable for its camp qualities and bizarre narrative situations. Maibaum delivered a treatment on 14 February 1968, followed by a full script on 11 March, a second draft on 8 April and a third on 3 June. While still recognizably based on the book, his screenplay introduced several new ideas that took *Logan's Run* in a different direction.

Maibaum set the action in Los Angeles in 2107 – imagining it as a futuristic city in the style of *Just Imagine* with sky-lanes and paravanes – and revised the account of the youth revolution by creating a leader in the person of a hippy demagogue called Chaney Moon, whose oratory is 'somewhere between Hitler and Stokeley Carmichael'. According to official history Moon was the first to accept voluntary euthanasia, and his body is preserved in a giant mausoleum where recordings of his speeches are played: 'For the first time in the history of mankind we forced their scientists before we liquidated them to computerize the pursuit of happiness ... Never again will age corrupt and enslave the young! Never again will anyone be permitted to grow old!' Maibaum drew a parallel between this society and the Soviet Union, describing 'a huge plaza, thronged with people, reminiscent of Red Square in Moscow', while the body of Chaney Moon is 'preserved like Lenin for the edification of the masses'.[10]

Maibaum made several important plot changes. He added what amounts to an orgy in Zanadu, a parlour for pleasure seekers ('Try the Hungarian twins in the Slavic Salon') and has Logan experiencing a bad 'lift' from consciousness expanding drugs. Maibaum imposed a more disciplined structure onto the narrative, though it remains rather episodic. He replaced the Pleasure Gypsies with a gang of futuristic Hell's Angels known as Devilstickers and removed the scene of Jessica being tortured and raped by Rutago. In his second draft the Devilstickers became the Sky Boarders on their flying surf boards. He added a scene where Logan and Jessica find the ruins of the White House and sleep in the Lincoln Bedroom. And he reinserted a scene from the novel not in the Johnson-Nolan screenplay where a robot army re-enacts the Battle of Fredericksburg. The robot General Lee turns out to be Ballard in disguise. However, the most significant change is to the ending. Sanctuary is no longer an off-world colony but a cave filled with refugees 'reminiscent both of early Christians in catacombs and internees of World War II concentration camps'. Ballard's true identity is revealed, but this time he is not Francis but none other than Chaney Moon, who turns out to have been 'the first runner': 'For years I hid away – watching the horror and cruelty perpetrated in my name – and my false, unnatural creed.'[11] Ballard/Moon sends Logan back into the city to destroy the Thinker.

Logan's Run looked set for production in 1968, but at this point a combination of circumstances contrived to halt the film in its tracks. First it had to contend with the censors. *Logan's Run* was one of the last scripts considered by the PCA: the increasingly outdated Production Code would be abandoned at the end of 1968 and replaced by a ratings system that categorized films as suitable for 'General', 'Mature' or 'Restricted' audiences. Geoffrey Shurlock told MGM 'it is our considered opinion that this is the type of story which suggests the kind of picture that, under the new Code regulations, will have to be advertised bearing the label SUGGESTED FOR MATURE AUDIENCES'. This was due to the 'excessive' and 'unacceptable' amount of nudity. Shurlock was particularly concerned about a scene in a 'Sex Hygiene Room' that 'calls for a man and a woman to stand nude before a class of children' and 'the sequence in which Logan and Jessica pose, in the nude, as models for the sculptor'.[12] 'The sex hygiene sequences would have to be handled with great discretion to be approved in the finished picture', he reiterated after reading a full screenplay. Shurlock also disliked the orgy ('It is difficult for us to see at this stage how this could be approved in the finished picture') and the suggestion of sado-masochistic practices ('In the so-called Zanadu sequence, the showing of a rack of jewel handled whips seems to delve into the area of sado-masochism, and as such, we feel it should be omitted').[13]

Furthermore, a rift was also opening within the production team. Richard Rush, the director attached to the project, disliked the screenplay.[14] Rush was not in sympathy with Maibaum's tongue-in-cheek approach, seeing *Logan's Run* instead as 'a social allegory ... It becomes a very American statement about the dangers in any society that sacrifices individual human rights. An audience senses the parallel ...' Rush suggested some major revisions, tightening the structure and exploring Logan's character in greater depth. He saw Logan as 'somewhat analogous to the Nazi storm trooper who falls in love with a Jew'. It was Rush who realized the significance of the scene in the ice cave: 'The critical thing which happens in the ice palace is while Logan and Jessica are posing, they experience the awakening of strange taboo emotions toward each other, a rekindling of romantic, possessive instincts.' And he felt the film should suggest underlying dissent with the regime in order to make the denouement more plausible: '[One] should get the feeling that there are flaws and cracks in the structure which will pay off in grand style at the end when, with Logan's help, the entire society will revolt and crush the establishment and re-establish their individual freedom – which is the natural ending of the picture.'[15]

Pal and MGM were now caught in an impasse: whether to go ahead with *Logan's Run* as it stood or to commission a full rewrite that would delay the start of production. Maibaum declined to revise the script. The dilemma was explained by studio executive Lewis Morton:

> I feel that there is a good deal to be said for Rush's point of view in the sense that genuine social context and analogy to present day problems would in my opinion enhance the potential of the picture. From a practical standpoint, however, I think you'll agree that the changes Rush suggests will in fact require a rewrite of the script before it can be properly budgeted. This immediately presents problems of both time and money. Whereas I hope Dick Maibaum could bring himself to go along with Rush, if only to protect his credit, I'm by no means certain of this.[16]

Pal, for his part, was sceptical of Rush's vision for the film: 'Could be awfully heavy-handed especially in contrast with the fluffy Maibaum approach and might take even more time than my estimate of 2–3 months to rewrite. And until then we won't know if it's better or worse than the Maibaum original.'[17]

The production of *Logan's Run* had stalled due to competing creative and economic demands. Pal wanted to go ahead with the Maibaum script but the studio had developed cold feet. By the spring of 1969 Pal was becoming frustrated with the continuing lack of progress. He feared, not without reason given the success in the interim of both *Planet of the Apes* and *2001*, that *Logan's Run* was in danger of missing the boat:

> As I have repeatedly stressed – a new era of Science Fiction and especially the type of Science Fiction that deals with the future is here. It seems that every studio in town is preparing one or more of such motion pictures ... One of the above now may not hurt us, but the accumulation of so many certainly would or might even kill the chances of *Logan's Run*. Ever since I bought in this project I have repeatedly emphasized that time was of the essence, but to no avail. Last May when the screenplay was completed we were ahead of the pack. Today we are in the middle of it, but still can win out provided we are allowed to proceed with production immediately.[18]

However, there was still no green light from the studio. This was almost certainly due to the chronic instability at the top of MGM during 1969–70 when no fewer than three studio heads came and went in quick succession. Pal later said: 'I became friendly with one management and this probably went against me with the next management. By the time I got friendly with the next management, they were out, and a new one came in.'[19]

Pal still refused to give up on what had become a pet project. He now explored the possibility of selling *Logan's Run* as a package to another company. American International Pictures reportedly offered $200,000, but MGM refused to sell for less than the $350,000 it reckoned to have invested in the film to date.[20] Another interested party was a West German company, Filmkunst, which planned to shoot it in Europe in 1970. Again, however, 'no deal with MGM could be made'. Peter Hahne of Filmkunst told Pal regretfully that 'it is very unfortunate that the picture cannot be realized. It is a very good story and I believe that the script also turned out very well.'[21] With MGM unwilling either to make the film themselves or to sell it to anyone else, Pal severed his connection with the studio and instead produced *Doc Savage: The Man of Bronze* (1975) for Warner Bros.

In the early 1970s *Logan's Run* seemed to have been consigned to the realm of what the film industry calls 'development hell'. Johnson tried to revive the project as a vehicle for Robert Redford, while producer Irwin Allen also showed an interest in making it.[22] In 1974, however, *Logan's Run* was handed to Saul David, the producer of *Fantastic Voyage* and *Our Man Flint* (1965), who had joined MGM from 20th Century-Fox. The studio's renewed interest in *Logan's Run* came in the wake of its success with two SF subjects, *Westworld* and *Soylent Green*, in 1973.[23] Stanley R. Greenberg, the scriptwriter of *Soylent Green*, was announced as the writer of *Logan's Run*, though the only record of his input is an incomplete treatment in the MGM Script Files. It was Greenberg who devised the idea of Carousel – a deathly merry-go-round where citizens believe they are being offered the chance of 'renewal' if they reach the top – that replaced the 'Sleepshops' of previous scripts. And Greenberg also devised a different reason for Logan's decision to seek Sanctuary when he is brainwashed by the computer: 'It is my duty to find Sanctuary and to kill Bannister.'[24]

In the event, however, the task of preparing the new screenplay of *Logan's Run* was handed to David Zelag Goodman, best known for the controversial *Straw Dogs* (1971), who effectively rewrote it from scratch. In the wake of films like *A Clockwork Orange* (1971) and *Soylent Green* it no longer seemed appropriate to treat *Logan's Run* as a spoof: Goodman's version was earnest and serious. Goodman maintained the idea of Carousel from Greenberg's treatment but raised the age of 'lastday' to thirty: this was a practical decision to widen the range of possible casting options. (In the film Logan is played by 33-year-old Michael York and Jessica by 23-year-old Jenny Agutter.) He developed the relationship between Logan and Francis, characterizing Francis as a younger man somewhat in awe of Logan. He maintained Logan's visit to the New You surgery and the scene in the ice cave where Logan and Jessica pose naked for Box. The Skyboarders and Civil War robots were dropped altogether, as was the character of Ballard/

Chaney Moon. Instead Logan and Jessica find a nameless Old Man living in the ruins of the Capitol Building with a colony of cats. At this point Logan realizes that Sanctuary is a myth: 'So many people wanted it to exist – so many who didn't want to die – that they evidently made it come into existence – *in their imaginations*.' Logan fights Francis, who has tracked him from the city, on the floor of the Capitol and kills him. Logan then resolves to destroy the Master Computer: 'I'm going back to destroy the way we live. I'm going to destroy the colour variant machines – and the machines that record people's age. That'll put an end to it. The entire city will be a Sanctuary.'[25]

Goodman wrote half a dozen drafts between April 1974 and March 1975 that further refined the script. He added more 'buddy' scenes between Logan and Francis at the start.[26] In one draft the Old Man shows Logan how to drive a reconstructed Rolls-Royce.[27] He added to the symbolism of the scenes in the Capitol – by now it seemed likely that the film would be released during the American Bicentennial in 1976 – when Francis wields a flagpole bearing the Stars and Stripes during his fight with Logan.[28] And he had Logan, at the climax, telling those entering Carousel: 'Don't be afraid! You won't die! No one has to die at thirty!! You don't have to blink out into Lastday's darkness at Carousel!! You can live longer and grow old ... I've seen it!'[29] Some of these changes were made solely to differentiate Goodman's script from previous versions so that he could be credited as sole author of the screenplay.[30] The scene in the ice cave, however, remained ever present. By early 1975 the British director Michael Anderson was attached to the film. Saul David chose Anderson on the basis that he had directed the film of Orwell's *1984* (1955) and had a feeling for realistic science fiction.[31] Anderson was a versatile director capable of handling the logistics of major productions: his other films included *The Dam Busters* (1955), *Around the World in Eighty Days* (1956) and *Operation Crossbow* (1965). Ironically he had just completed *Doc Savage* for George Pal.

The last major rewrite of *Logan's Run* occurred immediately prior to production. In March 1975 it was decided that Francis was not a strong enough antagonist and that his relationship with Logan should be changed: 'Francis is the older of the two men and the harder ... But something about Logan appeals to him and he has come to depend on Logan for an admiration and warmth he wouldn't admit to anyone.'[32] This was reflected in the final shooting script of 30 April 1975, which also revised the scene where Logan is assigned to find Sanctuary. In order for him to pose as a runner, Logan's 'life clock' is advanced against his wishes. 'Do I get my four years back?' he demands; there is no reply. In Goodman's previous scripts Logan had voluntarily relinquished his four years. A weakness in

18. Logan and Jessica meet the android Box. The ice cave sequence of *Logan's Run* (1976) was heavily cut by the censors (Source: British Film Institute).

all previous versions – the reason for Logan's conversion from Sandman to runner – had been remedied.[33]

Logan's Run finally went before the cameras in the summer of 1975. The production discourse of the film emphasized spectacle over content. The film occupied five sound stages at MGM's Culver City studios and the sets were described as 'the most expensive erected at the studio since its great early days of awe-inspiring musical spectaculars'.[34] It was shot in the Todd-AO widescreen process and was one of the first films to utilize Dolby stereo sound. It employed state-of-the-art visual effects: the credits included 'laser consultant' (Christopher Outwater) and 'Holograms by [the] Multiplex Company'.[35] The locations included a sewage disposal plant at El Segundo and the 135-acre Dallas Market Center that doubled as the city interior.[36] The notion that the architecture of the future would resemble a giant shopping mall might suggest a lack of imagination by the producers: consequently the 'look' of the film now seems rather dated. The final negative cost of *Logan's Run* was $9 million. It grossed $25 million in North America, which suggests that overall it made a profit.[37]

However, there was still one more twist before *Logan's Run* reached the screen. The Classification and Ratings Administration felt that the film 'contains an excessive amount of sexually oriented footage' and insisted upon the removal of two scenes if the film were to be rated 'PG' (parental guidance suggested) rather than a more restrictive 'R' (requiring under-sixteens to be accompanied by an adult).[38] As some three-quarters of all ticket sales at this time were to the 12–19 age group, the studio acquiesced in order to secure the 'PG' that would maximize ticket sales. The scenes concerned were the 'love shop' and the ice cave. A few seconds remain of the love shop – elaborately choreographed with nude dancers by ballet director Stefan Wenta – as Logan and Jessica are pursued by Francis. The removal of the sculpture scene where Logan and Jessica pose for Box is more damaging to the film: this had developed from a gratuitous nude scene to a tender romantic moment. Its absence, and the clumsy re-editing of the rest of the ice cave sequence, has an adverse effect on narrative logic. A few brief moments of nudity remain – a long shot of Jenny Agutter changing into fur robes in the ice cave and frontal images of Box's previous victims preserved in ice – but the release print of *Logan's Run* was far less explicit than any of the screenplays had been.

The reception of *Logan's Run* was mixed. *Variety* thought it 'a rewarding futuristic film that appeals both as escapist adventure as well as intelligent drama'.[39] But the *New York Times* found the plot incomprehensible: 'Just why and for what particular purpose Logan makes his run is anything but clear ... Had more attention been paid to the screenplay, the movie might have been a stunner.'[40] Little can reviewers have known how many revisions the script of *Logan's Run* had gone through over the previous nine years. William F. Nolan's view of the film was diplomatic: 'Many changes have been made, many sections of the book eliminated or transposed, but that's to be expected. The loss of Ballard, head of our Sanctuary people, disturbed me – and I liked our ending better than theirs. Still, I'm pragmatic about Hollywood. As an adaptation, it could have been much, much worse.'[41]

Logan's Run is an example of a film that was overtaken by events: a film of the 1960s made in the 1970s. The original concept – that a revolution of the young creates a dictatorship – is entirely lost in the film, which provides no historical context beyond an opening caption stating that in the twenty-third century 'the survivors of war, overpopulation and pollution are living in a great domed city'. The references to overpopulation and pollution tie the film in to trends in 1970s SF such as *Soylent Green*, but detach it from its original context of the rise of youth culture and protest movements. And the counter-cultural references that informed the original were gradually diminished through many rewrites and the intervention of the Classification and Ratings Administration. It is significant, for example, that while the film still includes some references to casual sex, there is no mention of recreational drug use – a reflection of the conservative reaction against the counter-culture by the mid-1970s. Furthermore, the motifs introduced into the film that did not feature in the book were mostly derivative of other films. *THX 1138* (1970) had already featured an individual rebelling against a futuristic police state and fleeing its sterile city, while *Westworld* and its sequel *Futureworld* (1976) explored the dark side of the pleasure society. And the shot of Logan and Jessica approaching the Lincoln Memorial in Washington DC is a pale imitation of the iconic ending of *Planet of the Apes*. In the last analysis *Logan's Run* simply did not have anything new to say.

Like *Planet of the Apes*, *Logan's Run* begat a short-lived television series, which ran for 14 episodes in 1977. By then, however, the cultural landscape of popular SF had been transformed by the extraordinary success of *Star Wars*. Consequently *Logan's Run* has been entirely overshadowed in the history of SF cinema by George Lucas's epic space opera. And, while there has been much speculation over a remake of *Logan's Run*, this has yet to come to fruition. *Logan's Run* represents something of a missed opportunity: a film that might have transformed the genre into 'James Bond in Tomorrowland' but which in the event became just another visually stylish but ultimately rather portentous statement about the future. It is nevertheless tempting to imagine just how different the subsequent history of SF cinema might have been had *Logan's Run* been made as the spoof adventure that George Pal and Richard Maibaum had intended in 1968.

Notes

[1]   William F. Nolan and George Clayton Johnson, *Logan's Run* (New York: Buccaneer Books, 1995 [1967]), p.ix.
[2]   Quoted in Wallace A. Wyss, 'Conception', *Cinefantastique* 5: 2 (1976), p.6.
[3]   Nolan and Johnson, *Logan's Run*, pp.64–5.
[4]   Margaret Herrick Library, Academy of Motion Picture Arts and Sciences (AMPAS), Turner/MGM Scripts Box 1708 f.L-870: *Logan's Run*. A Thriller by William F. Nolan and George Clayton Johnson. Undated, but with handwritten note: 'DOES NOT incorporate final book-ms changes 5/5/66.'
[5]   UCLA George Pal Collection Box 17 f.5: Clark Ramsay to Lewis Morton, 4 February 1969.
[6]   AMPAS Turner/MGM Scripts Box 1709 f.L-872: *Logan's Run*. Screenplay by George Clayton Johnson, William F. Nolan. First draft, 7 December 1966.
[7]   AMPAS Turner/MGM Scripts Box 1709 f.L-874: *Logan's Run*. Screenplay by George Clayton Johnson, William F. Nolan. Second draft, 21 February 1967.
[8]   Maibaum had worked on the first four Bond films – *Dr No* (1962), *From Russia With Love* (1963), *Goldfinger* (1964) and *Thunderball* (1965) – and would write thirteen in total.
[9]   AMPAS Turner/MGM Scripts Box 1708 f.L-876: *Logan's Run*. Treatment by Richard Maibaum, 14 February 1968.
[10] AMPAS Turner/MGM Scripts Box 1710 f.L-878: *Logan's Run*. Screenplay by Richard Maibaum, 11 March 1968.

11 Suggestions for the casting of the old and young Chayney Moon included Kirk and Michael Douglas, Lloyd and Jeff Bridges, Robert and James or Christopher Mitchum.

12 UCLA George Pal Collection Box 17 f.5: Shurlock to Robert Vogel, 13 March 1968.

13 Ibid: Shurlock to Vogel, 25 April 1968.

14 Rush specialized in low-budget motorcycle movies such as *Thunder Alley* (1967) and *Hells Angels on Wheels* (1968). He is best known as director of *Freebie and the Bean* (1974) and *The Stunt Man* (1980).

15 UCLA George Pal Collection Box 17 f.5: 'Notes and suggested changes – "Logan's Run" ', memorandum by Dick Rush, 8 November 1968.

16 Ibid: Lewis Morton to Clark Ramsay, 8 November 1968.

17 Ibid: handwritten note on Rush's memorandum of 8 November 1968.

18 Ibid: Pal to 'All Concerned', 18 March 1969. Among the films that Pal identified as being in preparation were *Colossus* (Universal), *When the Sleeper Wakes* (American International) and *Kyle* (Fox – 'a futuristic suspense thriller'). He reported that '*Brave New World* is being seriously considered by one studio', while Warner 'has "XTY-1021" based on a prize-winning student film expanded into a full length movie, featuring a young runaway from the mechanized society.' The only realized films from his list were *The Forbin Project* (aka *Colossus*, Universal, dir. Joseph Sargent, 1969) and *THX 1138* (Warner Bros., dir. George Lucas, 1970).

19 Quoted in Frederick S. Clarke, Steve Rubin and Wallace A. Wyss, 'Production', *Cinefantastique*, 5: 2 (1976), p.16.

20 Ibid: p.18.

21 UCLA George Pal Collection Box 17 f.5: Peter Hahne to Pal, 8 October 1969.

22 Wyss, 'Conception', p.9.

23 *Westworld* (MGM, dir. Michael Crichton, 1973); *Soylent Green* (MGM, dir. Richard Fleischer, 1973).

24 AMPAS Turner/MGM Scripts Box 1711 f.L-888: *Logan's Run*. 'Sequence and notes from the Opening through The New You.' Stanley R. Greenberg, 26 February 1974.

25 AMPAS Turner/MGM Scripts Box 1711 f.L-890: *Logan's Run*. Screenplay by David Z. Goodman, 10 May 1974.

26 AMPAS Turner/MGM Scripts Box 1711 f.L-891: *Logan's Run*. Screenplay by David Z. Goodman, 15 July 1974.

27 AMPAS Turner/MGM Scripts Box 1711 f.L-892: *Logan's Run*. Screenplay by David Z. Goodman, 26 August 1974.

28 AMPAS Turner/MGM Scripts Box 1711 f.L-894: *Logan's Run*. Screenplay by David Z. Goodman, 21 October 1974.

29 AMPAS Turner/MGM Scripts Box 1712 f.L-895: *Logan's Run*. Screenplay by David Z. Goodman, 25 February 1975.

30 AMPAS Turner/MGM Scripts Box 1713 f.L-898: Moya Moria to Carl Bennett, 13 November 1974.

31 Clarke *et al*, 'Production', p.18.

32 AMPAS Turner/MGM Scripts Box 1713 f.L-908: 'Logan's Run – Projected Rewrite', 18 March 1975, initialled 'SD' (Saul David).

33 AMPAS Turner/MGM Scripts Box 1713 f.L-904: *Logan's Run*. Screenplay by David Z. Goodman, 30 April 1975.

34 BFI Library microfiche for *Logan's Run*: 'Production Notes. Logan's Run: A Saul David Production', n.d.

35 '3D Pix making A Comeback Via Laser Technology in "Logan's Run" ', *Variety*, 17 May 1975.

36 'Dallas' Architecture Meets Metro's 23rd century Sci-Fi Pic Needs', *Variety*, 23 July 1975.

37   http://www.imdb.com/title/tt0074812/business (accessed 18.10.2010. The domestic rental (the amount returned to the distributor) amounted to $9.5 million. Overseas figures are not available, but it is likely they would have been similar to the domestic revenues.

38   Saul David, *The Industry: Life in the Hollywood Fast Lane* (New York: Times Books, 1981), p.260.

39   *Variety*, 16 June 1976.

40   *New York Times*, 18 June 1976.

41   Quoted in Wyss, 'Conception', p.9.

NO TIME FOR SORROWS:
STAR WARS (1977)

There is a moment towards the end of the original *Star Wars* when Princess Leia (Carrie Fisher) – newly rescued from the Death Star by Luke Skywalker (Mark Hamill) and Han Solo (Harrison Ford) – is met by an elderly rebel general (Eddie Byrne): 'You're safe' he declares, 'When we heard about Alderaan, we feared the worst.' She dismisses any thought of her vaporized home-world: 'We have no time for sorrows, Commander. You must use the information in this R-2 unit to help plan the attack. It's our only hope.' From one point of view the exchange is just a loose end in the glittering fabric of *Star Wars*; a symptom of the eagerness of the young writer/director George Lucas to cut to the chase and amaze his audience with the final round of swoops, bangs and flashes without digressing into what it might actually mean to see one's home world destroyed. Yet the moment, by its very incongruity, speaks of something beneath: a wider need within the film to avoid confronting trauma, including the historical trauma so readily apparent to contemporaries in America at the moment of its making. The film's setting, 'a long time ago in a galaxy far, far away', was deliberately doubly removed from the realities of its audience. Anything could happen. Moreover, its producer Gary Kurtz assured the press at the time of its release that it was not even science fiction but science fantasy: a dream world that merely borrowed the creative licence from science fiction.[1] Yet by being about nothing and abstracted from its time, *Star Wars* could also be about everything and profoundly rooted in its time. It operates as both an archive of popular culture and a frozen moment of historical consciousness, an insect caught in amber as it flees from a predator. Contrary to Leia's claim, *Star Wars* had plenty of time for a particular kind of sorrow: nostalgia for a lost world of entertainment and for family relationships gone awry.

Star Wars was always – in the first instance – about film. George Lucas sought to push the boundaries of the medium forward to new heights of spectacle, and simultaneously to take the medium backwards to a lost innocence. He explained the film as his attempt to recapture the world that had fascinated him as a child growing up in rural Modesto, California in the 1950s. The science fiction medium was part of those memories – with old *Flash Gordon* serials on television and *Forbidden Planet* in the town cinema – but the genre also provided an ideal mechanism to incorporate the other genres of his youth. This film could also be a western, a pirate movie, a war film and more. But *Star Wars* was not just evoking the images of these films, it set out to recapture the awe of the cinematic experience and even more importantly, the moral experience of an old-time adventure. The reviewer in *Variety* spoke for many when he proclaimed: 'Like a breath of fresh air, *Star Wars* sweeps away the cynicism that has in recent years obscured the concepts of valor, dedication and honor.'[2]

Considering *Star Wars* in historical context prompts the question of why the concepts of 'valor, dedication and honor' were so mired in cynicism and – by the same token – why genres like the war film and the western could not be visited directly. The creative process that led to *Star Wars* began in 1971 at a dark moment in American history. The Vietnam War was grinding to a bloody end in which the United States seemed like the bad guy – perpetrator of massacres and carpet bombings – while the first revelations of the Watergate scandal were raising profound questions about the integrity of the highest office in the land. George Lucas later recalled that his first model for the character of the emperor was Richard Nixon himself.[3] Hollywood had for the most part avoided talking about the Vietnam War directly. Rather it had used existing genres to open questions about morality by proxy. The upbeat western of the 1950s had morphed into the anti-western, in which the racism of westward expansion and brutality of the frontier environment were clear. In 1970 Vietnam incidents like the massacre at My Lai were dramatized by analogy in films like *Soldier Blue* or *Little Big Man*. By the same token in the wake of Vietnam the Second World War had undergone a re-evaluation. The war lost its clear moral lines. The year 1970 brought *Patton*, which displayed flaws in the allied leadership, *Catch 22*, which satirized the military, and *Kelly's Heroes*, which had the American fighting man malingering and more interested in personal enrichment than winning the war. It was still possible to make a straight war film but very hard to sell one. Audiences stayed away from that year's *Tora! Tora! Tora!* Part of the reason for the change was generational. The creative baton was being passed from a generation who had actually experienced the war to their sons who knew it only from stories charged with a family context. The Second World War was the father's war and even without the experience of Vietnam, a generational dynamic dictated a certain amount of revisionism. The generation split would also mark the *Star Wars* saga.

The early 1970s were also a difficult time for the American film industry. Film was just one more American industry in decline. Retreating in the face of television, the cinema had sought to provide something that the small screen could not: violence, realism and explicit sexuality. This was the era when pornography went mainstream. Hollywood projected the cynicism of the era straight back to the public. Writing shortly after the release of *Star Wars*, Pauline Kael noted 'Today movies say the system is corrupt, that the whole thing stinks ... When movie after movie tells audiences they should be against themselves it's hardly surprising that people go out of the theatres drained, numbly convinced that with so much savagery and cruelty everywhere, nothing can be done.'[4] George Lucas had already attempted to find a way back from the cultural impasse, scoring a hit with *American Graffiti* (1973), but his initial impulse was to tackle the absurdities of the era head-on with a black comedy about the Vietnam War, which became *Apocalypse Now* (1979). At some point during the early stages of that project he changed his mind and nostalgia prevailed. He parted company with the project and promptly disappeared into his own world of light sabres and droids, though some of *Apocalypse Now* went with him.

Star Wars began as a straightforward attempt to remake *Flash Gordon*. On learning that the rights were too highly priced, Lucas resolved to create a story of his own.[5] In 1971 he offered the concept of modern riff on *Flash Gordon* to United Artists as part of a two-film deal along with *American Graffiti*. The title *The Star Wars* was duly registered with the Motion Picture Producers Association. Lucas did little with the project until early 1973 when he completed the editing of *American Graffiti*. His first steps were to generate a clutch of exotic yet distinctive names for his characters; a list of planets followed. This basic vocabulary would be shuffled and reshuffled throughout the writing process, though some was dropped. He thought better of calling his emperor 'Cos Dashit' and of having the character reference 'essence of Bum-Bum'. Many drafts turned on the struggle to possess the Kiber crystal, a stone with the power to amplify a mystic energy: The Force. Luke Skywalker had the much less sympathetic moniker of Luke Starkiller until the very eve of production. Multiple treatments and full scripts followed. Despite the reshuffling of names, the writing process is remarkable for the lack of resemblance between the different drafts. However, the notion of a space adventure in a universe unconnected to earth was consistent, mixing combat in ships with hand-to-hand swashbuckling as warriors from different generations fight to defeat tyranny.[6]

The writing process was a trial, but Lucas made a massive leap forward in early 1975 when he commissioned former Boeing artist Ralph McQuarrie to create designs for the core characters in the third draft. Responding to Lucas's script and a sheaf of old comic books that the director left with him, McQuarrie developed the look of key characters, including the droids and Darth Vader (whom he decided should have a complex face mask).[7] The images helped to solidify Lucas's ideas, giving a distinctive 'lived-in' look to the film. For all the fantasy of the story, *Star Wars* would work to sell its audience on the veracity of its setting by showing plenty of wear and tear. A year before release Lucas spoke about this aesthetic: 'What is required for true credibility', he told the *Los Angeles Times*, 'is a used future.'[8]

The technical challenges and linguistic oddities of the early drafts concerned both Universal and United Artists who passed on their options to make the film. The project was taken up by Alan Ladd Jr at 20th Century-Fox. The story is often told as one of Lucas persevering with the unloved SF genre. The reality was that there was something of a SF boom in progress. Many studios had SF projects on the blocks and Paramount was already working on plans to resurrect *Star Trek* in motion picture form. Lucas's producer Gary Kurtz surmised that Fox was looking for a successor to its profitable *Planet of the Apes* franchise.[9] But Lucas intended to go beyond the state-of-the-art. His script called for enormous sound stages, armies of model makers and animators, and computer controlled camerawork that would allow multiple effects to be built seamlessly into a single scene. His answer to the challenge of television was the rediscovery of overwhelming spectacle. Resolving to film in the UK, he recruited many of the British technicians who had worked on *2001: A Space Odyssey*, relocating some of them to the USA to develop the bespoke special effects house: Industrial Light and Magic. The result allowed Lucas to defy the audience's expectations and create a world in which the spaceships had bulk and scale, and moved with speed into and between the worlds rendered on the screen. The worlds presented were utterly alien and external but at the same time familiar and internal to the audience. He aimed to work with their cultural memories.

The dominant cultural memory in *Star Wars* was that of the SF of the past. The opening crawl to establish the back story was pure *Flash Gordon* – not least the conceit of identifying the film as 'Episode Four: A New Hope'[10] The film had the requisite spaceships, exotic aliens and robots. C3PO's design evoked Maria in *Metropolis* (1927) and his claim to fluency in over 6 million forms of communication echoed Robby's skills in *Forbidden Planet* (1956).

19. A *Star Wars* (1977) tribute to Frank Herbert's *Dune*: Lost on Tatooine, C3PO (Anthony Daniels) wanders past a skeleton of something very like a sand worm (Source: British Film Institute).

R2D2 owed something to the small robots in *Silent Running* (1971). The production design recycled the sort of images that had graced the covers of SF novels and magazines for decades. There were also nods to classic texts: the giant worm skeleton seen in the desert of Tatooine was a tribute to Frank Herbert's novel *Dune* (1965). Herbert later grumbled that the film owed too much to his book and undercut its ultimate adaptation for the screen by David Lynch, released in 1984.[11] Lucas also credited Edgar Rice Burroughs's John Carter of Mars stories (launched 1912, and source of the word 'Sith') and E.E. 'Doc' Smith's Lensman saga (published between 1934 and 1950, and source of word 'Coruscant' used for a planet later in the cycle).[12] *Star Wars* stepped directly into the existing vocabulary of blasters, hyperspace and star systems, and charmed aficionados with its deft evocation of a wider cosmos than anything seen before on the screen; accompanied by off-hand remarks about 'Clone Wars', the 'spice mines of Kessel' or 'bulls-eyeing wamp rats'. Lucas was similarly profligate with his on-screen creations. Creatures apparently worthy of an entire story in their own right appeared for just a few moments. Many hours of stop-motion photography went to create the side-sequence in which holographic monsters manoeuvre in a hi-tech board game. While Lucas and Kurtz protested that their film would not be science fiction, they were careful to market the film to the SF fan community, trusting that word of mouth would create a valuable pre-release buzz. Travelling on Lucas's own dime, Gary Kurtz and Mark Hamill duly appeared at the SF and comic book conventions including the World Science Fiction Convention in Kansas City some months before release with the C3PO and Darth Vader costumes, models of spacecraft, the Ralph McQuarrie pictures, and plenty of give-away buttons. The anticipated fan buzz began.[13]

Into his SF setting Lucas mixed elements from various genres. He described an early draft of the film as a blend of *Lawrence of Arabia* and James Bond,[14] but the adventure and fantasy genre were especially influential, including a princess in peril, wizards in hiding, tin men, magic swords and ancient orders of knights. There were numerous nods to King Arthur. Though the final cut lost scenes in which Luke Skywalker was teased by his peers in much the same way as the future king in T. H. White's *The Sword in the Stone* (1938), during its final polish the script had acquired an Arthurian joke. When C3PO first calls Luke 'Sir', Luke requests 'Call me Luke'. The robot misunderstands and inadvertently uses the chivalric: 'Sir Luke'. Knighthood is not otherwise mentioned in the saga, though the title of 'Lord' is much used. Even more prominent was America's own mythology: the western. This was referenced in Luke's desert home planet, with its settlers living in fear of nomadic tribesmen; a desperado filled cantina and the gunslinging Han Solo. There were even homages to particular films. Most obviously Luke's discovery of his family's deaths echoes a similar sequence in John Ford's *The Searchers* (1956). Charles Champlin in the *Los Angeles Times* coined a hybrid science fiction-Arthurian-wild west term for *Star Wars*: 'the once and future space western'.[15]

Reviewers at the time loved spotting these allusions, but some influences were underplayed or even missed altogether. The generational aspect of *Star Wars* provoked little comment, yet the film plainly reflected a generation's estrangement from its elders. With the principal exception of the good substitute father, Ben Kenobi, Luke Skywalker's world was thoroughly polarized by age. Even before the revelation of Darth Vader's true identity, the father generation was shown keeping boys on the farm, enforcing segregation in bars, blowing up planets, and marching around like Fascists. Lucas was reflecting the disillusionment of his contemporaries, who had come of age in the 1960s, as well as speaking for himself. The father figures in the first film were all rough contemporaries of his own father – George Lucas Sr – and were a little old to be potential parents of Luke Skywalker.[16] The SF setting allowed Lucas not only to push back against his father's generation but also to appropriate that generation's great cause, the Second World War, as a model for their resistance.

Though he was too young to remember the war itself, Lucas later spoke of its continued presence as he was growing up. 'I loved the war', he recalled. 'It was a big deal when I was growing up. It was on all the coffee tables in the form of books and on TV with things like *Victory at Sea*.'[17] One major trace of the war in *Star Wars* was in the costumes. The black formal uniforms of the imperial forces evoked those of Nazi Germany, Vader's helmet echoed the German 'coal scuttle' and his shock troops – described as dressed in 'fascistic white armoured suits' in the script – were not only known by the Nazi term as 'Storm Troopers' but carried a cylinder on the small of their back of the size and shape of a German gas mask canister. The costume designer John Mollo kept a guide to the uniforms of the Second World War on hand.[18] The Nazi uniforms were matched by Nazi acts, from precision assaults of the sort seen in newsreels of the attack on Poland, to full scale genocide: the extinction of an entire world merely to demonstrate the power of a battle station. The rebel campaign against the empire involved a number of Second World War tropes: Luke and Han man gun turrets like those on a Flying Fortress, and penetrate the Death Star in stolen uniforms as did the commando team in *The Guns of Navarone* (1961). The battle at the end mixes dogfight sequences that Lucas based on films like *Battle of Britain* (1969) and *Tora! Tora! Tora!* with a special bombing mission like those seen in *The Dam Busters* (1955) or *633 Squadron* (1964). The final film even matched *The Dam Busters'* structure with dramatic cuts between the action in space and the anxious group waiting for news back at base, with closely matching dialogue. Lucas had literally taped these sequences from the television, transferred them to film and edited them into the sort of scenes that he needed as a guide for his animators, whose models were already Second World War hybrids as they were frequently built from cannibalized model kits.[19]

There were other subtle tributes to the Second World War film, as with the subplot in which Han Solo insisted on his maintaining neutrality and self-interest until the last moment, conformed to a familiar pattern in the films made on or depicting the eve of US entry into the war, most notably *Casablanca* (1942). The most curious borrowing from the war was a lift from the Nazi propaganda film *Triumph of the Will* (1935) for the final scene in which the conquering heroes are honoured by massed ranks of rebels. Lucas defended the final scene as 'what happens when you put a large military group together and give out an award'.[20] He later staged a much more anarchic celebration to mark the ultimate fall of the emperor in *Return of the Jedi* (1983).

As well as generational politics, *Star Wars* was marked by the ethnic politics of its time. Ethnic representation and misrepresentation remained a charged issue in the wake of the Civil Rights movement and its sequel in Black Power. This posed a problem for a project that sought to evoke the adventure genres of the past, which dealt liberally in currency of bwanas/sahibs and

20. Feudal Japan meets Nazi Germany in space: John Mollo's costumes for *Star Wars* (1977) (Source: British Film Institute).

effendis and their native allies, enemies, and background characters. Even so, Lucas considered a multicultural line-up for the film: he thought of finding a Eurasian princess Leia and he nearly cast an African American, Glynn Turman, as Han Solo. In the last analysis it was the issue of depicting inter-racial romance that frightened him into his 'all white' line-up. He told his biographer: 'I didn't want to make *Guess Who's Coming to Dinner* (1967) at that point, so I sort of backed off.'[21] Yet race remained ubiquitous in *Star Wars*. The production designers raided collections of ethnographic objects and languages to create their new 'others'. The Sand People used Fijian war clubs; the Jawas spoke speeded up Zulu and Swahili, while the low-life Gredo used an electronically distorted Quechua dialect of Peru.[22] The SF setting allowed the representation of difference in exaggerated forms – strong, instinctive, dark skinned (or furry) buddies, effeminate servants and smelly desert scavengers/slave traders – that could proliferate without fear of offence. More than this, the film allowed its audience to glory in a world of difference.[23]

One racial 'other' held a special fascination for Lucas and, given the success of the film, one may suspect that many people in 1970s America shared it. The director was strongly drawn to East Asia and to Japanese culture in particular. The script was heavily influenced by Akira Kurosawa's film *The Hidden Fortress* (1958) and Lucas considered casting Japanese star

Toshiro Mifune as Obi Wan or, as Alan Ladd Jr recalled, even working with an entirely Japanese cast.[24] East Asia was present in the costumes (designer John Mollo also kept books on Japanese armour to hand); there were pseudo-Asiatic names and terms (including the word Jedi, borrowed from the Japanese term for the Kurosawa-style period drama: *jidaigeki*); there was a pseudo-Asiatic culture with mystic monks urging their disciples to 'reach out' with their feelings. The abstraction of *Star Wars* allowed Americans to imagine themselves in samurai adventures without being limited to tales of westerners shipwrecked in feudal Japan in the manner of the protagonist in James Clavell's novel *Shogun* (1975), which was a runaway bestseller during the making of *Star Wars*. No less significantly, *Star Wars* allowed Americans to identify with analogues of the Vietcong, without obliging them to rejoice in the destruction of their own countrymen or considering the role of the United States in Asian history more widely, with its missionaries, military interventions and two atomic bombs.[25]

The film also had a place in the gender politics of the 1970s. Lucas wrote the part of Princess Leia as an active agent rather than a passive damsel in distress. She was a twin of the hero in structure long before the cycle revealed her to be so in fact. The closing scene placed her powerfully centre stage with the ability to choose between her rescuers. Yet much was left out of *Star Wars* and it seemed as though Lucas would be intimidated by too much female empowerment. Despite the promise of Tom Jung's art work on the poster, Leia's sexuality was repressed: a breach with tradition in the genre. Moreover, there were few other women to be found in the piece. *Star Wars* was scant female liberation.[26]

The final and most far-reaching element within *Star Wars* did attract the critics' comments: the film's strong religious and mythic dimension. Lucas had been raised as a Methodist and had internalized notions of good, evil, redemption and transcendence from that tradition. He sharpened this by revisiting the biblical epics of the 1950s – especially *Ben Hur* (1959) – during the writing process. The second and third drafts (both 1975) open with a pseudo-biblical quote: '... and in the greatest despair shall come a savior, and he shall be known as The Son of the Suns'. The source given was *The Journal of Whills*, 3: 127, a reference to the imagined origin of the saga.[27] The third draft has characters underlining the religious dimension of their culture with the religious oath: 'holy maker'.[28] In the final film the blessing 'May the Force be with you' mirrors 'May the Lord be with you', used in many Christian liturgies. Obi Wan's parting line to Luke 'the Force will be with you always' echoes the final words of Christ in the Gospel of Matthew: 'I will be with you always, even to the end of the age.'[29] One advantage of the complete abstraction of *Star Wars* from earth is that it enabled the evocation of a universal religion (quite literally) without stepping on any one group's toes. An emphasis on religious commonalities was not alien to the Normal Rockwell world of George Lucas's youth. The idea of a Golden Rule uniting all people of faith was often emphasised in the era – witness Rockwell's painting evoking the principle of 1961 – and was variously embedded in Modesto, from the religious tolerance in the Boy Scout manual (Lucas was a member) to the respect for the many pathways to the Supreme Being at the local Masonic Lodge.[30]

Whatever influences Lucas absorbed from his youth were overlaid with student reading in eastern and archaic religions. The idea of 'The Force' was adapted from the 'Life Force' in the writings of Carlos Castenada.[31] There was a deep engagement with the work of scholar of myths, Joseph Campbell who Lucas first read as a student and re-read during the re-drafting of his scripts. Lucas crafted his protagonist Luke Skywalker as the latest incarnation of Campbell's 'Hero with a Thousand Faces': the youth on a journey to discover his own destiny and renew his own culture. Other mythic archetypes also emerged. Han Solo filled the shoes of the trickster hero, a Ulysses able to convert his ship into a Trojan horse at a moment's notice.[32] But the significance of these borrowings from religion and myth was not merely to create a story. As any reader of Campbell would understand, myth is not just entertainment or an instructional allegory. A myth is an agent of re-creation with the power to restore a community. Lucas really wanted to save the world. To this end he also drew on the mythic dimensions of the genres he incorporated into the film: the heroism of the classic space serial; the simplicity of the black hat/white hat duels of the Western; the drive to overcome absolute evil of Second World War propaganda; the promise of redemption of the religious epic. Lucas bound all these elements into one with the intent to giving his audience the experience of believing once again. 'I wanted to make a kids' film that would strengthen contemporary mythology and introduce a kind of basic morality' he told his biographer Dale Pollock. 'Nobody's saying the very basic things; they're dealing in the abstract. Everybody's forgetting to tell the kids, "Hey this is right and this is wrong." '[33]

The final months of work on *Star Wars* were tense. Twentieth Century-Fox pulled the plug on the budget before Lucas was satisfied and he thought of the film as 'abandoned' rather than complete. Lucas's friends were dubious that the final film would work, though the addition of John Williams's rousing score helped. Meanwhile the Fox publicity machine swung into action, marketing the film for six months or so before release using the tagline 'a long time ago in a galaxy far, far away', and pledging 'coming soon to a galaxy near you'.[34]

The studio released the film mid-week on Wednesday 25 May 1977. The opening was an overwhelming success. Lucas forgot the date had moved forward and was himself caught in the crowds outside Mann's Chinese Theatre in Hollywood. His formula had worked. The audience's adulation was a testament to the extent that Lucas was answering a public need. Fox analysts found that much more than any other picture, people came to *Star Wars* because of word of mouth recommendations. News reports spoke of lines looping round city blocks; people going to see the film several times; and canny investors calling their brokers from crowded lobbies to order 20th Century-Fox stock. Within a matter of weeks the film had made back its production cost and Fox stock had risen 70 per cent.[35]

For most American critics, *Star Wars* was a welcome shot in the arm for the country and the business of film-making. They adored its escapism and its playful tributes to the films of the past, though a few doubters felt it was too derivative or simplistic.[36] Some reviewers spoke explicitly of the recent and traumatic past. Pete Hamill in the *Chicago Tribune* proclaimed:

> It's a perfect film for a time when no Americans are dying anywhere in a war, when no American bombs are landing on anyone, when no President is facing indictment, or impeachment. If it has anything to say it is this: for now the American wars are over on the earth, and now they are happening out there in the galaxy of the imagination. And that's just where they should be.[37]

Many reviewers and members of audiences who were interviewed for the press coverage of the film commented on its moral impact. Gene Siskel in the *Chicago Tribune* hailed the film as a work of moral value in Platonic terms that expresses 'ideals like goodness and virtue so that we are able to imagine them once again'.[38] Similarly the critic of the *LA Herald Examiner* wrote: '*Star Wars* is the Saturday matinee of our lives rolled into one irresistible fantasy seductive enough to make lifetime movie addicts out of the young and born-again innocents out of the rest of us. Director George Lucas gives us back our dreams.'[39] It did not take long for clergymen to begin preaching sermons that took *Star Wars* as their text.[40] Lucas has observed that representatives of every major religion have at some point claimed *Star Wars* as embodying their approach.[41] The studio began to receive letters about how *Star Wars* had changed audience members' lives, suggesting that the initial response to *Star Wars* should be read as an episode in the religious as much as the economic history of the United States.[42]

Although some of the context for *Star Wars* was specific to the United States, enough was shared to ensure that the western world reacted similarly to the film. International audiences had endured their own crises of faith, their own economic doldrums and had shared the same cynical cinematic diet as Americans. By the time the film got its international release in the autumn and early winter of 1977, they had also been thoroughly primed with media accounts of *Star Wars* mania in the USA. British schoolboys knew the music, had seen the stills, and even read the novelization before getting a chance to line-up in the winter rain to see the film. Derek Malcolm in *The Guardian* wrote that *Star Wars* offered 'enormous and exhilarating fun for those who are prepared to settle down in their seats and let it all wash over them. Which I firmly believe ... is more or less exactly what the vast majority of the cinema-going public want just now.'[43] International box office returns suggested that he was correct.[44]

There were some reservations. The racial politics of *Star Wars* initially passed without comment but on 17 July a black actor – Raymond St. Jacques – who confessed he had seen the film four times without noticing, wrote to the *Los Angeles Times* to complain about the absence of black faces in George Lucas's future or other films like *2001* and *Logan's Run*. He noted that the only African-American in the piece was the voice of pure evil. 'Why in the Force's name' he asked 'must our film creators continue to perpetuate the destructive ideals that put man against man, brother against brother and nation against nation?'[45] The paper received a flood of follow-up mail, which it dubbed 'the black-lash over *Star Wars*'. Some readers noted the secondary roles assigned to the non-human others as racism by proxy. 'I'm also concerned with the Wookie', wrote one lady, '... where was his medal at the end?'[46] The sequels/prequels included African-American characters, but did not escape accusations of tokenism.

Other observers were appalled by the hype around *Star Wars*. The film spawned a bewildering array of merchandising deals and it seemed that Lucas would be making his fortune from that rather than mere box office receipts. The *Star Wars* novelization was available even before the release of the film; the T-shirts, trading cards and spin-off comic books followed swiftly thereafter and the toys arrived in time for Christmas 1977 in the United States. The merchandise has never left the shops. The merchandise was not merely a parasitic coda to the films. The spin-off novels especially developed into a symbiotic parallel area of creativity whose success demonstrated the continued viability of the saga beyond the initial trilogy. But it was still big business. The film and its successors developed an odd relationship to global capitalism. From the early drafts Lucas had sniped at 'ruthless trader barons driven by greed and lust for power' in the screenplay, and yet the film became an object for global consumption and an element in the great game of the rise of a multi-national media empire.[47]

Star Wars also attracted criticism for its politics. Ironically, a text created by a confirmed liberal was seen as proto fascist and 'the cultural beginning of the Reagan era'.[48] Lucas countered by asserting the democratic content of the film and its presentation of the basic tale of the deterioration of a republic into tyranny and back to democracy.[49] The reality was that Star Wars was open enough as a text to be appropriated for multiple purposes. Any crusader could claim to be Luke Skywalker. President Reagan certainly tapped into the language of Star Wars, dubbing the Soviet Union of the early 1980s 'an evil empire'. His supporters used 'Star Wars' as the nickname for the Strategic Defense Initiative: a space-based anti-missile system. Lucas disliked this intensely and attempted to sue to prevent the term appearing in pro-Reagan commercials. He lost.[50] Later appropriators of the Jedi mantle included the Oklahoma City bomber, Tim McVeigh, who defended his mass murder of Federal workers and their children to a friend by comparing them to 'storm troopers in the movie Star Wars': 'They may be individually innocent, but because they are part of the evil empire they were guilty by association.'[51] In the political mainstream, Senator John McCain compared himself to 'Luke Skywalker trying to get out of the Death Star' during his bid for the Republican presidential nomination in 2000 and began wielding a light sabre at rallies.[52]

The runaway success of Star Wars meant that within days of its opening, the newspapers were speculating on sequels. Before the end of the year Lucas was at work on The Empire Strikes Back (1980). This second film brought complexity to the story, developing the romance between Han Solo and Princess Leia and challenging the simplistic externality of evil in the first film. Luke Skywalker learns that evil was not external to him but within: a dark side common to all. At the film's climax he feels this in the most fundamental way with the revelation that his nemesis, Darth Vader, was his father. It is clear from the script development that this plot twist came late in the creative process, but it provided the thread to tie an entire saga together.[53] The remaining films honed in on inter-generational issues. Luke's struggle with and successful redemption of his father provides the closure of the first three films in Return of the Jedi (1983). The engine of Anakin Skywalker's transition through the three prequels – The Phantom Menace (1999), Attack of the Clones (2002) and Revenge of the Sith (2005) – into the Darth Vader is also parental: he is separated from and then loses his mother, and is unable to bear a threat to his lover/mother substitute. The extent of Anakin's fall would be illustrated with an act of inter-generational violence: his killing of the younglings, the child Jedi in training.[54]

The transition from the first trilogy to the second reflected a shift in the family relationships of George Lucas and his generation. Lucas and his contemporaries really did have to come to terms with the realization that their fathers had made profound mistakes, both at home and in the wider world. The generation that won the Second World War had also rallied to Joseph McCarthy, turned a blind eye to segregation, sent its sons to fight a war in Vietnam, polluted the environment, and elected Nixon. By the new millennium the boomers had moved on. They were softening towards their fathers as their fathers moved first into old age and death, and then on into memory, and as the baby boomers experienced parenthood for themselves. It makes sense that Lucas, who lost his own father in 1991, would develop a new trilogy in which the dark father figure becomes the hero. By 2000 his generation, which had vilified its fathers in the 1960s and 70s, now hailed them as 'the Greatest Generation'.

The prequels had their share of contemporary comment. The final instalment in 2005 fixed the films politically with transparent attacks on President George W. Bush and the erosion of civil liberties associated with his War on Terror. The president's 'with us or against us' line was appropriated by Anakin (Hayden Christensen) and rejected by Obi Wan (Ewan McGregor): 'Only the Sith deal in absolutes'. 'This is how liberty dies,' the disillusioned Padmé (Natalie Portman) mourns, 'with thunderous applause.' The conservative blogosphere raged against Lucas in the aftermath and even attempted to organize a boycott of the film.[55]

What then is the legacy of *Star Wars*? The film certainly prepared the way for a legion of other films set in galaxies both far away and nearer to hand, including Disney's *The Black Hole* (1979) and Roger Corman's space version of *Seven Samurai/The Magnificent Seven*: *Battle Beyond the Stars* (1980).[56] George Lucas did not always welcome the imitation. Fox sued MCI over its *Star Wars*-inspired TV show *Battlestar Galactica* (1978–9), claiming that it stole the 'look and feel' of Lucas's work. The suit failed.[57] Although the SF genre was alive and well, *Star Wars* kicked it into hyper-drive. It emboldened producers to consider adapting the serious authors like Philip K. Dick. It changed the economics of motion pictures in general and SF pictures in particular, proving the value of merchandizing and marketing to a family audience. It also provided a technological base with spin-off companies like Industrial Light and Magic, Skywalker Sound and Pixar, which made more SF possible, affordable and better to look at. Even *Star Wars* became better to look at as Lucas cannily enhanced the effects in the original trilogy in 1997 and completed the films as he originally wished, as part of the lead up to the prequels.[58]

It is difficult to underestimate the centrality of *Star Wars* to the generation who grew up watching it. One only need glance at any American street at Halloween, or surf fan sites on the web, or scan toy shop or bookshop shelves or a videogame line-up to glimpse its ubiquity. The spin-off television series *Star Wars: The Clone Wars* (2009–) is bringing a new generation of fans to the franchise. Google has licensed the term 'Droid' as a name for its smart phone. Fan generated media continues to proliferate including fan-edits of the films that bite the hand of George Lucas by minimizing the appearances of unpopular characters (principally JarJar Binks). Fan-made *Star Wars* tributes abound on You Tube, including multiple episodes of *Chad Vader: Day Shift Manager* (the adventures Darth Vader's brother in a mini-mart) and such oddities as *Star Wars* scenes performed on the New York Subway. [59] The volume of this material is such that they have had their own fan film awards since 2002.[60] There have been tribute episodes of major television shows including *Friends* (airing 1996); several episodes of *The Simpsons*; a trilogy of extended parodies on both *Family Guy* (airing in 2007, 2009 and 2011) and *Robot Chicken* (airing in 2007, 2008 and 2010); and numerous references in the cult British comedy: *Spaced* (1999–2001). *South Park* pushed back against Lucas tweaking the saga in an episode in the 2002 season. Entire feature films have revolved around *Star Wars* fan culture such as *Fan Boys* (2008) or *Paul* (2011). There are over 8,000 storm trooper re-enactors (the 501st Legion), who march around in costume as if they were creating a genuine episode in Earth's military history.[61] There are conventions, theme park rides, an annual theme park festival (at Walt Disney World, Florida), and a *Star Wars* holiday celebrated by fans on 4 May as a play on 'May the fourth be with you'.

Although born in trauma, *Star Wars* has outlived the moment of genesis to become a cultural institution in its own right. *Star Wars* is now about itself. *Star Wars* films are held in sufficient public regard to justify further re-mastering and re-formatting, including a theatrical re-release of the entire cycle in a 3D format beginning in 2012. Fans complain and feel ignored or exploited, but continue to pay. The films still trade on nostalgia but it is no longer nostalgia for a lost world of pirates, westerns, samurai or wartime heroics. Today *Star Wars* trades on nostalgia for *Star Wars*.

Notes

1   See for example Kurtz to *Time* magazine, '*Star Wars*: The year's best movie', *Time*, 30 May 1977.
2   A.D. Murphy, '*Star Wars*', *Variety*, 24 May 1977.
3   Dale Pollock, *Skywalking: The Life and Films of George Lucas* (New York: Da Capo, 1999), p.145.
4   Quoted in Griel Marcus, 'The style of the 70's: Pop culture pop', *New York Times*, 5 June 1977, p.B6.

5   J. W. Rinzler, *The Making of Star Wars* (New York: Del Rey, 2007), p.4; Michael Kaminski, *The Secret History of Star Wars: The Art of Storytelling and the making of a modern epic* (Kingston, Ontario: Legacy Books, 2008), p.42.

6   Many of the draft scripts and treatments are now in the public domain and readily available online – see for example: www.benandgrover.com/scripts.asp Last accessed: 7 June 2012 Archive copies of the first draft may be found at the USC cinematic arts library and the Herrick library, which also holds the first treatment. For detailed accounts of the evolution of the screenplays see Kaminski, *The Secret History of Star Wars* and Rinzler, *The Making of Star Wars*.

7   Kaminski, *The Secret History of Star Wars*, p.98. McQuarrie's idea was that the Storm troopers and Vader should be able to operate in the vacuum of space.

8   Charles Champlin, 'Futurist film's tricks to treat the eye', *Los Angeles Times*, 20 June 1976, Calendar p.1.

9   Rinzler, *The Making of Star Wars*, p.12.

10 The unconventional opening was not without cost to Lucas. It broke the rules for credits established by the Director's Guild of America, resulting in a fine and prompted his resignation from the guild.

11 Writing just before his death, Herbert noted: 'David [Lynch] had trouble with the fact that *Star Wars* used up so much of *Dune*. We found sixteen points of identity between my novel and *Star Wars*. That is not to say that this was other than a coincidence, even though we figured the odds against coincidence and produced a number larger than the number of stars in the sky.' From the preface to Frank Herbert, *Eye* (New York: ibooks/Simon & Schuster, 1985), p.13. The passage was quoted in *Hollywood Reporter*, 10 October 1986, the writer speculating that had he lived, Herbert might have sued.

12 Pollock, *Skywalking*, p.142; Kaminski, *The Secret History of Star Wars*, p.471.

13 Chris Salewicz, *George Lucas*, (New York: Thunder's Mouth Press, 1999), p.69; Rinzler, *The Making of Star Wars*, p.291.

14 George Lucas to *Camplin* magazine, fall 1973, as cited in Kaminski, *The Secret History of Star Wars*, p.61. He was perhaps referencing the contrasting settings of the film – an epic rendering of a Lawrence-style desert shifting to Bond-ian high-tech fortress. Both models were in themselves descendants of a knight errant narrative.

15 Charles Champlin, '*Star Wars* hails the once and future space western', *LA Times*, 27 May 1977, p.X1.

16 George W. Lucas Sr was born in 1913; Peter Cushing (Grand Moff Tarkin) was born in 1913; Alec Guinness (Ben Kenobi) was born in 1914, Phil Brown (Uncle Owen) was born in 1916. Of the minor characters, Eddie Byne (General Willard) was born in 1911 and Ted Burnett (uncredited as Wuher the barman) was born in 1926. The actor eventually cast to play the face of Darth Vader/Anakin Skywalker – Sebastian Shaw – was the oldest, born 1905, though his age may have been a way to show the ravages of his injuries rather than to fix him in time. Mark Hamill was born in 1951 and Lucas in 1944. Lucas felt that some elements of *Star Wars* were a tribute to his father, specifically the entrepreneurism of Han Solo. See Pollock, *Skywalking*, p.166.

17 Pollock, *Skywalking*, p.36. Lucas's father did not serve in the war.

18 Pollock, *Skywalking*, p.160.

19 For Lucas's own account of this process see Stephen Zito, 'George Lucas goes far out', in *American Film*, April 1977, pp.8–13, anthologized in Sally Kline, *George Lucas Interviews* (Jackson, MS: University Press of Mississippi, 1999). The parallel dialogue is as follows: *Dam Busters*: 'How many guns do you think there are, Trevor?' 'I'd say they're about ten guns – some in the field and some in the towers.' *Star Wars*: 'How many guns do you think, Gold Five?' 'I'd say about thirty guns – some on the surface,

some in the towers.' And, *Dam Busters*: 'I'll fly across the dam as you make your run and try to draw the flak off you.' *Star Wars*: 'I'm going to cut across the axis and try and draw their fire.'

20   Rinzler, *The Making of Star Wars*, pp.296–7.

21   Pollock, *Skywalking*, p. 151. [recently seen as the teacher/rogue scientist in *Super 8* (2011)]

22   Pollock, Skywalking, p.179. The present author had the pleasure of viewing the *Return of the Jedi* with the renowned scholar of Tibet, Robin Kornman, who confirmed that the Ewoks speak a speeded-up Tibetan. Much of their dialogue translates as 'What's this? What's this? It's a microphone.'

23   By the 1980s Lucas was bold enough to present his ethnic stereotypes more directly, reviving the earth-bound adventure genre with the Indiana Jones films.

24   Pollock, *Skywalking*, p.151; Charles Champlin, *George Lucas: The Creative Impulse* (New York: Harry N. Abrams, 1997), p.42.

25   Lucas's comparison of the good guys to North Vietnam and the Empire to America is documented by Rinzler, *The Making of Star Wars*, p.16. Obsession with the victor's culture is a common reaction to defeat in war.

26   For an exploration of *Star Wars* and gender see Diana Dominguez,'Feminism and the Force: Empowerment and Disillusionment in a Galaxy Far, Far Away', in Carl Silvio and Tony M. Vinci, *Culture, identities and technology in Star Wars films* (Jefferson, NC: McFarland, 2007), pp.109–32.

27   The epigram echoes one traditional title for Jesus Christ – 'King of Kings' – taken from the First Epistle of Timothy 6: 15 and Revelations 17: 14 and 19: 16 and used to title biblical epics in 1927 and 1961.

28   This oath echoes C3PO's line in the eventual film on taking a bath: 'Thank the maker', which, when coming from a robot can either reference a deity or his manufacturer.

29   Matthew 28: 20.

30   On Lucas's scouting see Pollock, *Skywalking*, p.21. There is an affectionate picture of scouting in *Indiana Jones and Last Crusade*. There were two Masonic Lodges in Modesto when Lucas was growing up: Stanislaus Lodge No. 206 F&AM and Modesto Lodge No. 675 F&AM. Both met at the Masonic Hall located at 15th and J streets from 1917 to 1971. The lodges were very much a part of town life, and youth activities included dances organized by their youth groups DeMolay, Job's Daughters, or Rainbow Girls; however, according to the present secretary of Modesto Lodge 206 – Mike Americh – there is no record of George Sr having been a member of either lodge or of George Jr participating in the youth activities.

31   See especially Carlos Castenada, *The Teachings of Don Juan: A Yaqui Way of Knowledge* (Berkeley: University of California Press, 1968).

32   Joseph Campbell, *The Hero with a Thousand Faces* (Princeton: Princeton University Press, 1968).

33   Pollock, *Skywalking*, p.144.

34   Lobby cards and newspaper advertisements are preserved in the core collection of the Herrick library.

35   For a typical audience story see Lee Grant, '*Star Wars* out of this world', *Los Angeles Times*, 4 June 1977, p.B8; the stockbrokers are reported in Gary Arnold, 'Star Wars', *Washington Post*, 25 May 1977, p.B1. For a narrative of the opening see Rinzler, *The Making of Star Wars*, pp.292–296; Pollock, *Skywalking*, pp.185–186.

36   Nelson George, '*Star Wars*: A Space Morality Film', *New York Amsterdam News*, 4 June 1977, p.D3. Prominent negative reviews appeared in *The New Republic* and *New York Magazine* and in December 1977 in the UK from Barry Norman on the *Film 77* program on BBC TV. Norman contrasted the 'easy answers' of *Star Wars* with the complexity of the work of Howard Hawks who had just died.

37 Pete Hamill, 'Star Wars: dumb good times here again?' Chicago Tribune, 8 June 1977, p.A13.

38 Gene Siskel, 'Plato would have loved Star Wars', Chicago Tribune, 5 June 1977, p.16.

39 Richard Cuskelly, 'Star Wars, "I believe, I believe"', LA Herald Examiner, 25 May 1977, p.B1.

40 A priest's endorsement of Star Wars is cited in Siskel, 'Plato would have loved Star Wars', and the author himself heard more than one Star Wars themed sermon and school assembly in the UK in 1978.

41 Pamela Mason Wanger (dir.), George Lucas/Bill Moyers, The Mythology of Star Wars, (WNET New York, 1999) available on YouTube at www.youtube.com/watch?v=5HeXWoz6Ixo Last accessed: 7 June 2012.

42 A year later in April 1978 Gary Kurtz attempted to cool off the religious attention by speaking of Star Wars as a simple parable at LA's First Congregational Church. John Dart, 'Star Wars religious impact in parable form', Los Angeles Times, 1 May 1978.

43 Derek Malcolm, 'Lucas in the sky with diamonds', Guardian, 27 December 1977.

44 On foreign business see 'Star Wars overseas', Variety (weekly), 15 February 1978 and 'Star Wars overseas' Variety (daily), 3 February 1978. On success in Japan see Fox press release of 26 June 1978, Star Wars microfiche 10, core collection, Herrick Library.

45 Raymond St. Jacques, 'The great white void', Los Angeles Times, 17 July 1977, p.R2.

46 'The Blacklash over Star Wars', Los Angeles Times, 24 July 1977, Calendar, p.32.

47 For an exploration of this issue see Carlo Silvio, 'Trilogies and global capitalism', Silvio and Vinci, Culture, identities and technology in Star Wars films, pp.53–73. The quote is from the opening of the third draft from August 1975.

48 This argument is made in Tom Carson, 'Jedi uber alles', in Glenn Kenny, A Galaxy not so far away: Writers and artists on twenty five years of Star Wars (New York: Henry Holt, 2002), pp.160–171.

49 See Debbie Dykstra, 'George Lucas lets Ian McDiarmid and Hayden Christensen get their Revenge in Episode III' Science Fiction Weekly, 2005 accessed online at http://www.libertyparkusafd.org/Star%20Wars/primers%5CIan%20McDiarmid%20and%20Hayden%20Christensen%20get%20their%20Revenge%20in%20Episode%20III.htm accessed: 7 June 2012 This allegory was present for most of the development but not in the earliest versions of the story. The rough draft of May 1974 did not posit a good republic replaced by an evil empire, but good (old) and bad (new) empires.

50 For coverage of this lawsuit see 'Star Wars film makers sue over name in defense ad', Wall Street Journal, 13 November 1985; 'US judge bars Star Wars suit', New York Times, 14 November 1985; 'Lucas loses name battle', Variety (daily), 2 December 1985.

51 Jo Thomas, 'Friend says McVeigh wanted bombing to start an "uprising"',' New York Times, 13 May 1997, p.1.

52 James Bennet, 'Evangelist goes on attack to help Bush', New York Times, 22 February 2000, p.1.

53 On the Empire Strikes Back see J. W. Rinzler, The Making of The Empire Strikes Back (New York: Del Rey, 2010).

54 The origin of the bounty hunter Boba Fett was also tied to the loss of a father.

55 David M. Halbfinger, 'Star Wars is quickly politicized', New York Times, 19 May 2005, p.1.

56 For initial coverage of imitations see Joseph McBride, 'Star Wars latest pic to film itself in the vanguard of a film-making trend', Variety (daily), 10 June 1977, pp.1,5.

57 On the Battlestar Galactica suit see Lane Maloney, 'Galactica not in violation of Wars c'right, judge says', Variety (daily), 25 August 1980 pp.1,15; 'Star Wars, Galactica to battle in court', LA Herald Examiner, 12 January 1983; Lane Maloney, 'Litigation haunts two outer space pics; rule Universal is not a pirate', Variety (weekly), 27 August 1980. Battlestar's creator, Glen A. Larson, had first imagined his show in

1968, but was unable to sell it until after the success of *Star Wars*. Universal launched an equally unsuccessful counter suit that Lucas had violated the copyright of *Silent Running*.

[58] For a technological history see Michael Rubin, *Droidmaker: George Lucas and the Digital Revolution* (Gainsville, FL: Triad Publishing, 2006).

[59] For Chad Vader see the official site www.blamesociety.net/chadvader Last accessed: 7 June 2012. The subway film is: Improv Everywhere, *Star Wars subway car* online at www.youtube.com/watch?v=J5gCeWEGiQI Last accessed: 7 June 2012.

[60] For the awards website see www.atom.com/channel/channel_star_wars Last accessed: 7 June 2012.

[61] The Legion is now worldwide but originated in 1997 in the epicentre of Civil War re-enactment, South Carolina. They have excellent relations with Lucasfilm and as a tribute to their work for charity, Lucas wrote the legion into *Revenge of the Sith*. For the legion's website see: www.501st.com/ Last accessed: 7 June 2012.

RUST-BELT MESSIAH: *ROBOCOP* (1987)

The blockbuster SF cinema of the late 1970s and early 1980s demonstrated clearly what the new technology of the motion picture could achieve. The initial *Star Wars* trilogy, *Close Encounters of the Third Kind* (1977), *E.T.: The Extra-Terrestrial* (1982) and their ilk traded on the impact of their special effects. Yet vast resources were certainly not a prerequisite for innovation. In the parallel realm of comic books a new era was taking shape. Artists had begun to challenge the conventions of their genre and to win new audiences with darker visions of the present and the future. Masters of this renaissance included Frank Miller, who had brought a renewed edge to the Marvel universe and re-imagined Batman in *Batman: The Dark Knight Returns* (1986), and the creative energies associated with the British comics *2000AD* and *Warrior*, such as writer, Alan Moore. At the same time literary SF ruminated upon the relationship between human beings and technology, ricocheting off *Blade Runner* (1982) into the labyrinth of cyborgs and psychosis that was the emerging cyberpunk genre. These stories and sensibilities were slow to translate to the big screen. James Cameron's *The Terminator* (1984) led the first surge. *RoboCop* (1987) followed up. Violent, edgy, with a mythic almost biblical edge to the story and a visual approach torn straight from the pages of Frank Miller, *RoboCop* strode onto the screens of America in the summer of 1987 and blasted its way to box office success. It opened the way to further films in cyberpunk themes and with the same comic book visuals. But *RoboCop*'s interest lies in more than its style. The film set out to comment on its times as surely as any of the works of Swift. It is a fascinating document of late 1980s America, as the country awoke to the downside of the Reagan revolution.

RoboCop began in the mind of an employee of Paramount named Edward Neumeier. His task at the studio was to read and evaluate literary properties for possible purchase and production as feature films. As the 1980s progressed Neumeier became increasingly fascinated by the comic books and graphic stories that passed across his desk, featuring characters like Rom, Machine Man, Iron Man and, from the UK, Judge Dredd. Paramount was less impressed and so was his next employer Columbia. Moving into the realm of production first at Columbia and then Marty Ransohoff productions, Neumeier formed a plan to strike out on his own and write his own screenplay in the spirit of this new dark comic book art. In the summer of 1984 he completed his first treatment entitled: *RoboCop: The Future of Law Enforcement*. It made no secret of its influences. On the title page where some writers might have quoted a Nobel laureate, Neumeier quoted his own brand of heroes. Iron Man: 'I love it when the bad guys try to hurt me...Yeah, I eat this stuff up with a spoon...Go ahead. Be dumb enough to hit me.' Machine Man: 'Keep away! You're a blasted freak!' 'No, I'm a machine...A machine that just saved your life!' Judge Dredd: 'You're next punk.'[1]

Many elements of story, characters (including names), dialogue and even the tag line used in the initial treatment, survived to be used in the final film. The plot in the initial pitch, as in the final film was this: in the near future a corporation is seeking to regenerate the urban wasteland of Old Detroit and build 'Delta City'. They run the police force as a privatized business, but are having difficulty establishing the law and order they need to begin major construction. The number two at the company – Dick Jones – has thrown his weight behind the creation of a law enforcement droid called ED 209 to accomplish this, but during a boardroom demonstration, the fearsome robot accidentally kills a young executive. The CEO (known only as The Old Man) proclaims himself 'very disappointed' and an ambitious junior executive – Morton – sees his opportunity and proposes that the corporation try his pet project instead: RoboCop. Meanwhile a good cop named Murphy is gunned down by a ruthless gangster named Clarence Boddicker. From Murphy's point of view the audience sees doctors, flashbacks to family, then scientists and 'grids and gun sights' as he is rebuilt into a cyborg policeman: RoboCop. His face is hidden within a helmet and the memories of his former life are erased.

RoboCop is immediately assigned to the streets where he rapidly hunts down criminals and becomes a darling of the media. When he begins to remember his old life and investigates the gang responsible for his 'death' he becomes a threat to Jones (who is secretly the boss of this gang). Jones engineers the murder of Morton and then convinces the corporation that RoboCop has gone rogue. Massive force is deployed to destroy RoboCop. He is rescued by his female partner – Officer Lewis – who has recognized his true identity. Lewis takes him to an abandoned factory where RoboCop uses the remaining machinery to rebuild himself. He is seen without his visor. Reborn, he arrests Clarence and defeats the ED 209 robot. He then forces entry to the corporation's boardroom where he exposes Jones as the true villain and kills him. The movie ends with RoboCop back on duty, protecting the city at night.

There were some differences from the final film. In this first iteration RoboCop was powered by drug-like intravenous infusions – he was to be seen shooting-up with 'a stimulant cartridge' before going into action. There was also a key plot trajectory in which RoboCop was to be exposed to the 'evils' of alcohol by a grizzled old sergeant and to go off the rails – driven into despair by memories of his previous life and knowledge that he had lost his wife and son. In the initial treatment, when drunk and pursuing Clarence, he crashes a car into a school, killing teachers and wounding children, thereby losing public support. He is also misdirected by Jones into being the actual agent of the murder of Morton, and sexually harasses his partner Lewis. She recognizes the good still in him and perseveres to win him back to the side of true justice. The fall and redemption of the hero was a common enough trope in heroic literature from the biblical story of Samson to *Superman III* (1983). *RoboCop* would be a stronger story without it.[2]

Daunted by the prospect of developing a full screenplay Neumeier was open to collaboration on the next phase of the project. He found a suitable partner in much the same way that he had found his initial idea. Paramount set him reviewing student film projects in search of undiscovered talent. He saw a film by Michael Miner (then working as a music video director) and called him in to talk about a job. In the course of the interview he recognized so much of his own sensibility in Miner that he invited him to collaborate on writing the *RoboCop* screenplay.[3] Writing in their spare time, their initial first full screenplay was complete by January 1985. It kept the original trajectory but lost the alcohol component. Now, merely the obsession with tracking down Clarence and the gang who had ended his human life drove RoboCop to extremes. At the same time, the corporation had acquired a name: International Consumer Management; RoboCop's exploits included rescuing the mayor from a kidnap; and the story had a date: 1995. The result was strong enough for producer Jon Davison (best known for the 1980 comedy *Airplane!*), mindful of the success of *The Terminator* in the preceding months, to pick up the project and begin the process of hawking the screenplay around studios.[4]

Davison found an interested party in the shape of Orion Pictures, a production company founded in 1978 by a breakaway group of United Artists executives, which seemed on the up-swing, with a stable that included Woody Allen and Oliver Stone, and such critical successes as *Amadeus* (1984) and *Platoon* (1986). The script continued to evolve, with new scenes including Clarence's murder of Morton. A studio reader in the summer of 1985 liked the device of introducing plot information by cutting to TV newscasts but commented that the crimes averted by RoboCop seemed rather banal. While welcoming the psychotic edge now given to Clarence and his gang, the reader had some concern over the levels of violence, noting: 'At one point they blow up a pet store with puppies in it just for the fun of it. Excessive, maybe?' [5] Another executive commented: 'While some of the shootings are especially gruesome, I'm reminded of the huge box office success *The Terminator,* which held back nothing in this department, enjoyed.'[6]

Changes continued. By November 1985 the third draft of the screenplay had acquired the twist whereby Jones was protected from RoboCop by a secret directive. When the Old Man fires Jones during the final showdown, RoboCop becomes free to shoot him. The news broadcasts were to be accompanied by satirical commercials. It was, Orion's Celia Pool remarked, 'a good attempt to do a *Terminator* turn around with plenty of action...various twists like the partner being female, directive #4 and the vague haunting memories of Robo/Murphy keep an otherwise predictable plot interesting'.[7]

During the early months of 1986 the *RoboCop* screenplay was honed further, while Davison looked for a director. Davison had been introduced to the project by director Jonathan Kaplan but he jumped ship to direct the now forgotten *Project X* for 20th Century-Fox, leaving Davison in need of a replacement.[8] Davison wanted someone inexpensive who could bring the class and edge of the art house to the project. First choice was the British director Alex Cox who had recently caused a splash with *Repo Man* (1984). When Cox (and several other candidates) declined Orion approached Dutch director Paul Verhoeven whose works included the war drama *Soldier of Orange* (1980) and who had just completed the raw historical drama *Flesh and Blood* (1985) in Europe for the studio. Verhoeven was initially reluctant, but on reflection saw the potential to do something new.[9] He later recalled: 'It was the comic-book feel of *RoboCop* that attracted me to the picture...I like comic books, in part, because they're stylized. Although *RoboCop* is an action-adventure, it has the very stylized feel that reminds me of a comic.'[10] He brought on board the German cinematographer Jost Vacano with whom he had worked on *Soldier of Orange,* and who was best known for his Oscar-nominated camerawork on *Das Boot.* Davison later confessed that Vacano had the added advantage – as a European – of being employable at less than union rates.[11]

During the production process, Verhoeven demonstrated his affinity with the comic book/graphic novel form, picking up a pen and sketching storyboards for himself to supplement the work of the team's main storyboard artist, John Dahl. Sequences drawn by Verhoeven included the memorable 'melting man' scene in which the gangster Emil is doused in toxic sludge and begins to fall apart until, lurching in front of a car, he is hit and reduced to a splash of green goo on the windshield. He also drew the corporate men's room confrontation between Morton and Jones, and the scene in which RoboCop – with memories of his former life returning – visits and tours his old family home and is haunted by flashbacks of how things had been.[12]

Verhoeven's particular interest was to flesh out gender relations including Murphy's married life. Verhoeven toyed with the idea of a full-on passionate love scene early in the film but settled on more discreet images in the house visit flashbacks. He was, however, adamant that the relationship between the male and female cops should be futuristic and abstracted from the inequality of the present. His shorthand for doing this was to devise a mixed locker scene in which men and women in various stages of undress banter in a matter-of-fact way while preparing to begin or end their shifts. The resulting sequence made his point. He added depth. Verhoeven looked to foreground the tenderness in the relationship between Murphy/Robo

21. 'Like a love scene …' Lewis (Nancy Allen) helps a repaired RoboCop (Peter Weller) readjust his targeting mechanism in *RoboCop* (1987) (Source: British Film Institute).

and Officer Lewis, saying of the sequence in which she helps repair him: 'The targeting grid adjustment should play as a love scene.'[13] But there were cheaper additions too. Verhoeven was also responsible for a scene in which Murphy's partner is overpowered after being distracted by glancing at the private parts of one of the gangsters when she disturbs him in the act of urinating.[14]

With Verhoeven in place, the team worked on production designs for the film. The look of RoboCop's costume – created by Rob Bottin, best known for the astonishing make-up effects in John Carpenter's *The Thing* – seemed a fairly transparent tribute to Judge Dredd. The other major piece of design was the ED 209 enforcement droid. The design came from Craig Davies, and stop motion effects king Phil Tippett brought it to life.[15]

Meanwhile work proceeded on the flesh and blood component of the film: the cast. The producers considered a number of actors for the

22. Inspired by comic books: Peter Weller in the armour designed by Rob Bottin for *RoboCop* (1987) (Source: British Film Institute).

lead role including Keith and David Carradine, Peter Coyote and Peter Fonda. Veteran producer Mike Medavoy sent a note with a number of names of his own, including that of Mark Hamill and a still little known Nicolas Cage.[16] Actors tested but baulked when they considered the rigours of the costume. Davison later recalled that over one hundred actors turned the role down. Added to that, the lead needed movement skills and a particular build. As Davison expressed it: 'Put Arnold Schwarzenegger in the RoboCop suit and he'd look like the Pillsbury doughboy.'[17] Fortunately, screen-testing threw up a young actor with a background in theatre and dance named Peter Weller, who was glad to take the part. Weller had already attracted the attention of SF fans with the title role in *The Adventures of Buckaroo Banzi: Across the 8th Dimension* (1984). Weller – a perfectionist for his art – took the role really seriously. He read all he could about robotics and hammered out eight pages of script and casting suggestions for the team.[18] Weller commenced a series of 12 two hour lessons with a New York-based mime artist, named Moni Yakim, to perfect his movement. In the final film Yakim received on-screen credit for 'Robomovement'.[19]

Murphy/RoboCop's partner – the spirited female cop Lewis – proved only marginally easier to cast. Names raised early on included Jamie Lee Curtis and Mary Elizabeth Mastrantonio and even someone with the marginal note 'Medavoy's girlfriend'. Many of them were unavailable.[20] The first choice was Stephanie Zimbalist, but she pulled out at the last moment to take TV work. After a moment of panic the team settled on Nancy Allen, an actress best known as the screaming girl in distress-type roles with flowing ringlets of blonde hair. Allen – daughter of a cop – attacked the role with gusto. She cut her hair and stepped convincingly into the part.[21]

Production began in the early summer of 1986. Dallas won out as the location because of the availability of both run-down neighborhoods and a glittering corporate downtown in that city. With a heavy costume and sweltering summer heat filming was a trial for Weller. Temperatures inside the suit regularly reached 115°. Filming slowed to allow Weller more breaks and improved ventilation. Moni Yakim flew down to revamp the entire concept of 'Robomovement' to fit the limits of the suit which, as Weller recalled, 'transformed the character.' There were other issues too. Weller and Verhoeven initially experienced creative differences but after an uncomfortable weekend these were resolved. Davison was sufficiently concerned by their spat to develop a contingency plan in case he had to replace Weller. The surviving production files include a hurriedly written list of alternative candidates for his role including the names of Tom Berenger, Michael Madsen and Willem Defoe, with a note of Peter Weller's measurements as any replacement needed to be exactly the same size as the fiberglass costume. Davison's fears proved unjustified and production continued apace.[22]

The budget remained a tight $11 million. Orion could not afford to get caught up in the story as Dore Schary had in *Forbidden Planet*. A couple of scenes disappeared and some props became much simpler than originally imagined. The initial treatment called for a complicated future police car for RoboCop like the 'Batmobile': in the event the 'Turbo Cruiser' ended up at the wheel of a matt black Ford Taurus with a couple of data screens to indicate the future setting.[23] These were not serious setbacks. An early scene intended to establish Clarence Boddicker's character by showing the murder of a cop, was deftly replaced with news coverage of the event. The cuts had their compensations. The final pruning back of the screenplay resulted in a pared down and polished final product in which not a line seemed to be wasted. The film cost only $13.1 million: $4 million less than the industry average at that time and around half the budget of Steven Spielberg's SF offering that year: *Inner Space*.[24]

From the first draft *RoboCop* had the quality of a modern myth. The good cop – Murphy – emerged as a Christlike figure who experiences a horrific death and resurrection and goes on to redeem Detroit. One parallel with the death and resurrection of Jesus, especially as recounted in the Gospel of Luke, is that neither the resurrected Murphy nor Jesus are immediately recognizable to their former colleagues. In both cases a characteristic hand gesture triggers recognition – the act of blessing a meal, in the case of Jesus; and the trick of spinning his sidearm, copied from a TV show to amuse his son, in the case of Murphy.[25] Murphy is also photographed towards the end of the story walking through a large puddle of water. In that moment he appears to be walking on water, an iconic accomplishment of Jesus mentioned in three Gospels. In this same spirit, early drafts of the script give Murphy an explicitly religious back-story. Flashbacks of key moments of his life, which Neumeier suggested should pass in front of his eyes before death, were to include images of Murphy in church. That was not part of the final film, though the sequel would suggest that it was Murphy's Irish-Catholic refusal to contemplate suicide that made him capable of withstanding the emotional stresses of his transformation.

But *RoboCop* was more than just a terrific story with elements of religion/myth. It was angled explicitly to comment on its own times. The core scenario – the redevelopment of Detroit – articulated one of the great issues of the age: the painful decline of the traditional manufacturing sector in the USA, symbolized here as elsewhere by the auto industry.[26] While the economy had rebounded from the crisis of the late 1970s, the new jobs were in different parts of the country. Pundits spoke with grim resolution about the 'rust belt'. Ironically, *RoboCop*'s location work underscored the shift. While the abandoned mill used in the opening and conclusion of the film was shot at the Wheeling-Pittsburgh plant in western Pennsylvania, the main production needed to mix urban decay with ultra-modern. Most of the filming took place in Dallas, the iconic city of the sun-belt, home to the booming elements in the 1980s economy, and – thanks to the television show of the same name – a place symbolic of the excesses of American 1980s corporate life. None of *RoboCop* was actually filmed in Detroit.[27]

The film would foreground the issue of crime in the American inner city. In so doing it was articulating a perennial theme in the cinema of the era. Since the mid-1970s Hollywood had presented the city as a zone of chaos in which the police were out of their depth and the letter of the law was inadequate to the challenge. Films like *Dirty Harry* (1971), *Death Wish* (1974) and their sequels valorized the rogue cop and the vigilante.[28] *RoboCop* trod the same beat and self-consciously sought to tap the same audience, even while satirizing the approach by rendering it in absurd extremes.

One major issue in the 1980s was that of so-called 'white flight': the abandonment of the inner city to racial minorities. Detroit was an especially black city with the proud heritage of MoTown music and such iconic citizens as boxer Joe Louis. This was an aspect of the 1980s city that the film-makers chose not to extend into the future. One executive at Orion feared it might be otherwise. In February 1986 Bill Bernstein wrote a hurried memo to Mike Medavoy in February 1986 under the erroneous impression that all the villains in the film would be African-American. He was not solely motivated by a desire to avoid the defamation of his fellow citizens, but had an eye on the bottom line: 'the film should play strongly to a traditional black audience – especially in large urban areas'. Colleagues assured him that race would not be an issue and indeed the final film is scrupulously racially balanced with African-Americans faces represented among the criminals, the citizenry, the cops and the corporate-types too.[29] One element of ethnic comment survived the scrutiny of 'the suits': the decision to make the hero cop an Irish-American. The identification of Irish-Americans with law enforcement in fact and fiction was such that the implied ethnicity of Murphy provided an anchor point linking the present and the future. *Just Imagine* also had an Irish future cop. Perhaps there was something comforting in knowing that however the world might change in the future, the police would still be Irish.[30]

Other 1980s social issues in the film included the challenge of drugs. This had grown since the 60s, to become, by the 70s – in President Nixon's terminology – 'public enemy number one'. The 80s saw an understanding on the part of social scientists that drugs and urban decay were inter-related. The decade also brought campaigns to turn back the tide of drugs, most famously with First Lady Nancy Reagan urging the youth of America to 'just say no'. Peter Weller suggested that the film should remain current with the evolution of the problem: 'A more interesting lethal and addicting choice of drugs, and one becoming more prevalent in the world now, is if Clarence et al smoke cocaine stuffed into small cigarettes and pipes (now called 'crack') and no one has done it yet. Snorting is passé and urbane and common.'[31] Soon no one would need an actor to teach them the word 'crack'. Yet *RoboCop* wore its social comment lightly. Its best points were made through humour. The film sought out two main targets: corporate America and the ever dumbing-down media.

The 1980s saw a rapid transformation in the landscape of the American media as cable television took hold. Hundreds of channels became the norm in the American household and, as competition for viewers heated up, anxious television executives aimed for the lowest common denominator. News seemed a particular casualty. Media critics like Neil Postman lamented the death of the traditions of Edward R. Murrow, as bulletins became shorter, more fixated on the appearance of the anchors and dominated by violence and salacious fluff.[32] *RoboCop* used spoof news broadcasts both to efficiently establish the key elements of life in future Detroit and to satirize the state of broadcast news. From the anchor's catchphrase – 'You give us three minutes and we'll give you the world' – the satire was biting and right on target.[33] Even a historic story like the death of two former presidents in an accident is delivered with an up-beat glib detachment. Early drafts of the script included a gag about an accident on the HISS – a Highspeed Interstate Subway System. The item was dropped perhaps for reasons that reflected the American present. One Orion executive noted in a critique of the script: 'We question somewhat the likelihood of major funds being allocated to set up technologically advanced public transport systems in the USA.'[34]

Besides the news, *RoboCop* also spoofed America's taste in popular entertainment and the willingness of the TV channels to deliver it. The most successful show in *RoboCop*'s future is 'It's Not My Problem' hosted by a prurient moustachioed 'cheaky chappy' named Bixby Snyder. Snyder seems a descendant of the British comedian Benny Hill, whose blend of slapstick and innuendo topped ratings in the late 1980s. Snyder's catchphrase: 'I'll buy that for a dollar' was an SF in-joke. It was a tribute to the classic short story The Marching Morons by C. M. Kornbluth from 1951, where, in a future inhabited only by people of low intelligence, the top entertainer is a bawdy comedian who uses the catchphrase 'Would you buy it for a quarter?'[35] Towards the end of *RoboCop* Snyder shifts from the entertainment slot to the news as he is arrested for trading sex for job security with underage co-stars. Thus the media consumes itself.

The final elements of media satire were in the mock commercials that punctuate the news. These provided an effective mechanism for displaying the nature of the future society. A family laughs uproariously during a board game about nuclear war; an unctuous doctor promises a great deal on an artificial heart; a car – the 6000 SUX – is advertised with an absurdly wasteful fuel consumption: 'an American tradition'. The audience can recognize the world being evoked.

The other – and arguably the prime – target of satire in *RoboCop* was corporate America. By the mid-1980s the American mega corporations were riding high. Whether in Hollywood or Wall Street, mergers were everywhere and stock prices soared. The world had leaned the term 'yuppie' and applied it to the young men and women who filled the corporate ranks. Buoyed by the de-regulation and tax cuts of the Reagan administration, corporate greed seemed to define the era for many observers. 1987 would also see Oliver Stone's *Wall Street* with its mantra 'greed is good'. Corporate villains were not new to American SF. In the previous decade the genre had seen the Soylent Corporation in *Soylent Green* (1973), the Weyland-Yutani Corporation in *Alien* and *Aliens* and The Tyrell Corporation in *Blade Runner*. Yet a viewer who knew those films and had no knowledge of American business in the 1980s could tell from *RoboCop* that something had changed. The corporate villains of *RoboCop* were not remote like the God-like Tyrell at the helm of the Tyrell corporation in *Blade Runner* or abstract like Ripley's employer in *Alien*. *RoboCop* depicted the American corporation as a hive of Machiavellian machinations: a greasy pole that the ruthless climbed with utter disregard for their fellows. The clichés of corporate life were there: sycophantic applause in the board room; the triumphant acquisition of the key to the executive washroom. Corporate evil is rendered in lurid tones. The principal villain, Dick Jones, would not only engineer the murder of his rivals, he would also be revealed to be the man behind the city's organized crime. To the executives at Orion it all seemed plausible. They hailed the screenplay as a 'logical outcome to current events': an American response to Australia's *Road Warrior*, in which the quasi-aboriginal tribes of the post-apocalyptic outback replaced by 'a casaba of killer yuppies and privately subsidized street gangs'.[36]

The corporation depicted was initially to be called ICM (for International Consumer Management) a single letter removed from the archetypal giant of the tech industry IBM. It would be a sprawling octopus with tentacles everywhere including mines, oil, entertainment, weapons and military services. 'We practically ARE the military', Jones would boast towards the end of the movie. The idea in the film that a private corporation could do a better job of policing Detroit than the city's own police was no abstract fantasy. It was a rendering of the era's economic orthodoxy: privatization. The only problem with calling the evil corporation ICM was that these initials were the same as those used by the powerful Hollywood talent agency International Creative Management. When a representative of Tobor Pictures wrote to see if ICM might give permission for the usage she was told unequivocally not. Robert Chuck of ICM noted that, like the ICM in the movie, they operated from a skyscraper labelled with the initials of the corporation in giant shining letters, and that while the ICM of the story was involved in military and heavy industrial work; it also had an entertainment division. 'We do believe that our interest and reputation could be damaged by your use of the ICM initials and logo' stated Chuck. 'We cannot consent to such usage' he concluded.[37] The writers obligingly switched ICM to OCP (Omni Consumer Products), which had an appropriately corporate ring and was an anagram of the word 'cop'.[38]

Despite ripping the façade of the corporation, it is arguable that *RoboCop* fudged its critique by shying away from a negative portrayal of 'the Old Man' at the helm. His insensitive response to the malfunction of ED 209 notwithstanding, the Old Man is essentially a benign father figure. He ends the movie by acknowledging the humanity of RoboCop in the simplest way: asking his name. Some critics have seen the Old Man/Jones dichotomy as a reworking of the God/Lucifer relationship in Milton's *Paradise Lost*, but it seems a fairly universal impulse in humanity to believe that the man at the top is benign. Russian peasants famously lamented 'if only the Tsar knew what his ministers are doing'. There was an obvious 1980s example of the same dynamic. Despite persistent social problems during the Reagan period, the image of the President himself seemed somehow untainted – at home at least. The Coen brothers had their character Hi (Nicolas Cage) say of Reagan in *Raising Arizona* (1987): 'They say he's a good man. Perhaps it's his advisers who are confused.' By the time of *RoboCop*'s release, the misdeeds of Reagan's Dick Jones equivalents were a matter of public record. In the fall of 1986 the world had learnt that the White House had covertly funded Contra rebels in Nicaragua with money raised from the secret sale of arms to Iran. Indicted and found guilty, Admiral John Poindexter and White House staffer Colonel Oliver North became household names. The president rose above the affair as though coated with Teflon. America's belief in goodness at the top remained. Neumeier was either reproducing this tendency in the screenplay or gently spoofing it.

There were a couple of moments of explicit political satire in the film. The film plainly took aim at the Reagan-ite rush to privatize government services. The news broadcasts announced first the launch and then the spectacular failure of one of the policy icons of the Reagan era: the space-based anti-ballistic missile platform that the White House dubbed the 'strategic defense initiative' and Senator Edward Kennedy contemptuously called 'Star Wars'. Not only does the platform malfunction in the film, wipe out Santa Barbara and thereby kill two unidentified retired presidents, there is a possibility that one of them might actually be meant to be Reagan himself since his plans to retire to the vicinity of Santa Barbara were already well known. Early versions of the script cast the net even more widely. The writers originally planned to include a major subplot about corruption in city government and a connection between the construction workers' trade union and the mafia. Readers considered this subplot to be both unnecessarily complicated and unwise as it might create the impression that the film was hostile to the working man. One Orion executive also worried about the news broadcasts explicitly identifying the insurgents as 'pro-Marxist' noting: 'Does it suggest that the underlying point of the view of the movie is right wing?'[39]

With a boost from a marketing campaign that included random appearances by actors in RoboCop armour around the country, *RoboCop* opened well at the box office. It beat out all rivals on its first weekend, taking over $8 million.[40] The critical reception was, however, mixed. Despite the last minute cuts necessary to obtain the R rating,[41] many reviewers felt that the film was simply too violent and were alarmed by the enthusiasm of the audience for that violence. One called the film 'an inhuman assault on the senses'.[42] Pauline Kael of the *New Yorker* lamented that the main thing being resurrected was not Murphy the cop, but Verhoeven's career. She was unimpressed: 'He's come back as a man without sensibility, RoboDirector.'[43] British columnist Simon Hoggart, writing in *The Observer* argued that the film's success revealed a disturbing American taste for guns and gore, and speculated that the film might be 'a hugely successful European joke at the expense of the new world'.[44] He might equally have pointed to the film's anti-corporate credentials and wry critique of TV news as evidence that America was pushing back against the cultural rot of the era. Some got the point. The *Village Voice* praised RoboCop's 'satire of the Reaganaut present'.[45] John Powers in *LA Weekly* found the film 'filled with guttersnipe subversiveness', and noted how 'compared to most of our current cinema, *RoboCop*'s Hobbesian satire looks rather progressive'.[46] While the SF community generally embraced the film, there were exceptions. Veteran writer Harlan Ellison launched a stinging attack on the film as 'vicious' and 'a film about, and intended for, no less than brutes ... made by, and for, savages and ghouls'. He called the writers 'literary grave robbers' for appropriating Judge Dredd and announced that he had walked out halfway through the film, during the city hall scene, which he saw as a parody of the murder of Harvey Milk in San Francisco in 1978.[47] International audiences were similarly polarized. French critics flipped at the philosophical implications. Most British critics saw the satire. Maggie Alderson of the London *Evening Standard* walked out after twenty minutes lamenting: 'I want my money back; I want my time back – and most of all I want my innocence back.'[48] Audiences continued to vote with their feet and the film eventually grossed in excess of $50 million.

RoboCop opened the door to further films in the same spirit.[49] Verhoeven himself followed up with *Total Recall* and a screenplay loosely based on a story by *Blade Runner*'s Philip K. Dick and starring *The Terminator*'s Arnold Schwarzenegger. *RoboCop 2* (1990) reunited Peter Weller and Nancy Allen under the direction of Irvin Kershner, who had delivered the much-admired *Star Wars* sequel *The Empire Strikes Back* in 1980. The new film was not, however, written by Miner and Neumeier. Orion passed on their script and instead hired the man behind the boldest of *RoboCop*'s influences, Frank Miller, whose un-filmable script was pulled into shape by the well-established screenwriter (and director of *The Hellstrom Chronicle*) Walon Green. Miller remained on set throughout production to tweak the final product.[50] *RoboCop 2* developed the theme of a police strike. It also maintained the element of satire with the same mock-ads for products like an extreme sun block for the post-Ozone layer era. Levels of violence remained a concern for some viewers, more especially after a murderer named Nathaniel White claimed that one of his killings was in direct imitation of a scene in *RoboCop 2*.[51] The producers weathered the criticism and media attention soon drifted elsewhere. *RoboCop 3* reached the screen in 1993 without Weller, or the wit or vision of the original and ended the immediate film cycle.

RoboCop had a life beyond the big screen. The film inspired by comic books returned the favour. A Marvel adaptation appeared at the time of its first release and the film spawned a full-blown Marvel comic book series in 1990, written by two stars of British comics Alan Grant and Lee Sullivan.[52] Frank Miller created a 'crossover' comic book for the publisher Darkhorse called *RoboCop versus the Terminator* (1993). There were TV series, both live-action (1994) and animated; a stage show; a theme-park ride and video games. In 2000 Officer Murphy returned in a four-part TV movie called *RoboCop Prime Directives*.[53]

RoboCop launched Verhoeven's career and he was smart to recognize a public identification with SF material. Ten years later, Verhoeven, executive producer Jon Davison and writer Ed Neumeier teamed up again to tackle a classic SF novel, Robert Heinlein's *Starship Troopers*. That tale of 'grunts' in a future war included some of the hallmarks of *RoboCop*: a mix of action, media satire, and a view of future male-female working relationships that included shared combat roles. There was also a suggestion of a joke at the expense of the audience, as though Verhoeven and Neumeier had taken a bet to see how militaristic or straight out fascistic a film they could create without America minding. Even with Neil Patrick Harris gracing the closing scenes of the movie in what amounted to a Nazi officer's uniform, America didn't blink. It was a suggestion perhaps that a suitably remote enemy and sufficiently outrageous provocation would see the US as gung ho for blood as any Empire of the past. 'War', Verhoeven explained on the DVD commentary, 'makes Fascists of us all'.

In the 21st century RoboCop still thrives as a comic book character. He has earned his place in the comic pantheon alongside Judge Dredd and Ironman, who inspired him. A quarter century on from *RoboCop*'s release, the themes seen in the original film remain prescient. Privatization has marked America's military and prisons, if not its police. The film's critique of the news media and banality of advertising seem as apposite now as then. Perhaps that is why reports have continued to surface for a big-budget *RoboCop* reboot, which, following the success of *Avatar* (2009), is now planned for 3D. A still greater compliment to the potency of the story came from Detroit where, in 2011, as a real post-industrial regeneration of the city began, citizens launched a campaign to erect a statue of RoboCop. Officer Murphy lives on.[54]

Notes

[1]   Margaret Herrick Library, Academy of Motion Picture Arts and Sciences, John Davison papers (hereafter AMPAS Davison): *RoboCop* script, f.1, treatment by Neumeier, 30 August 1984.

[2]   Ibid: The harassment is on p.11.

[3]   Lee Goldberg, 'Robowriters! Screenwriters Michael Miner and Edward Neumeier program the future in law enforcement. They call it ROBOCOP', *Starlog*, February 1988, pp.22–25, 75. See also Jack Mathews, 'The Word is out: good writing still pays off', *Los Angeles Times*, 1 September 1987, pp.c1, c9.

[4]   AMPAS Davison: *RoboCop* script, f.2, reader's report by Diana Birchall on screenplay by Miner/Neumeier, 23 January 1985. Davison formed a company called Tobor Pictures (a reversal of robot).

[5]   AMPAS Davison: *RoboCop* script, f.3, noted on *RoboCop* second draft by RS, dated 7 May 1985. This reader suggested that Officer Lewis should survive the story, which she did in later drafts.

6   AMPAS Davison: *RoboCop* script, f.11, Commentary on draft by Marty Barkan, 16 March 1986.

7   AMPAS Davison: *RoboCop* script, f.4, Memo by Celia Pool on *RoboCop*, 5 November 1985. Another reader – Susan Cohn – suggested that the ads be more tightly tied to elements of the film, such as the corporation, and noted that there could only be one PRIME directive. AMPAS Davison: *RoboCop* script, f.5, noted by Susan Cohn, 23 January 1986.

8   Ann Thompson, 'Risky business: Robo-producer', *LA Weekly*, 31 July 1987.

9   Lee Goldberg, 'Robowriters!' According to the commentary on the Criterion DVD, Verhoeven actually discarded the script and his wife rescued it from the bin and made him read it again.

10   Eric Niderost, 'Paul Verhoeven, War, Remembrance and RoboCop', *Starlog*, September 1987, pp.36–9.

11   Ann Thompson, 'Risky business: Robo-producer', *LA Weekly*, 31 July 1987.

12   AMPAS Davison: *RoboCop* storyboards, f.45 for melting man, f.54 for the men's room, f.56 for the home visit.

13   AMPAS Davison: *RoboCop* script, f.8, Paul Verhoeven's notes for the third draft, n.d.

14   AMPAS Davison: *RoboCop* storyboards, f.51, boards drawn by Verhoeven.

15   AMPAS Davison: *RoboCop* drawings, f.24, Ed 209. See also Phil Tippett to Visual Effects Award Committee (AMPAS), 20 January 1988, as filed at AMPAS Core Collection files, production, *RoboCop* (credits, visual effects notes).

16   AMPAS Davison: *RoboCop* casting, f.18, Dennison and Selzer casting notes, January 1986.

17   Ann Thompson, 'Risky business: Robo-producer', *LA Weekly*, 31 July 1987.

18   AMPAS Davison: *RoboCop* script, f.12, note from Paul Weller to Verhoeven and Neumeier, 21 March 1986. None seem to have been followed.

19   AMPAS Davison: *RoboCop* casting, f.18, Davison to Yakim, n.d. Also studio publicity material for *RoboCop* held in Herrick Core Collection.

20   Ibid: Dennison/Selzer casting memo, 21 May 1986.

21   Ibid: Memo headed 'people considered in last minute scramble to replace Stephanie Zimbalist ...', n.d. The document notes that Melissa Gilbert 'passed' and includes a contact number and note of salary for Geena Davis. On Allen, see studio publicity packet for *RoboCop* in Herrick Core Collection, p.13.

22   Ibid: list of 'actors considered when it was contemplated to replace Weller during shooting ...', c.August 1986; Peter Weller to Cull, 30 October 2012.

23   The script also called for more complex data screens and animated maps. AMPAS Davison: *RoboCop* storyboards f.57 is a storyboard drawn by Verhoeven himself for an animated map sequence that Davison notes 'we couldn't afford'.

24   Ann Thompson, 'Risky business: Robo-producer', *LA Weekly*, 31 July 1987.

25   The 'guntrick' motivation – Murphy imitating his son's favourite TV show – was introduced in the revised third draft of the script. AMPAS Davison: *RoboCop* script, f.6.

26   Other films using the auto industry as a metaphor for the American condition include *Gung Ho* (1986) and Michael Moore's *Roger and Me* (1988).

27   On the Pennsylvania location, see 'Pennsylvania', *Hollywood Reporter*, 6 November 1986. Aware of the suffering of the rust belt, Davison donated $10,000 to the unemployed steel workers' fund during the location work.

28   The link to *Dirty Harry* is noted in AMPAS Davison *RoboCop* script, f.11: Commentary on draft by Marty Barkan, 16 March 1986.

29 AMPAS Davison: *RoboCop* script, f.9, Bernstein to Medavoy, re *RoboCop*, 11 February 1986. He was corrected in a memo from Ann Rodman to Medavoy of 12 February 1983, filed in Davison, *RoboCop* script, f.10.

30 This was commented on in the UK press see: John Munro, Sean O'Hagan, Nigel Floyd, 'Murphy's Law', *New Musical Express*, 6 February 1988, pp.24–5. It is worth noting that the same year as *RoboCop* – 1987 – saw the release of *The Untouchables* in which Sean Connery won an Oscar for his portrayal of an old-time Irish cop.

31 AMPAS Davison: *RoboCop* script, f.12, Note from Paul Weller to Verhoeven and Neumeier, 21 March 1986.

32 Neil Postman, *Amusing Ourselves to Death: Public Discourse in the Age of Showbusiness*, Penguin, New York, 1985.

33 Legal researchers noted that this was a parody of the current slogan of LA news radio station KFWB, which was asking for just 22 minutes. AMPAS Davison: *RoboCop* legal, f.27, de Forest research to Davison, 2 April 1986.

34 AMPAS Davison: *RoboCop* script, f.7, noted on 2nd draft by Frances Doel (Orion), n.d.

35 The tribute was noted in AMPAS Davison: *RoboCop* legal, f.27, de Forest research to Davison, 2 April 1986.

36 AMPAS Davison: *RoboCop* script, f.13, Commentary on 4th draft by Ann Rodman, 30 June 1986.

37 AMPAS Davison: *RoboCop* legal, f.27, Chuck (ICM) to Allegra Clegg (Tobor), 10 March 1986.

38 One paper noted that the OCP logo bore a 'startling resemblance' to the logo for Cannon Films. *LA Herald-Examiner*, 2 July 1987.

39 AMPAS Davison: *RoboCop* script, f.7, notes on 3rd draft by Frances Doel, n.d.
    Lee Goldberg, 'Robowriters!'

40 'RoboCop in first place in box office sales', *New York Times*, 22 July 1987; Jack Matthews, 'The marketing of a mechanical hero', *Los Angeles Times*, 21 July 1987, pp.1, 9.

41 Lee Goldberg, 'Robowriters!' For press comment, see 'Orion seeks postponement of "RoboCop" X-rating appeal', *Variety*, 13 May 1987; 'Orion awarded an R for its "RoboCop"', *Variety*, 15 May 1987; 'Morning report: movies', *Los Angeles Times*, 20 May 1987.

42 Peter Rainer, 'RoboCop an inhuman assault on senses', *LA Herald Examiner*, 17 July 1987, p.10.

43 Pauline Kael, 'RoboCop', *New Yorker*, 10 August 1987, pp.72–3.

44 Simon Hoggart, 'Below the Belt', *Observer* (London), 30 August 1987, p.19.

45 David Edelstein, 'Heavy Metal', *Village Voice*, 21 July 1987, p.58.

46 John Powers, 'Murphy's Law', *LA Weekly*, 17 July 1987, p.41.

47 Harlan Ellison 'Watching: Installment 27', *Fantasy and Science Fiction*, January 1988, anthologised in Harlan Ellison, *Harlan Ellison's Watching*, (Los Angeles: Underwood-Miller, 1989' pp. 273–274.

48 Maggie Alderson, 'Who really wants to see this?' *Evening Standard*, 16 February 1988, p.7.

49 Todd David Schwartz, 'RoboCopies... or RoboCoincidences?' *Los Angeles Times*, 13 March 1988.

50 Green to author, 25 April 2011.

51 'Accused sex killer: I killed like RoboCop', *New York Newsday*, 6 August 1992, p.1. The story was somewhat garbled, confusing the two films and getting the date of the release of the original wrong by two years. White specified that he was imitating the character Cain. For a further negative review from Ellison, see Harlan Ellison, 'Watching: Installment 43', *Fantasy and Science Fiction*, October 1990, pp.54–60.

52 'RoboCop goes up-scale', *Los Angeles Times*, 14 December 1989.

53 On the ride see Matt Rothman, 'RoboCop targets theme park crowd', *Variety*, 30 October 1992.

54 Jon Oosting, 'RoboCop fans raising money for statue in Detroit', MLive.com, 10 February 2011, online at www.mlive.com/news/detroit/index.ssf/2011/02/robocop_fans_raising_money_for.html Last accessed: 7 June 2012.

THE IMAGE AS HERO: *AVATAR* (2009)

The screen is black. We hear a drum beat, pan pipes and the wail of a female singer; evocative of a distant place, an unknown culture and intense emotion. The screen erupts in colour and movement. We plunge down through clouds and swoop over a jungle. Even in 2D the effect is of diving into another world, but in 3D the sense of immersion is overwhelming. Thus audiences were pitched headlong into the world of James Cameron's *Avatar* and the cinema of science fiction reached an undoubted milestone. *Avatar*'s significance was manifold. It bore testament to the culture of its era. It showcased an anti-corporate and anti-military sensibility; it embraced the values of sustainability, indigenous rights and environmentalism; it recalled and extended some of the great science fiction of the past, but its true triumph lay in the visual realm.

In his 1960 survey of the literary genre of science fiction entitled *New Maps of Hell,* the British writer Kingsley Amis observed that much science fiction had 'the idea as hero'.[1] Ideas were in the foreground, so characters and their development frequently became a secondary consideration. *Avatar* had its share of ideas and a heroic central character, but which was really the hero? If we understand a hero in terms of function as the prime focus of our attention, our point of entry into the story, that which is most celebrated in the experience of consumption, and the thread that links the events presented, then the answer is no. Neither the ideas nor the protagonist were the hero of *Avatar*. *Avatar* has the *image* as hero. The film was conceived, created, marketed and consumed around the notion of immersive spectacle. Its success – becoming the biggest grossing motion picture of all time – promised to change the way in which films were made and exhibited, influencing not only the SF genre but films and the film business in general.

Avatar takes place in 2154, a future in which humans have exhausted the Earth and, greedy for new resources, are mining a rare mineral named 'unobtainium' on the distant and exotic moon of Pandora (studio backstory locates it in the orbit of a planet called Polyphemus, in the Alpha Centuri-A system, 4.4 light years from earth). To facilitate their quest, humans have developed a technology allowing them to survive on the planet and interact with the tall blue natives – the Na'vi – by inhabiting genetically engineered bodies called Avatars, which are a hybrid of their human operator and native DNA. A paraplegic veteran marine named Jake Sully (Sam Worthington) unexpectedly becomes an Avatar operator when his identical twin brother is murdered in a random robbery. Jake travels to Pandora and is exhilarated to recover his mobility through his Avatar body. He is initially shunned by the senior scientist, Grace (Sigourney Weaver), but is welcomed by the head of security Colonel Quaritch (Stephan Lang). The Colonel promises to arrange a surgical cure for his disability if Jake will become his spy among the natives. On his first expedition into the Pandoran environment Jake becomes separated from the rest of his group. He is rescued from wild animals by a Na'vi female named Neytiri (Zoe Saldana). Neytiri brings Jake to the 'home tree' in which her people live and he persuades the tribe to allow him to stay and learn Na'vi language and ways. Jake settles into a routine of long sessions inside his Avatar body with occasional briefings to Quaritch. Over a few months he wins the admiration of Grace, he comes to respect the Na'vi and he falls in love with Neytiri. He is initiated into the tribe and mates with Neytiri. When the humans encroach on Na'vi territory, Jake attacks their machinery. Enraged, Quaritch captures Jake, Grace and the rest of the humans sympathetic to the Na'vi, and moves to destroy the home tree. Jake is allowed to warn the Na'vi to leave, but is rejected by Neytiri. He is re-imprisoned by the humans who plan an all-out attack. He and his colleagues escape and re-enter their Avatar bodies but Grace is fatally wounded. Jake manages to tame a ferocious flying creature that gives him messianic status among the Na'vi. Neytiri and Jake are reconciled. Jake rallies Na'vi from many regions and mounts a coordinated rising against the humans, in which even the animals of the planet join. The Na'vi are victorious. Refusing to accept defeat, Quaritch fights Jake's Avatar and attempts to destroy his human body. Neytiri arrives in time to save Jake and kill the Colonel. The hostile humans leave Pandora. Jake participates in a ceremony that uses the power of one of Pandora's sacred trees to transfer his consciousness permanently into his Avatar body. The film ends as Jake opens his eyes for the first time in his new permanent Pandoran body.

Avatar was the culmination of the vision of one man: James Cameron. It sprang from his imagination. It reflected his personal ideology. It was driven by his ambition. It sold to the public in part because of his track record as a film-maker. *Avatar* began with Cameron's childhood SF reading in Ontario, Canada and developed in his later teenage years in the Southern California suburb of Brea: 'I've dreamed of creating a film like this, set on another world of great danger and beauty since I was a kid reading pulp science fiction and comic books by the truckload, and sitting in math class drawing creatures and aliens behind my propped up textbook.'[2]

It was an SF classic that first drew Cameron, as a teenager, towards a career in film. Kubrick's *2001: A Space Odyssey* (1968) left the 15-year-old so disoriented that he vomited outside the theatre but from that point on he was obsessed with special effects.[3] Brimming with plans for films and fabulous spacecraft of his own, Cameron was a lacklustre student. He dropped out of college and drifted into various odd jobs, but never abandoned his ambition to place remarkable images on the big screen. Around 1976 he and a friend began drafting a screenplay for an elaborate SF epic called *Xenogenesis*. He painted fantastical concept art, full of floating creatures and glowing forests, to accompany the script. When his mother mentioned having dreamt of a12-foot-tall blue-skinned woman, Cameron added a painting of a tall blue girl amid long orange grass to the portfolio. It was the first glimpse of Neytiri.[4] Cameron knew he had much to learn, and spent his spare time teaching himself the technology of film in the cinema library at the University of Southern California. The release of *Star Wars* in 1977 brought his ambition to a head. 'I was really upset when I saw *Star Wars*', he recalled. 'That was the movie that I wanted to make. After seeing the movie I got very determined. I decided to get busy.'[5] Cameron was able to find work building models on one of the projects reaching for the coattails of *Star Wars*: Roger Corman's *Battle Beyond the Stars* (1980). He built a spaceship that resembled the female torso so beloved by Corman, and ended that project a fully-fledged art director.[6] Further art direction and then a low-budget project as director – *Piranha II* – followed. Cameron's breakthrough came in 1984 as writer/director of *The Terminator*. Its style and intensity belied the low budget, launched his career and confirmed the stardom of his star, Arnold Schwarzenegger. Hitches included a run-in with Harlan Ellison over the alleged plagiarism of the story. Cameron settled out of court and conceded a screen credit.[7] He followed up with *Aliens* (1986), *The Abyss* (1989) and *Terminator 2: Judgment Day* (1991), which showed his mastery of cutting edge effects and record-breaking budgets. The undoubted high point of the latter film was the effect allowing the T-1000 robot to melt into liquid and then re-form into solid shape. His comedy about terrorism *True Lies* (1994) troubled some critics but did well at the box office, however, it was the success of *Titanic*

(1997) that sent Cameron into the stratosphere. The film broke box office records worldwide.

Even before *Titanic* audiences knew what to expect from Cameron. Effects were the central part of his brand, but a particular kind of characterization was not far behind. Cameron was associated with strong female characters like Ripley (Sigourney Weaver) in *Aliens* or Sarah Connor (Linda Hamilton) in the *Terminator* films; he clearly had a bone to pick with the military-industrial complex and inserted militaristic corporate villains into *Aliens* and *Terminator 2*. The inflexibility of the military mind was presented in *The Abyss*.[8] As a writer he also devised the anti-military subplot of *Rambo: First Blood Part II* (1985).[9] The corporate plutocrat was seldom as vilified as in the person of Cal Hockley (Billy Zane), the villain in *Titanic*. There were also characteristic Cameron supporting characters: little utopias of teamwork and mutual support seen in the salvage crews depicted in *The Abyss* and in the modern day sequences of *Titanic*. He was a genre in his own right, which placed him in the unique position of being able to mount a multi-million dollar production based on his own reputation and not, as the increasingly risk-averse Hollywood of the era usually preferred, that of a previously published novel, play, film, television programme, video game or – as in the case of Disney's *Pirates of the Caribbean* series – theme park ride.

In 1995, after completing *True Lies*, Cameron resolved to embark on a spectacular new science fiction project that would use the emerging technology of computer-generated imagery to render an alien world in unparalleled detail, but still tell a compelling story. The framework came easily. Cameron later recalled:

> When I sat down to write the first draft of *Avatar* in 1995 it burst forth like a river through a breaking dam, seeming to write itself in just three weeks. The reservoir behind that dam had been filling since I was a child, with images from a thousand science fiction novels and hundreds of movies. Every piece of fantasy art ever created, every *Analog* and *Eerie* magazine cover, all fed into that reservoir. In addition, my real life experiences under the ocean, from the profusion of life in the coral ecosystem to the alien forms lurking at the edges of our submersible's lights miles down in the blackness, found their way in the swirl of ideas that fed *Avatar*.[10]

Three weeks later he had an 80-page 'scriptment' outlining both the essential story of the final film and the core creatures and settings.[11] The sticking point was technology. As Cameron recalled, he wanted to get away from the latex aliens who were the staple of *Star Trek* and create creatures with skin that was like real skin and eyes that were of a non-human size and location. It was a tall order requiring technology far in advance of the mid-1990s state-of-the-art. Disappointed, Cameron decided that it was easier to re-float the *Titanic* and to wait for technology to catch up with his vision.[12] Whispers of his project reached the trade press. In August 1996 the *Hollywood Reporter* revealed his plan to deploy 'synthetic stars' – 'at least six photorealistic CGI (computer-generated imagery) actors' – in an epic love story set on another world. Production was slated to begin when *Titanic* was complete.[13]

Following the success of *Titanic* Cameron worked on a series of marine documentaries developing revolutionary 3D cameras as he went. He created a short-lived dystopian TV show – *Dark Angel* – and flirted with a film about the colonization of Mars, but continued to nurse the idea of *Avatar*. [14] Motion capture technology developed for the *Star Wars* prequels and Peter Jackson's *Lord of the Rings* trilogy finally opened the door. Jackson's Weta Workshop in New Zealand became the special effects house for the project, though *Avatar* would require a battery of new techniques. Cameron later compared making *Avatar* to 'jumping off a cliff and knitting the parachute on the way down'. The effects needed five hundred times more computer space than *Titanic*.[15]

The film required not merely convincing alien characters and movement but convincing movement and language. Rather than electronically modulate existing exotic earth language as George Lucas had done in *Star Wars*, Cameron resolved to create one as had been done for the Klingon culture in the *Star Trek* franchise. One of Cameron's first commissions was to Paul Frommer, a linguistics professor based at the University of Southern California, to design a credible alien language for the film. The result was sufficiently natural that some words became proverbial on the set, especially '*Skxawng*' the Na'vi word for moron.[16] Cameron's instruction for the design of the wider environment and its creatures was to begin from Earth-bound reference points but to overlay them with alien characteristics. 'We wanted to remove the creatures and flora from being Earth-like just enough to remind you that you're on another world,' he recalled, 'but at the same time, you'd find then accessible.' Most of the creatures had a fairly obvious earth equivalent – a panther, a horse, a monkey, a dog – even if the Pandoran version displayed extra legs. The same principle applied to the alien movement, dance and material culture seen in the film, and the music too. The choreographer Lula Washington worked from existing indigenous dances, while the movement coach Terry Notary drew inspiration from domestic cats.[17] The score by James Horner used plenty of drums, ethnic chants and vocalizations, but fell back on grand orchestral techniques for its key moments. The home tree would fall to the strains of Mahlerian horn motifs.

The future setting had the potential to also alienate the audience from the humans represented. To ease this distance Cameron wove in familiar sights, objects and costume elements into the human settings. Such things had been done before in SF cinema. Kubrick playfully included the PanAm, Howard Johnson and American Express brands in his vision of 2001 to show its proximity to the era of the original viewer. Other filmmaking placing familiar objects and brands in future settings have done so as mercenary product placement, but something more complex happened in *Avatar*.[18] Contemporary objects were used to establish character. Jake has a twentieth century wheelchair not some super high-tech design and talks about 'a shot of tequila' rather than some future beverage like *Star Trek*'s synthahol. In her human form Grace (50-something in the script) bellows for a cigarette while her Avatar (30-something in the script) is lithe and athletic in her Stanford sweatshirt; Trudy (Michelle Rodriguez) the tomboy pilot fist-bumps her buddies; the mining boss Selfridge (Giovanni Ribisi) wears a corporate shirt and tie and practices his putting on the command bridge. The script specifies that his golf balls are Titleist. The script also specifies that the AMP robot suits are made by Mitsubishi. Sometimes these links to our own time convey an ideological connection. The Native American dream-catcher in Selfridge's trophy cabinet is an obvious reminder of an earth parallel to the events depicted. Some audiences will have connected to lessons of their own childhood when in the ruins of the Na'vi school Grace picks up a copy of the Dr Seuss book *The Lorax* (1971). 'I love this one ...' she says. The book tells of a greedy entrepreneur who ignores the warnings of a moustachioed sprite – the Lorax of the title – and ruins an entire ecosystem by cutting down the Truffula trees. For many children this book was their first lesson in ecology. Sometimes the link is unsettling. Later in the film as the battle fleet prepares to attack, Quaritch is seen nonchalantly sipping a drink – presumably coffee – from a stainless steel 'to go' cup in a lead vehicle. The link back to our time is uncomfortable. For Quaritch cultural genocide is all in a day's work. Can the coffee-drinking viewer with a similar cup at home but be disturbed by a connection to the villain of the film?

By mid-2009 *Avatar* was complete: it only remained to be seen whether audiences shared Cameron's vision. *Avatar*, like *Star Wars*, was deeply imbedded in the SF tradition. Cameron, like Lucas, was fuelled by memories of comic books and encounters with the art and adventures from John Carter of Mars onwards. Cameron, however, seemed to have kept reading and his work reflected themes and ideas from the 1990s and beyond, especially an interest in the boundary between the human and the machine. The term

'Avatar' was ancient, originating in Hindu mythology, but it had been given a new resonance as humans gained the ability to pilot characters in digital environments. It was popularized by its use in Neal Stephenson's novel *Snow Crash* (1992). *Avatar* paralleled Ursula Le Guin's famous novella *The Word for World is Forest* (1972) in its depiction of an alien forest people, and borrowed the idea of a paraplegic human finding liberation though mental projection into an engineered alien body from Poul Anderson's story 'Call Me Joe' (1957).[19] Fans of Soviet SF noted 'tributes' to the work of the Russian SF writers Arkady and Boris Strugatsky, who had also dubbed their alien world Pandora.[20] The look of the aliens and their environment was an outgrowth from half a century of SF illustration. The massive planets overhead, vast vehicles, and impossibly tall, thin and attractive aliens were familiar from the cover art of a thousand novels. The work of Roger Dean sprang especially to mind. The idea of creating a film in which the humans were the villains was not new. Groups of humans had often threatened alien heroes, witness *The Day the Earth Stood Still* (1951), *Escape from the Planet of the Apes* (1971), *E.T.: The Extra Terrestrial* (1982) and many others, but no one had previously created a world on screen in which the works of humanity were so vilified.[21]

There were elements of fantasy fiction and cinema in *Avatar*. The *Wizard of Oz* (1939) allusion in the line 'You're not in Kansas anymore' spoke to both the dislocation of the characters within the film as they first set eyes on the alien planet, and also located the film in the tradition of Hollywood fantasy: a film remembered for its transition from black and white to colour. There is a fairy-tale quality in the idea of venturing into the woods. The Na'vi have an elfin appearance. The exhilarating sequences in which Jake flies on his banshee tap into a deeply embedded and apparently universal human dream of flight. Cinematic renderings of this include *Superman* (1978) with its tag-line 'You'll believe a man can fly', multiple sequences of the *Star Wars* saga, E.T. and his friends on their flying bicycles, and Harry Potter on his broomstick.

Avatar was also a Western. At one point Grace even delivers a Western cliché: 'Time to get out of Dodge.' There are numerous cues associating the Na'vi with Native Americans. Their bows and arrows; their war paint; their horsemanship; their war cries; their culture of balance and reverence for nature; their use of a travois to transport their wounded – all reflect Plains Indian culture. The dialogue in the film in which Jake speaks of coming to regard his dream world to be real and his real world as a dream parallels the reported philosophy of the Sioux leader Crazy Horse.[22] Cameron cast iconic Cherokee actor Wes Studi in the role of Eytukan the tribal chief. The actor's distinctive accent and delivery was recognizable even with the Na'vi language dialogue.

There was more to the parallel than just the Na'vi culture. *Avatar* built particularly on the sub-genre of western in which a white man is thrust into the midst of a Native American tribe, learns to understand them and finishes up as a respected member of their community or even their leader. The most recent example of this for *Avatar*'s audiences was *Dances with Wolves* (1990) – and parallels are made stronger through *Avatar*'s use of Jake's 'reports to diary' to tell the story. There were also echoes of *Little Big Man* (1970) and *A Man Called Horse* (1970), or from an earlier era *Broken Arrow* (1950). Ruptures with the older iterations of the sub-genre included the successful inter-racial (or in the case of *Avatar* inter-species) relationship. In the archetypal rendering the native bride perishes, providing a motive propelling the hero into the final act of the drama. *Dances with Wolves* had dodged the issue by making the protagonist's love interest a fellow outsider. Disney's *Pocahontas* (1995) broke the taboo.

The story of a white man 'going native' was much older than the Western. The English-speaking public had long been fascinated by characters like 'Chinese' Gordon/Gordon of Khartoum (1833–85) or T.E. Lawrence 'of Arabia' (1888–1935) who developed powerful affinities with non-white peoples and led them in battle, or Sir James Brooke (1803–68), the British adventurer who became Rajah of Sarawak in 1841. Such stories had inspired classic imperial fiction with stories like Joseph Conrad's *Lord Jim* (1900) or modern analogues like Pierre Schoendoerffer's *Farewell to the King* (originally published in French in 1969), and all of them had been filmed. Cameron has identified two variants from the genre as particular favourites of his boyhood: Edgar Rice Burroughs's transposition of the concept into space in the Barsoom/John Carter of Mars novels and Rudyard Kipling's story 'The Man Who Would Be King' from 1888.[23] Besides adapting such stories, Hollywood had devised its own stories of white men 'exalted amongst the heathen' with films like *The Last Samurai* (2003). There was an inherent racism to such films with its implication that the greatest Sioux, Arab or Samurai warrior could be incarnate within the lily white skin of Kevin Costner, Peter O'Toole or Tom Cruise. Some critics would trace this prejudice forward into *Avatar*.[24]

Cameron also cited the influence of a small clutch of films depicting the rainforest and its people on his film including John Boorman's *The Emerald Forest* (1985) and the epic adaptation of Peter Matthiessen's novel *At Play in the Fields of the Lord* (1991).[25] The influence here was not merely visual but extended to the attitudes underpinning the film. *Avatar* firmly endorsed the notion of the value and even superiority of indigenous life and the idea, as the UK tag line for *The Emerald Forest* had it: 'They still know what we have forgotten.' For Cameron the great insight of the Amazonian and other archaic cultures was their insistence on the connectedness of the individual to the environment and of each creature one to another, the theory that has become known as Gaia. When accepting his Golden Globe, Cameron explained: '*Avatar* asks us to see that everything is connected: all human beings to each other, and us to the earth.'[26] He was able, within *Avatar*, to posit an actual mechanism for this – a naturally evolved spiritual equivalent to the internet in which creatures could commune with one another and at their death be uploaded into a collective afterlife within the great reservoir of soul energy that was the planet's deity Eywa. It was the most thoroughly realized extraterrestrial theology since the Force of *Star Wars*. It was ironic that the endorsement of traditional spirituality and aboriginal values required unprecedented feats of technological wizardry, but Cameron had already made *T2* into what he called 'a violent movie about peace',[27] and succeeded in turning the story of the RMS *Titanic*, which had always before been told as a warning against trusting too much to technology, into a celebration of the technology of the screen. Few would notice the irony.

Cameron's story had obvious implications. It was obviously a plea against racism. We are shocked when Selfridge dismisses the Na'vi as 'blue monkeys'. By the same token it was a plea on behalf of the rights of indigenous peoples around the world. It was also an endorsement of the sustainable management of resources. Within the film Neytiri explains to Jake that he should take no more from the environment than he needs and when he dies he returns to the ecosystem. Against this is set the negative example of the greedy human mining corporation. Like the Dr Seuss book *The Lorax*, seen in the school, *Avatar* challenged its audience to recognize the folly of taking too much from the world and behave differently. A parable of sustainability was utterly in step with the spirit of its age. The popular discourse was full of concern over the insatiable appetite of oil companies and other extractive industries, and the damage that the reckless consumption of fossil fuels was doing to the environment. The story had particular significance at a time when the United States remained aloof from the international agreements designed to stabilize the climate, and politicians, bankrolled by energy corporations, routinely second-guessed the science underpinning the mounting concern. By 2009 sustainability had begun to operate as a moral code in its own right: a system of ethics by which an individual or an entire society could be judged. Cameron's message was both timely, and of its time. His associated attack on corporations was also topical. During the final months of production, the US economy went into a serious downturn, prompting widespread questioning of the ethics of Wall Street. The peak of this re-evaluation of the corporate sphere was years away but few commentators on *Avatar* would mourn hurt feelings in the corner offices of corporate America.

Cameron's story also reflected a message of anti-militarism. This theme had figured in his earlier films as a counter-cultural echo of the Vietnam War that had loomed large in Cameron's youth. New spins in *Avatar* included a twinning of the military/marines and the Na'vi tribal structures as when Jake presents himself as a member of the 'Jarhead Clan'. In the years since *Titanic* militarism had taken on a new significance. It was no longer just how America once behaved; it was back with major interventions in Afghanistan and Iraq. Cameron's critique partly drew on Vietnam-era images and stereotypes. His instructions to designers for the vehicles drew on Vietnam hardware. He described the Sampson craft – shown swooping over the jungle canopy with door guns at the ready – as like a Huey helicopter.[28] The Valkyrie shuttle was influenced by the Vietnam-era F-4 phantom on the outside and the C-130 Hercules inside. The final attack uses a Vietnam-type daisy cutter bomb.[29] Vietnam also influenced the characterization and dialogue. Colonel Quaritch is a generic hyper-masculine, seething marine whose idiom reflects that documented in *Full Metal Jacket* (1987). Selfridge's reference to 'winning hearts and minds' is lifted straight out of the vocabulary of Vietnam.[30] But there were more modern references too. The attack on home tree is described as a 'shock and awe' campaign, deploying the phrase from contemporary military theory used to describe the massive bombardment of Baghdad at the opening of the second Gulf War in 2003.[31] Quaritch vows to 'fight terror with terror' and moves into a pre-emptive attack.[32] What is especially disturbing is his desire to use cultural knowledge to target his final attack. Having already destroyed the home tree, Quaritch plans to attack the focal point of the Na'vi religion and their point of connection to their spiritual plain: the tree of souls. 'This will blow a hole in their racial memory' he gloats. The idea of culturally-informed tortures and attacks was part of the second Gulf War, underpinning stories of abuse at Abu Grahib and elsewhere with dogs and sexual humiliations calculated to hurt the 'Arab mind'. As his fleet moves into attack, the music switches to some vaguely Middle Eastern riffs. Iraq is not far away.

And yet for all these themes, *Avatar* was based around the image. The film was marketed and consumed in the first instance as an immersive experience: rendered in three dimensions and on an epic scale: sometimes on an IMAX screen. The key point of *Avatar* was to see it and be overwhelmed by it. Much of the discussion of the film was around simply the experience of the images. The theme of an immersive experience was a major theme in the story as well. Jake is able to immerse himself in the world of Pandora through the technology of the Avatar, and we learn that within the Na'vi culture the idea of seeing is a crucial concept. The Na'vi expression 'I see you' is used to mean a total appreciation of the addressee and their place in

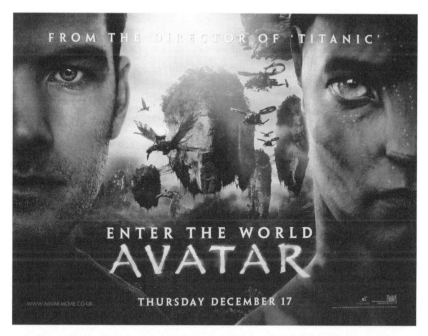

23. 'Enter the world *Avatar*': the promise of an immersive experience as the prime selling point in a poster for *Avatar* (2009) (Source: British Film Institute).

the interconnected ecosystem that is Pandora. 'Sky people cannot learn; they cannot see' says Neytiri. 'Teach me to see' Jake begs in reply. When progress is slow, Tsu'tey the young warrior leader says disparagingly: 'A rock sees more ...'. But Jake triumphs and learns to see like a Na'vi. The final image of the film is a close-up of one of Jake's eyes – as now permanently inhabiting his new Avatar body – he opens it to look out at his world for the first time. Lest anyone miss the point, the credits roll over a song: 'I see you'.

Having completed the film Cameron faced a major challenge in marketing it. While his reputation guaranteed a certain level of expectation, there was no obviously bankable star involved in front of the camera. More than this, the film's visual impact and financial achievement would be maximized if it played in 3D format on screens where exhibitors could charge a premium price for a ticket, but the necessary technology was still being installed. In June and July Fox screened excerpts of the film to conventions of US and European cinema exhibitors hoping to spur the conversion of more screens to the 3D format. Cameron himself introduced scenes to the SF community at Comicon.[33] To encourage demand among general audiences, the studio held a lottery to distribute free tickets to see scenes from the film on 131 IMAX screens around the country on 21 August: 'Avatar day'. Similar screenings took place that day on 300 screens internationally. Thousands saw the clips and millions more people downloaded the trailer online.[34] Gimmicks to reach the young male audience included the release of special tins of Coke Zero printed with a code that, when held up to a webcam, created an image of one of the vehicles from the film, which could be piloted by manipulating the can.[35] By December the necessary number of 3D screens had been prepared and the audience was primed.

The initial reviewers of Avatar were blown away. Variety hailed the film as 'eyepopping' and noted that it was 'the most expensive and technically ambitious film ever made'.[36] The New Yorker's David Denby called it 'The most beautiful film I've seen in years.'[37] In the Los Angeles Times Kenneth Turan, who had been tough on True Lies and Titanic, called the film 'a dazzling revelation' that 'restores a sense of wonder to movie going that had been missing'. Turan also noted the likely implications of so spectacular a showcase of the 3D format, dubbing the film: 'The Jazz Singer of 3D film making.'[38] In the New York Times Manohla Dargis agreed, observing: 'With Avatar James Cameron has turned one man's dream of the movies into a trippy joy ride about the end of life – our movie going life included – as we know it.'[39] There were few detractors in the initial round of reviews though Time magazine doubted the film could make as much money as Titanic as it lacked an equivalent to 'DiCaprio appeal'.[40] Reviewers internationally were similarly impressed, though as the astonishing appeal of the film from Chile to China became apparent, a noticeable backlash began – sour grapes perhaps – and it became fashionable to deride the script, if not the images on the screen. Conservative critics latched on to the 'un-American' aspects of the film. Cameron triumphed at the Golden Globe awards but his peers engineered a poetic ego check at the Oscars, awarding the best director and best picture awards to his ex-wife Kathryn Bigelow and her Iraq war movie The Hurt Locker.[41]

The extraordinary vividness of the immersive world of Avatar was disturbing to some members of its audience. Even the preview had one reviewer longing to return to Pandora.[42] The full film sparked full-on depression in some viewers. The fan website Avatar Forums received more than a thousand posts from people experiencing 'Avatar blues', a sorrow not to live in the world depicted in the film. Some fans confessed to suicidal thoughts. Others wrote of disgust for the human race and disengagement from reality.[43] Other controversies included an attack on the film from a Seattle-based pastor, Mark Discoll, who called the film 'the most demonic, satanic movie I've ever seen' largely because of its representation of 'pagan theology'. Even the Christian blogosphere was largely unconvinced by his argument.[44]

One of the most interesting results of *Avatar* was the use of the film's images by indigenous rights campaigners around the world. Following the film's big win at the Golden Globes the pressure group Survival International issued a compendium of statements from indigenous people drawing parallels between the film and their real lives, including testimony from a Kalahari bushman and the Yanomami Indians of the Amazon and a leader of the Penan people of Borneo who said: 'The Na'vi people in Avatar cry because their forest is destroyed. It's the same with the Penan. Logging companies are chopping down our big trees and polluting our rivers, and the animals we hunt are dying.'[45] Elsewhere in the world the mantle of *Avatar* was claimed by spokesmen for the Dongria Kondh people in India's eastern province of Orissa, who were struggling to prevent their sacred mountain from being excavated by the foreign mining company Vedanta.[46] Expatriate groups representing both Tibetan and the Uyghur people of Xinjiang claimed that their situation was analogous to that of the Na'vi. The *Irish Times* reported rumours that the Chinese government might have cut short the film's run because of an overlap between the plot and the general issue of 'land-grabs by unscrupulous developers, aided by corrupt officials'.[47] A few weeks later on 12 February 2010 Palestinians

24. On the coattails of *Avatar*: Palestinians from the village of Bil'in protest against the Israeli barrier dressed as Na'vi, 12 February 2010 (Source: Bil'in Popular Committee).

from the village of Bil'in actually donned blue paint and body suits and paraded up and down beside the 'Peace Barrier' in a photo opportunity for the international media. Israeli security forces dispersed the demonstration with tear gas in an incident that was soon posted on *Youtube* where it scored many more hits than previous videos of conventional protests at the same location.[48] James Cameron endorsed some of these parallels and worked to draw particular attention to the problems facing the peoples of the Amazon. In April 2010 he travelled to the region and announced that the people were facing a real-life *Avatar* situation. Fifty Amazonian leaders attended a special screening in Quito, Ecuador.[49]

Twentieth Century-Fox was swift to capitalize on the success of *Avatar*. It marked the first anniversary of its release with the re-release of an extended special edition with nine minutes of extra footage. The DVD version added 18 minutes.[50] The added length did not deter audiences, even in a 2D format the Blu-ray/DVD became an immediate global bestseller, shifting 30 million copies worldwide in a matter of weeks.[51] Cameron also signalled that *Avatar* would not be his only excursion to Pandora. In October 2010 he contracted to make two sequels due in 2014 and 2015. This artist, *Hollywood Reporter* quipped, was plainly 'staying in his blue period'.[52]

Avatar had demonstrated the potency of SF genre and the potential of the 3D process to deliver a new level of immersion in the story. Across the industry new projects were green-lit and others retooled to match the increased expectations of a post-*Avatar* audience. The processes pioneered on *Avatar* were now in the marketplace. It only remained to be seen where Cameron and his successors would take audiences next.

Notes

[1]   Kingsley Amis, *New Maps of Hell: A Survey of Science Fiction* (New York: Harcourt, 1960), p.137.
[2]   Quoted in studio publicity packet, archived in Margaret Herrick Library Core Collection.
[3]   Christopher Heard, *Dreaming Aloud: the life and films of James Cameron* (Toronto: Doubleday, 1997), p.6; Marc Shapiro, *James Cameron: An Unauthorized Biography* (Los Angeles: Renaissance Books, 2000), pp.32–33; Rebecca Keegan, *The Futurist: The Life and Films of James Cameron* (New York: Crown, 2009), pp.10–11.
[4]   Keegan, *The Futurist*, pp.232–33; Jody Duncan and Lisa Fitzpatrick, *The Making of Avatar* (New York: Abrams, 2010), p.13. The dream is mentioned in Michael Ordoña, 'Eye-popping "Avatar" pioneers new technology', *San Francisco Chronicle*, 13 December 2009, online at www.sfgate.com/cgi-bin/article.cgi?f=/c/a/2009/12/11/PK4B1B0EHD.DTL&ao=2#ixzz1b77w0iZ5Last accessed: 7 June 2012.
[5]   Heard, *Dreaming Aloud*, pp.9–10; Shapiro, *James Cameron*, pp.54–55.

6   Keegan, *The Futurist*; pp.20–25; Heard, *Dreaming Aloud*, pp.13–25.

7   Shapiro, *James Cameron*, pp.126–31.

8   For a survey of scholarship on Cameron see Alexandra Keller, *James Cameron* (New York: Routledge, 2006).

9   Heard, *Dreaming Aloud*, pp.40–1.

10 From Cameron's epilogue to Lisa Fitzpatrick, *The Art of Avatar: James Cameron's epic adventure* (New York: Abrams, 2009), p.105.

11 The *Avatar* scriptment has not been published. Duncan and Fitzpatrick, *The Making of Avatar*, p.14. Note its similarity to the final film except that Jake was initially called Josh Sully and Neytiri was Zuleika.

12 Keegan, *The Futurist*, pp.146–7, 236; see also studio publicity packet, archived in core collection, Herrick Library.

13 Paula Parisi, 'Cameron's future actors could send in the clones: synthetic stars planned for his Avatar'.
    Hollywood Reporter, 8 August 1996.

14 Keegan, *The Futurist*, pp.208–30; on the Mars project see pp.212–22.

15 For a detailed account see Duncan and Fitzpatrick, *The Making of Avatar*.

16 Ben Zimmer, 'On Language: *Skxawng*', *New York Times*, 6 December 2009, p.MM.20.

17 Studio publicity packet, archived in core collection, Herrick library.

18 Hence the Levi jeans in *Star Trek V* (1989); the Taco Bell restaurants in *Demolition Man* (1993); the futuristic BMW in *Minority Report* (2002) and the notorious posters for Sugar Puffs cereal in *Daleks – Invasion Earth 2150* (1966). For a commentary see Charlie Jane Anders, 'The History of Product Placement in Science Fiction'; *io9 We Come from the Future*, posted 13 October 2008: http://io9.com/5061426/the-history-of-product-placement-in-science-fiction Last accessed: 12 June 2012.

19 For commentary on some of these borrowings, see Gary Westfahl, 'All energy is borrowed: a review of Avatar', *Locus On-line*, 20 December 2009, www.locusmag.com/Reviews/2009/12/all-energy-is-borrowed-review-of-avatar.html Last accessed: 7 June 2012.

20 Luke Harding, 'James Cameron rejects claims Avatar epic borrows from Russians' sci-fi novels', *Guardian*, 14 January 2010, p.25.

21 At one point in the development of *Star Wars* George Lucas had declared that in his film 'The space aliens are the heroes, and the Homo Sapiens naturally the villains'. George Lucas to *Camplin* magazine, fall 1973, as cited in Michael Kaminski, *The Secret History of Star Wars: The Art of Storytelling and the making of a modern epic* (Kingston, Ontario: Legacy Books, 2008), p.61.

22 The widely-read history Dee Brown, *Bury My Heart at Wounded Knee* (New York: Henry Holt, 1970) notes: 'Since the time of his youth, Crazy Horse had known that the world men lived in was only a shadow of the real world. To get to the real world, he had to dream ...' (p.289 in the 2001 paperback edition).

23 Duncan and Fitzpatrick, *The Making of Avatar*, p.15.

24 For a survey of this criticism see Jesse Washington, '*Avatar* critics see racist theme', *Huffington Post*, posted 11 January 2010, www.huffingtonpost.com/2010/01/10/avatar-critics-see-racist-theme_n_418155.html Last accessed: 7 June 2012.

25 Geoff Boucher, 'James Cameron: Yes, *Avatar* is *Dances with Wolves* in space...sorta' *Los Angeles Times Hero Complex blog*, posted 10 August 2009, http://herocomplex.latimes.com/2009/08/14/james-cameron-the-new-trek-rocks-but-transformers-is-gimcrackery/ Last accessed: 7 June 2012

26 Associated Press '*Avatar* glory at Golden Globes', *Guardian online*, posted 18 January 2010, www.guardian.co.uk/culture/2010/jan/18/golden-globes-avatar-james-cameron Last accessed: 7 June 2012.

27 Keegan, *The Futurist*, p.132.

28   Lisa Fitzpatrick, *The Art of Avatar: James Cameron's epic adventure* (New York: Abrams, 2009), p.23.

29   Duncan and Fitzpatrick, *The Making of Avatar*, p.72.

30   Dialogue cut from the script even duplicated some idiom heard in *Full Metal Jacket*.

31   The term was devised by Harlan K. Ullman and James P. Wade of the National Defense University in 1996.

32   While the invocation of 'terror' is Bushian, the phrase 'terror with terror' was coined as a critique of the US by Hugo Chavez of Venezuela during the attack on Afghanistan in 2001. Quoted in John Pilger, 'Latin America: The attack on democracy', *New Statesman*, 24 April 2008.

33   Carl DiOrio, 'US exhibitors get glimpse of *Avatar*', *Hollywood Reporter*, 17 July 2009; Marc Graser, 'The Eyes Have it: 3D wins the day at Comic-con', *Variety* (daily), 24 July 2009, pp.1, 14.

34   Keegan, *The Futurist*, pp.151–53; Michael Cieply and Dave Itzkoff, 'Blockbuster trailer: the selling of Avatar', *New York Times*, 22 August 2009, p.C1; Pamela McClintock and Justin Kroll, 'Fox beats 3D drums', *Variety* (daily), 24 August 2009, pp.1, 11.

35   Marc Graser, '*Avatar* will give auds a reality check', *Variety* (daily), 20 November 2009, pp.1, 34.

36   Todd McCarthy, 'An Eye-popping world', *Variety* (daily), 11 December 2009, p.1.

37   David Denby, 'Going Native', *New Yorker*, 4 January 2010, pp.76–7.

38   Kenneth Turan, 'A dazzling revelation', *Los Angeles Times*, 17 December 2009, D.1, 9.

39   Manohla Dargis, 'A new Eden both cosmic and cinematic', *New York Times*, 18 December 2009, pp.C1, 6.

40   Mike Goodridge, 'Avatar', *Time*, 18 December 2009 p.20.

41   Susan King, '*Hurt Locker* wins best picture', 7 March 2010.

42   Michael Cieply, 'Fan fever rising for debut of Avatar', *New York Times*, 25 April 2009, pp.C1, 6. The reviewer in question was Joshua Quittner, the tech writer for *Time* magazine.

43   Jo Piazza, 'Audiences experience *Avatar* blues', *CNN Entertainment*, posted 11 January 2010 http://articles.cnn.com/2010–01-11/entertainment/avatar.movie.blues_1_pandora-depressed-posts?_s=PM:SHOWBIZ Last accessed: 7 June 2012.

44   Mark Moring, 'Avatar the most satanic film I've ever seen …' *Christianity Today*, posted 26 February 2010, http://blog.christianitytoday.com/ctentertainment/2010/02/avatar-the-most-satanic-film-i-1.html Last accessed: 7 June 2012.

45   Survival International, '"*Avatar* is real" say tribal people', 25 January 2010, online at www.survivalinternational.org/news/5466 Last accessed: 7 June 2012.

46   www.cnngo.com/mumbai/none/video-indian-tribals-appeal-james-avatar-cameron-943069#ixzz1agOcUYYr Last accessed: 7 June 2012.

47   Cliford Coonan, 'Sci-fi epic Avatar tops China's movie hit list', *Irish Times*, 20 January 2010. See also Tigiarya Taro, 'Opinion: Avatar's Pandora is Tibet', posted 28 January 2010, *Canada Tibet Committee Newsroom*, www.tibet.ca/en/newsroom/wtn/8394 Last accessed: 7 June 2012.

48   For the Youtube video see www.youtube.com/watch?v=KStnbXWfnuk Last accessed: 7 June 2012. For discussion see Henry Jenkins, 'Avatar activism', *La Monde Diplomatique*, 15 September 2010, http://mondediplo.com/2010/09/15avatar Last accessed: 7 June 2012.

49   Alexi Barrionuevo, 'Amazon tribes find ally right out of Avatar', *New York Times*, 11 April 2010, p.1, 4; 'Avatar in the Amazon', *ONTD: Oh no they didn't*, 3 February 2010 http://ohnotheydidnt.livejournal.com/43687307.html Last accessed: 7 June 2012.

50   The DVD restored scenes that further developed the character of Jake – who is shown defending a girl in a bar fight on a polluted and broken earth – and Grace, with the story of the failure of her school and a massacre that killed Neytiri's sister, see Peter Debruge, 'New hues in Avatar', *Variety* (daily), 16 November 2010, pp.1, 17.

51   Mark Graser, 'Fox pumps its Blu crew', *Variety* (daily), 6 December 2010, p.1.

52   Jay A. Fernandez and Georg Szalai, 'Cameron staying in his blue period: Helmer inks for a pair of Avatar sequels', *Hollywood Reporter*, 28 October 2010, pp.1, 14.

Afterword

The historical study of any set of films throws up tantalizing glimpses of what might have been. The cinema of science fiction has its own 'what ifs'. What if *Logan's Run* had been developed as a spoof? What if Toshiro Mifune had played Obi Wan Kenobi in *Star Wars* and Han Solo had been black? Imagine a drug dependent RoboCop or *Planet of the Apes* with no Statue of Liberty ending. What potential images spill forth from the MGM contract for *2001: A Space Odyssey* that specified Alfred Hitchcock, David Lean or Billy Wilder as alternate producer-directors? But these case studies are important not because of any revelation of what might have been in fictional worlds, but to the extent of their illumination of the real world, past and present. Our objective in the volume was to use the cinema of science fiction as a window on its times, though in the process we have also illuminated key corners of and interconnections within the genre.

To study any genre is to lay bare its interconnections. The work of the founder of the hard science genre, H. G. Wells, and the pioneer of a more fantastic approach, Edgar Rice Burroughs, is still being adapted directly, witness Steven Spielberg's *War of the Worlds* from 2005 and Disney's film of *John Carter* in 2012. Themes and aesthetics hinted at in passing in *Just Imagine, Things to Come* and *Forbidden Planet*, blossom in later films. Film-making technology similarly grew by accretion. Kubrick's *2001* emerges as the watershed of the genre: an indispensible impetus to its expansion on the screens of the 1970s and an inspiration for work long thereafter. But every film treated here had its impact within the genre. With *The Hellstrom Chronicle* we even saw SF jumping beyond fiction to shape a documentary, only to then spark its own round of responses in more usual territory with the film *Phase IV* and Frank Herbert's novel *Hellstrom's Hive*.

These case studies have highlighted a number of tensions with the screen genre of science fiction. As noted in the introduction to this volume, despite clear lines of authorship and inspiration, the literary genre and its cinematic analogue have seldom sat well together. H. G. Wells himself had at best a mixed relationship with the film industry. These cases suggest that it has been downhill ever since. Authors have claimed to be forgotten, exploited and outright plagiarized by the process of adaptation or inspiration within the genre. Frank Herbert felt ripped off by *Star Wars* and allegations of plagiarism soon gathered around *Avatar*. Part of this is a process inherent to the creation of a genre, when it is still unclear where the boundaries of originality lay, hence the suit against *Just Imagine*, claiming that the idea of a trip to Mars was proprietary. But the problem has remained. The Fox suit against *Battlestar Galactica* claimed unsuccessfully that the 'look and feel' of *Star Wars* was intellectual property. James Cameron's claim during his dispute with Harlan Ellison over the origins of *The Terminator* that notions like time travel and robot assassins belonged to the genre and not any one writer remains moot, even if the studio conceded credit to the veteran author.[1]

A second point of tension within these essays has been the relationship between television and the motion picture. We have seen movies drawing on SF television as with the *Quatermass* adaptations; we have seen television inspired by SF movies as with the influence of *Forbidden Planet* on *Star Trek*. We have also seen television launching spin-off series from SF cinema as with the adaptations of *Planet of the Apes, Logan's Run*, the *RoboCop* TV films and links (of opportunity or imitation) between *Star Wars* and *Battlestar Galactica*. It has been a singular symbiosis, with TV learning from the SF cinema and embracing its technological breakthroughs, while the SF cinema plainly traded on its ability to deliver a spectacle that the small screen could not.

A third point of tension is that between SF film-makers and their audiences. The usual issues of following or leading taste are complicated within the genre by the emergence of SF fandom. While the initial forays in the genre did not have a niche audience in mind, by the post-war period it was clear that film-makers could count on a core audience for the SF genre. We have seen that the studio boss behind *Forbidden Planet* had a gentle prod from two young fans to seek out SF material, but he did little to market the finished film to the SF community beyond arranging for a novelization of the screenplay. Something changed in the mid-1960s. Fandom reached a critical mass and new types of fandom emerged. The format and characters on *Star Trek* inspired a new generation of fans (disproportionately female) to write and circulate their own fiction inspired by the series. *Star Trek* fandom became a model for the wider consumption of the genre.[2] By the mid-1970s a smart producer like *Star Wars*'s Gary Kurtz understood the benefits of pre-marketing his film to comic and SF fans. This became a tried and tested formula. Initially fans were just a key audience to be reached and exploited by the film-maker: the outermost tendrils on a grapevine leading to a wider audience. Fans have developed a more active role, sometimes sustaining a cycle in hiatus as with the *Star Wars* fans of the late 1980s, who loyally purchased spin-off novels; sometimes pushing back against elements within a film or cycle. *Star Wars* fans were vocal in their criticism of the character of JarJar Binks in *Star Wars Episode I: The Phantom Menace,* and in their indignation over Lucas's continued tweaking, and reformatting of the series.

Producers have increasingly sought to manage fandom, regulating fan fiction and seeking to both cater to and cultivate demand through the presentation of their story across multiple platforms. In recent years specialist companies have sprung up whose sole role is in developing tools to provide consistency within the authorized spin-off media.[3] The Internet has amplified the role of the fan, creating an echo chamber that can build or undermine the reputation of a film long before a professional critic gets sight of it. *Avatar* was a milestone in online marketing, but it will be fascinating to see where a digitally-empowered audience and an Internet savvy producer might take the genre next.

One final point of tension and exchange within this book is that between the United States and Great Britain. With cases from both sides of the Atlantic, the SF genre emerges as a transatlantic conversation. America certainly reacted to Wells but, as *Quatermass* shows, British producers drew on US themes too. Several of the films discussed in this book were effectively joint enterprises. *2001: A Space Odyssey* was a product of British technicians if not British finance; British accents abound in the future depicted in *Logan's Run* and many other locations. The original *Star Wars* trilogy bore a British imprint from talent in front and behind the camera, where the course of industrial relations was not always smooth. The truly abysmal relations between James Cameron and his British crew on *Aliens* lie beyond the scope of this volume. Visual influences open another set of links with the British comic book scene inspired by America, which, in turn, returned the favour and provided a welcome infusion of fresh ideas in the late 1980s as is seen in *RoboCop* and more recent films, including the splendidly subversive *V for Vendetta* (2006). The net could be cast yet wider to include the influence of, and exchanges with, European and Soviet Bloc writers, artists and film-makers as well as exchanges with Japan.

But what of the themes within these films? Many of the themes that emerged from the research might have been predicted. Science fiction has been the principal creative space in which humans have engaged their anxieties over the development of science, technology and urbanization, and the SF cinema has showcased these themes. Fears over the destructive-ness of future war are prominent in *Things to Come, 2001,* the *Planet of the*

Apes cycle and even *The Hellstrom Chronicle*. Today the post-apocalypse is as routine a setting for contemporary SF as the Wild West or Merrie England for previous generations of film-goers. Recent examples have included *The Book of Eli* (2010) or Neil Marshall's vision of a savage future Scotland behind a rebuilt Hadrian's Wall in *Doomsday* (2008). It is equally evident that SF cinema provides a space and a language for contemporary issues to be addressed. Questions of race, gender and identity appear fairly consistently, and many cases here also reflect specific concerns at the moments of production, from Prohibition in *Just Imagine* through to the indigenous rights and environmentalism of *Avatar*.

SF cinema has used many genres as a source material, especially since the mid-1970s. If fact, future/outer space settings have become a location where unfashionable genres can be reworked. Genres absorbed into SF include the western, and – less obviously – the imperial adventure genre. George Lucas himself mourned the departure of the mystic east and uncharted lands on earth and posited outer space as the obvious substitute.[4] Certainly *Avatar* bore a close relation to an imperial romance. Perhaps the most surprising genre to find within SF is the religious epic. Both SF and religion concern themselves with the great questions of purpose and collective destiny. The religiosity of *Forbidden Planet* was a token of its times, but by *2001*, something more was happening. In an age of secular popular culture SF cinema provided a collective experience of awe and mystery. *Star Wars* explicitly aimed to teach morality and provide a myth to inspire; *RoboCop* reworked Christian themes of death and resurrection; *Avatar* dramatized the animist religious world of the rainforest, rendering it existentially true on Pandora at least. The persistence and success of these themes reflects both their endurance within the imagination of the writer and the need of audiences to glimpse the infinite.

As to the genre itself: SF has plainly grown, achieving prominence and in some seasons even dominance in popular culture. There have been fertile generic fusions. SF/horror has done especially well. Familiar cycles have been successfully 'rebooted' with new sensibilities, including both *Doctor Who* (2005–) and *Battlestar Galactica* (2004–2009) on television; and *Star Trek* (2009) and a new *Planet of the Apes* in 2011 on movie screens. Other developments since 2000 have included a resurgence of films organized around a single near future social or technological concept – inheritors of Wells's *Invisible Man* – like the memory wipe in *Eternal Sunshine of the Spotless Mind* (2004) or the disturbing scenario of young people waiting to be used as spare parts in the low-budget British film *Never Let Me Go* (2010). Such films have demonstrated that an idea can still be hero on the big screen. Ideas and images converged in spectacular fashion in *Inception* (2010).

As CGI technology has removed the technical barriers to what can be put on the screen, the barrier seems to increasingly become internal to the film-makers themselves. Despite having all of outer space and all of time to explore, film-makers have tended to turn inwards, as if acknowledging that it is the interior life that gives meaning to all the rest in the first place. Thus the protagonist in *Contact* (1997) travelled into deep space but only meets aliens in the form of her dead dad; thus the *Star Wars* cycle became an exploration of the fall and redemption of the father. Even the most elaborate visions of future worlds have been routed in the experience of this world. From *Just Imagine* onwards, film-makers have sought to create creatures and environments that are extensions of those known from earth rather than truly launch into extra-*terra incognita*. Like their biodiversity, their politics remains a reworking of their own time. For the historian – as we have argued – this provides abundant material for further study. For the film-maker it should be a challenge to think anew and go beyond what has been. Perhaps the time has come to actually return to science for inspiration. Steven Spielberg has been thinking along these lines. In 2006 he announced plans to collaborate with Cal Tech professor of astrophysics Kip Thorne on a 'scientifically accurate' film in which explorers travel through a wormhole. The film – currently titled *Interstellar* – is scheduled for release in 2014 by Paramount. Since the success of *Avatar* it has been reconfigured to be 3D.[5]

After a century or more of SF cinema there is still a universe to discover. Let the next phase of that exploration begin.

Notes

[1]   Scholars interested in pursuing this legal theme might also examine the lawsuit filed by Francis Ford Coppola against author/scientist Carl Sagan over the intellectual property underpinning *Contact* (1997).

[2]   On the evolution of SF fandom see John Tulloch and Henry Jenkins, *Science Fiction Audiences: Watching Star Trek and Doctor Who* (London: Taylor and Francis, 1995).

[3]   For an insight into this see Peter Caranicas, 'Bibles hold tentpole revivals: bis moved backstory to forefront', *Variety* (weekly) 29 July 2009, pp.5,11, profiling a company called Starlight Runner Entertainment that generates the 'bible' (the anthology of backstory, mythology and design) necessary to ensure the consistent development of trans-media extensions of an SF or fantasy property in toy and game form.

[4]   Stephen Zito, 'George Lucas goes far out', in *American Film*, April 1977, 8–13, anthologized in Sally Kline, *George Lucas Interviews* (Jackson, MS: University Press of Mississippi, 1999).

[5]   Kip Thorne interview with Cull, 5 February 2010 see also Michael Fleming, 'Nolan to write Spielberg film', *Variety.com* 22 March 2007, www.variety.com/article/VR1117961655?refCatId=13 Last accessed: 7 June 2012.

Filmography

Just Imagine

USA. Fox Film Corporation. 1930.

Director: David Butler. *Producer:* Ray Henderson. *Story, dialogue, music and lyrics:* Buddy De Sylva, Lew Brown, Ray Henderson. *Director of photography:* Ernest Palmer. *Art director:* Stephen Goosson. *Costume design:* Sophie Eacher, Dorothy Tree, Alice O'Neill. *Editor:* Irene Morra. *Special effects:* Ralph Hammeras. *Musical director:* Arthur Kay. *Choreography:* Seymour Felix. *Running time:* 113 mins.

Cast: El Brendel (Single O), John Garrick (J-21), Maureen O'Sullivan (LN-18), Marjorie White (D-6), Frank Albertson (RT-42), Hobart Bosworth (Z-4), Kenneth Thompson (MT-3), Wilfred Lucas (Z-10), Mischa Auer (B-36), Sidney De Gray (AK-44), Joseph Girard (Commander), Joyzelle Joyner (Looloo/Booboo), Ivan Linow (Loko/Boko).

Things to Come

UK. London Film Productions. 1936.

Director: William Cameron Menzies. *Producer:* Alexander Korda. *Screenplay:* H. G. Wells. Based on *The Shape of Things to Come* and *The Work, Wealth and Happiness of Mankind* by H. G. Wells. *Director of photography:* Georges Périnal. *Production designer:* Vincent Korda. *Assistant art director:* Frank Wells. *Costume design:* John Armstrong, Rene Hubert and the Marchioness of Queensbery. *Supervising editor:* William Hornbeck. *Editors:* Charles Crichton, Francis Lyon. *Special effects director:* Ned Mann. *Special effects photography:* Edward Cohen. *Assistant special effects:* Laurence Butler. *Music:* Arthur Bliss. *Running time:* 100 mins.

Cast: Raymond Massey (John Cabal/Oswald Cabal), Edward Chapman (Pippa Passworthy/Raymond Passworthy), Ralph Richardson (The Boss), Margaretta Scott* (Roxana/Rowena), Cedric Hardwicke (Theotocopulos), Maurice Braddell (Dr Harding), Sophie Stewart (Mrs Cabal), Derrick de Marney (Richard Gordon), Ann Todd (Mary Gordon), Pearl Argyle (Catherine Cabal), Kenneth Villiers (Maurice Passworthy), Ivan Brandt (Morden Mitani), Patricia Hilliard (Janet Gordon), Anne McLaren (Child), Charles Carson (Great grandfather), John Clements (Airman), Patrick Barr (World Transport Official).

The War of the Worlds

USA. Paramount. 1953.

Director: Byron Haskin. *Producer:* George Pal. *Screenplay:* Barré Lyndon. Based on the novel by H. G. Wells. *Associate producer:* Frank Freeman Jr. *Director of photography:* George Barnes. *Art direction:* Hal Pereira and Al Nozaki. *Costume designer:* Edith Head. *Editor:* Everett Douglas. *Special effects:* Gordon Jennings, Wallace Kelley, Paul Lerpae, Ivyl Burks, Jan Domela, Irmin Roberts. *Explosions:* Walter Hoffman. *Astronomical art:* Chesley Bonnestell. *Music:* Leith Stevens. *Running time:* 83 mins.

Cast: Gene Barry (Clayton Forrester), Anne Robinson (Sylvia Van Buren), Les Tremayne (General Mann), Robert Cornthwaite (Dr Pryor), Sandro Giglio (Dr Bilberbeck), Lewis Martin (Pastor Collins), Jack Kruschen (Salvatore), Ivan Lebedeff (Dr Gratzman), Housely Stevenson Jr (Aide to General Mann), Paul Frees (Radio announcer), Sir Cedric Hardwicke (Narrator).

The Quatermass Experiment (US title: The Creeping Unknown)

UK. Hammer Film Productions. 1955.

Director: Val Guest. *Producer:* Anthony Hinds. *Screenplay:* Val Guest, Richard Landau. Based on the BBC television serial by Nigel Kneale. *Director of photography:* Walter Harvey. *Art director:* J. Elder Wills. *Wardrobe:* Molly Arbuthnot. *Editor:* James Needs. *Special effects:* Les Bowie. *Music:* James Bernard. *Running time:* 78 mins.

---

* Margaretta Scott is billed as 'Margueretta Scott' on both the film credits and in publicity materials, though in other film roles has always been 'Margaretta Scott'.

Cast: Brian Donlevy (Professor Quatermass), Jack Warner (Inspector Lomax), Richard Wordsworth (Victor Caroon), Margia Dean (Judith Carroon), David King Wood (Dr Briscoe), Thora Hird (Rosie), Lionel Jeffries (Blake), Harold Lang (Christie), Barry Lowe (Tucker), Jane Aird (Mrs Lomax), Gordon Jackson (Television producer), Frank Phillips (Television announcer), George Roderick (Policeman), Sam Kydd (Police sergeant).

Quatermass 2 *(US title: Enemy from Space)*

UK. Hammer Film Productions. 1957.

Director: Val Guest. *Producer:* Anthony Hinds. *Screenplay:* Nigel Kneale and Val Guest. *Story:* Nigel Kneale. Based on the BBC television serial by Nigel Kneale. *Production supervisor:* Anthony Nelson Keys. *Director of photography:* Gerald Gibbs. *Art director:* Bernard Robinson. *Wardrobe:* Rene Coke. *Editor:* James Needs. *Special effects:* Bill Warrington, Henry Harris, Frank George. *Music:* James Bernard. *Running time:* 85 mins.

Cast: Brian Donlevy (Professor Quatermass), John Longden (Lomax), Sydney James (Jimmy Hall), Bryan Forbes (Marsh), William Franklyn (Brand), Vera Day (Sheila), Charles Lloyd Pack (Dawson), Tom Chatto (Broadhead), John Van Eyssen (The P.R.O.), Percy Herbert (Gorman), Michael Ripper (Ernie), John Rae (McLeod), Jane Aird (Mrs McLeod), Betty Impey (Kelly), Michael Balfour (Harry), Howard Williams (Michaels), Marianna Stone (Secretary), Gilbert Davies (Banker), George Merritt (Superintendent).

Quatermass and the Pit *(US title: Five Million Miles to Earth)*

UK. Hammer Film Productions. 1967.

Director: Roy Ward Baker. *Producer:* Anthony Nelson Keys. *Screenplay:* Nigel Kneale. Based on the BBC television serial by Nigel Kneale. *Director of photography:* Arthur Grant. *Production designer:* Bernard Robinson. *Art director:* Ken Ryan. *Editor:* James Needs. *Special effects provided by:* Bowie Films. *Music:* Tristram Cary. *Running time:* 97 mins.

Cast: Andrew Keir (Professor Quatermass), Barbara Shelley (Barbara Judd), James Donald (Dr Roney), Julian Glover (Colonel Breen), Duncan

Lamont (Sladden), Bryan Marshall (Captain Potter), Maurice Good (Sergeant Cleghorn), Peter Copley (Howell), Robert Morris (Watson), Edwin Richfield (Minister of Defence), Hugh Futcher (Sapper West), Sheila Steafel (Journalist), Hugh Morton (Elderly journalist), Thomas Heathcote (Vicar).

Forbidden Planet

USA. MGM. 1956.

Director: Fred McLeod Wilcox. *Producer:* Nicholas Nayfack. *Screenplay:* Cyril Hume. *Story:* Irving Block and Allen Adler. *Director of photography:* George J. Folsey. *Art direction:* Cedric Gibbons and Arthur Lonergan. *Costumes:* Walter Plenkett, Helen Rose. *Editor:* Ferris Webster. *Special effects:* A. Arnold Gilespie, Warren Newcombe, Irving G. Reiss and Joshua Meador. *Electronic tonalities:* Louis and Bebe Barron. *Running time:* 98 mins.

Cast: Walter Pidgeon (Dr Morbius), Anne Francis (Alta), Leslie Nielsen (Commander Adams), Warren Stevens ('Doc' Ostrow), Jack Kelly (Lt Farman), Richard Anderson (Chief Quinn), Earl Holliman (Cook), George Wallace (Bosun), James Drury (Strong), Bob Dix (Grey), 'and introducing Robby the Robot'.

2001: A Space Odyssey

UK. MGM. 1968.

Producer and director: Stanley Kubrick. *Screenplay:* Stanley Kubrick and Arthur C. Clarke. *Associate producer:* Victor Lyndon. *Director of photography:* Geoffrey Unsworth. *Additional photography:* John Alcott. *Production design:* Tony Masters, Harry Lange, Ernest Archer. *Art director:* John Hoesli. *Costume designer:* Hardy Amies. *Editor:* Ray Lovejoy. *Special effects:* Stanley Kubrick, Douglas Trumbull, Wally Veevers, Con Pederson, Tom Howard. *Music:* Richard Strauss, Johann Strauss, Aram Khachaturian, György Ligeti. *Running time:* 141 mins.

Cast: Keir Dullea (David Bowman), Gary Lockwood (Frank Poole), William Sylvester (Dr Heywood Floyd), Douglas Rain (Voice of HAL 9000), Daniel Richter (Moonwatcher), Leonard Rossiter (Smyslov), Margaret Tyzack (Elena), Robert Beatty (Halvorsen), Sean Sullivan (Michaels), Frank Miller (Mission controller), Penny Brahms (Stewardess).

Planet of the Apes

USA. Apjac Productions/20th Century-Fox. 1968.

Director: Franklin J. Schaffner. *Producer:* Arthur P. Jacobs. *Screenplay:* Rod Serling and Michael Wilson. Based on the novel *Monkey Planet* by Pierre Boulle. *Associate producer:* Mort Abrahams. *Director of photography:* Leon Shamroy. *Costume designer:* Morton Haack. *Editor:* Hugh S. Fowler. *Special effects:* L. B. Abbott, Art Cruikshank, Emil Kosa Jr. *Ape make-ups:* John Chambers. *Music:* Jerry Goldsmith. *Running time:* 112 mins.

Cast: Charlton Heston (Taylor), Roddy McDowall (Cornelius), Kim Hunter (Zira), Maurice Evans (Dr Zaius), Linda Harrison (Nova), James Whitmore (President of the Assembly), Robert Gunner (Landon), Jeff Burton (Dodge), James Daly (Honorius), Lou Wagner (Lucius), Woodrow Parfrey (Maximus), Buck Kartalian (Julius), Wright King (Dr Galen).

The Hellstrom Chronicle

USA. Wolper Productions/20th Century-Fox. 1971.

Director: Walon Green. *Producer:* David Wolper. *Screenplay:* David Seltzer. *Associate producer:* Sascha Schneider. *Director of photography:* Ed Spiegel (Hellstrom sequences). *Wildlife photography:* Helmut Barth, Walon Green, Ken Middleham, Gerald Thompson. *Additional photography:* Ferdinando Armati, Heinz Heilmann, Tony Coggans, J.-M. Bouffe. James Fronseca. *Editor:* John Soh. *Music:* Lalo Schifrin. *Running time:* 90 mins.

Cast: Lawrence Pressman (Nils Hellstrom).

Logan's Run

USA. MGM. 1976.

Director: Michael Anderson. *Producer:* Saul David. *Screenplay:* David Zelag Goodman. Based on the novel by William F. Nolan and George Clayton Johnson. *Associate producer:* Hugh Benson. *Director of photography:* Ernest Laszlo. *Art director:* Dale Hennesy. *Costume designer:* Bill Thomas. *Editor:* Bob Wyman. *Special effects designer:* L. B. Abbott. *Additional visual effects:* Fred Van Der Veer. *Choreography:* Stefan Wenta. *Music:* Jerry Goldsmith. *Running time:* 118 mins.

Cast: Michael York (Logan), Jenny Agutter (Jessica), Richard Jordan (Francis), Roscoe Lee Browne (Box), Farrah Fawcett-Majors (Holly), Michael Anderson Jr (Doc), Peter Ustinov (Old Man), Randolph Roberts (Second Sanctuary man), Lara Lindsay (Woman runner), Gary Morgan (Billy), Michelle Stacy (Mary), Gregg Lewis (Cub), Glen Wilder (Runner), David Westberg and Bill Couch (Sandmen).

Star Wars

USA. Lucasfilm/20th Century-Fox. 1977.

Written and directed by: George Lucas. *Producer:* Gary Kurtz. *Production supervisor:* Robert Watts. *Director of photography:* Gilbert Taylor. *Production designer:* John Barry. *Costume designer:* John Mollo. *Editors:* Paul Hirsch, Marcia Lucas, Richard Clem. *Special photographic effects supervisor:* John Dykstra. *Special production and mechanical effects supervisor:* John Stears. *Music:* John Williams. *Running time:* 121 mins.

Cast: Mark Hamill (Luke Skywalker), Harrison Ford (Han Solo), Carrie Fisher (Princess Leia Organa), Peter Cushing (Grand Moff Tarkin), Alec Guinness (Ben/Obi-Wan Kenobi), Anthony Daniels (C3PO), Kenny Baker (R2D2), Peter Mayhew (Chewbacca), David Prowse (Darth Vader), James Earl Jones (Voice of Darth Vader), Jack Purvis (Chief Jawa), Eddie Byrne (General Willard), Phil Brown (Uncle Owen Lars), Shelagh Fraser (Aunt Beru Lars), Alex McCrindle (General Dodonna), Drewe Hemley (Red Leader), Dennis Lawson (Red Two – Wedge), Garrick Hagon (Red Three – Biggs), Jack Klaff (Red Four – John 'D'), William Hootkins (Red Six – Porkins), Angus McInnis (Gold Leader), Jeremy Sinden (Gold Two – Tyree), Graham Ashley (Gold Five – Hutch), Don Henderson (General Taggi), Richard Le Parmetier (General Motti), Leslie Schofield (Commander #1).

RoboCop

USA. Orion. 1987.

Director: Paul Verhoeven. *Producer:* Arne Schmidt. *Screenplay:* Edward Neumeier, Michael Miner. *Executive producer:* John Davison. *Co-producer:* Edward Neumeier. *Director of photography:* Jost Vacano. *Production designer:* William Sandell. *Costumes:* Janet Lucas Lawler. *Second unit director:* Mark Goldblatt. *Editor:* Frank J. Urioste. *Special photographic effects:* Peter Kuran. *Music:* Basil Poledouris. *Running time:* 102 mins.

Cast: Peter Weller (Murphy/RoboCop), Nancy Allen (Lewis), Ronny Cox (Dick Jones), Dan O'Herlihy (The Old Man), Kurtwood Smith (Clarence Boddicker), Miguel Ferrer (Morton), Robert DoQui (Sergeant Reed), Ray Wise (Leon), Felton Perry (Johnson), Paul McCrane (Emil), Jesse Goins (Joe), Del Zamora (Kaplan), Calvin Jung (Minh), Rick Lieberman (Walker), Lee DeBroux (Sal), Marl Carlton (Miller), Edward Edwards (Manson), Michael Gregory (Lt Hedgecock), Angie Bolling (Murphy's wife), Jason Levine (Murphy's son).

Avatar

USA. Lightstorm Entertainment/20th Century-Fox. 2009.

Written and directed by: James Cameron. *Producers:* James Cameron, Jon Landau. *Co-producers:* Brooke Breto, Josh McLaglen. *Executive producers:* Laeta Kalogridis, Colin Wilson. *Director of photography:* Mauro Fiore. *Production design:* Rick Carter, Robert Stromberg. *Supervising art directors:* Todd Cherniawsky, Stefan Dechant, Kevin Ishioka, Kim Sinclair. *Costume designers:* Mayes C. Rubeo, Deborah L. Scott. *Editors:* James Cameron, John Refoua, Stephen Riukin. *Senior visual effects supervisors:* Joe Letten. *Visual effects producer:* Joyce Cox. *Visual effects supervisor for Industrial Light and Magic:* John Knoll. *Visual effects supervisors for WETA:* Stephen Rosenbaum, Eric Saindon, Dan Lemmon, Guy Williams. *Na'vi dance choreography:* Lula Washington. *Music:* James Horner. *Running time:* 162 mins (original release), 171 mins (extended version).

Cast: Sam Worthington (Jake Sully), Zoë Saldana (Neytiri), Sigourney Weaver (Dr Grace Augustine), Stephen Lang (Colonel Miles Quaritch), Michelle Rodriguez (Trudy Chacon), Giovanni Ribisi (Parker Selfridge), Joel David Moore (Norm Spellman), C.C.H. Pounder (Mo'at), Wes Studi (Eytukan), Laz Alonso (Tsu'tey), Dileep Rao (Dr Max Patel), Matt Gerald (Corporal Lyle Wainfleet), Sean Anthony Moran (Private Fike).

Index

Page numbers in **bold type** refer to an illustration.